AF505832

Clergy, ministers and priests

International Library of Sociology

Founded by Karl Mannheim

Editor: John Rex, University of Warwick

Arbor Scientiae
Arbor Vitae

A catalogue of the books available in the **International Library of Sociology** and other series of Social Science books published by Routledge & Kegan Paul will be found at the end of this volume.

Clergy, ministers and priests

Stewart Ranson

Institute of Local Government Studies
University of Birmingham

Alan Bryman

Department of Social Sciences
University of Loughborough

and

Bob Hinings

Institute of Local Government Studies
University of Birmingham

Routledge & Kegan Paul

London, Henley and Boston

First published in 1977
by Routledge & Kegan Paul Ltd
39 Store Street,
London WC1E 7DD,
Broadway House,
Newtown Road,
Henley-on-Thames,
Oxon RG9 1EN and
9 Park Street,
Boston, Mass. 02108, USA
Set in 10 on 11 Times Roman by
Kelly and Wright, Bradford-on-Avon, Wiltshire
and printed in Great Britain by
Lowe & Brydone

British Library Cataloguing in Publication Data

Ranson, Stewart

Clergy, ministers and priests. — (International
library of sociology).
1. Clergy — Great Britain
I. Title   II. Bryman, Alan   III. Hinings, Bob
IV. Series
301.5'8   BV660.2   77—30134

ISBN 0—7100—8713—6

For Helena, Sue and Mary

Contents

Illustrations

Preface

This book is a study of clerics from three English denominations, clergy from the Church of England, priests from the Roman Catholic Church, and ministers from the Methodist Church. Clerics have been relatively neglected as a topic of study in Britain. This is somewhat surprising when they are considered by many to be a group in crisis, a group in transition held in tension between conservative institutions and radical forces of change, exhorted to react and adjust. Here is a subject of intrinsic sociological interest.

This particular book grew out of much broader sociological study into the organisation structures of Churches. While at Aston and Birmingham universities, Bob Hinings had worked with Derek Pugh and David Hickson on a major research project which strove to elaborate and extend Weber's work on bureaucracy. This has since become known as the 'Aston' approach to the study of organisations. Having extended this work cross-culturally in Canada, Hinings brought together his interests in the sociology of organisations and the sociology of religion to examine Churches as organisations. This research utilised the theoretical model developed in the earlier projects.

The Social Science Research Council funded the project entitled 'The Organisation Structure of Churches' from 1970 until 1973. For all but the first six months of this period the project was based in the Industrial Administration Research Unit at the University of Aston (the home of the 'Aston' approach). Bruce Foster was a member of the team for the first eighteen months but then left academic life. Alan Bryman overlapped with Foster, working as a member of the IARU until the end of 1972. He then moved to the University of Birmingham and continued to be closely involved with the project. Stewart Ranson then became a full-time member of the team for the final funded year.

This book has been written between 1973 and 1976 with Hinings and Ranson at the Institute of Local Government Studies, University of Birmingham, and Bryman, since 1974, in the Department of Social Studies, University of Loughborough. Essentially, it is an extension of the central focus of the original project which was organisational. A book on this aspect will be appearing later.

We would like to thank our colleagues in the Industrial Administration Research Unit, especially Diana Pheysey, for general intellectual help and support. We are particularly indebted to Bryan Wilson, whose encouraging criticism helped to sharpen our thinking and correct the worst excesses of style. Of course, he bears no responsibility for the defects which inevitably remain. We are grateful for the early secretarial assistance of Jill Fussell. More especially, we owe a debt of gratitude to Pauline Grounds who typed the whole manuscript and whose initative and efficient manner helped considerably in producing the book.

1 Introduction

Religion has become a fashionable subject once more within sociology, and the practitioners an emergent force. Some have made
imperialist intellectual claims for the sociology of religion, believing
that it is central to any explanation of structural and cultural life:
'religion is not only a central concern of sociological theory it is *the*
central concern' (Hill, 1973). This claim seems strange when we
focus upon the contemporary demise of religion in a largely secular
world ostensibly stripped of its superstitious, miraculous and magical
trappings. But the importance of religion does appear to remain;
on the one hand, new faiths and rituals are continually emerging,
usually sect-like in character; on the other hand, many attribute
the contemporary social malaise to the receding salience of institutionalised religious beliefs and argue from a conviction that
religion is crucial to an understanding of the cohesion and trans-
formation of societies.

It has been the case, however, that whether the sociology of
religion has been a dormant or dominant interest in the past or
present, it has tended to be partial and selective in its treatment of
religious belief and behaviour, whether that treatment has been
substantive, theoretical or methodological. *Substantively* sociologists
either have written in a speculative and general vein about the place
of religion in society, or have produced detailed empirical analyses
of religious phenomena. There has been, of course, a particular
concern with sectarian organisation and behaviour, rather than
with 'mainstream' Churches (cf. Wilson (1970) as a good example),
and with aspects of individual religious behaviour. *Theoretically*,
as Robertson (1970) has pointed out, sociologists have been preoccupied, often inordinately, with classification rather than explanation. Such explanations as have been preferred tend to be functional

or cultural in character (cf. Glock and Stark, 1965; Luckmann, 1967). *Methodologically* sociologists have usually dealt with the immediate observables of individual religious behaviour, such as church attendance, and shied away from religious beliefs of individuals and structures of large religious organisations. Recently sociologists have begun to identify beliefs as a central problem for the study of religion (cf. Budd, 1973) together with the analysis of the organisational frameworks within which such beliefs are located (cf. Demerath, 1965; Eister, 1967).

This book is about Anglican, Roman Catholic and Methodist clergy, a relatively neglected topic within the sociology of English religion. One of the aims of the book is to adopt a more eclectic and theoretically ecumenical approach to its topic wherever possible. We have sought to elucidate the complexity of any explanation, to unravel the peculiar interrelationship of factors rather than the singular importance of one as against another. The intricate tangle of structural, cultural and demographic factors given in experience belies any simple account. Description must search for accuracy, explanation for balance.

II

The clergy are often considered as a group in crisis. Towler (1969) has pointed to the comprehensive manner in which the clergy are at present subject to social changes: 'they are lacking in manpower, their social status is declining and there is considerable uncertainty about their true role'. Theological creeds and ritual practices once entrenched and accepted without question are now threatened from secular sources outside the Church, but more disturbingly by incipient doubts and radical movements from within the Church itself.

Similarly, Harrison (1970) has suggested that the modern cleric engages in a greater variety of activities, which are inadequately defined and raise questions of legitimacy. Educationally the clergy are unprepared for many of these activities, which, in any case, are likely to be the preserve of other occupations.

Further uncertainties result from the reactions of the Churches themselves to the recognition of their changing position in society. Every major denomination has, in the past decade, produced a report or reports suggesting restructurings, amalgamations, new ways forward, etc. The Church of England has changed its system of government; in the wake of Vatican II the Roman Catholic Church is in the process of decentralisation, opening the way to more lay participation; the Methodist Church has considered restructuring the districts and reorganising its committee structure;

the Presbyterians and Congregationalists have amalgamated to become the United Reformed Church. Thus, apart from his role in relation to the wider society, the organisational and task role of the clergyman has been changing. His institutional position and support is less clear.

Along with this self-searching on organisation have gone commissions and committees on topics such as the nature of ministry, social welfare and responsibility, and the attitude of Churches to revolutionary movements. Also, there has been continuous exploration on the ecumenical front. Taken together all of this activity represents Churches searching for new identities, new stances.

The relative neglect of the clergy as a topic of study is, therefore, a little surprising. A group in transition, held in tension between conservative institutions and radical forces of change, exhorted to react and adjust, is intrinsically of sociological interest. Yet exactly what do we mean by the term 'clergy' as such? Most literature has adopted the term 'clergy' as a general concept to refer to religious functionaries of all denominations. This is inadequate and will not do. The term 'clergy' is possibly a misleading one, a blanket concept, masking and concealing far more than it reveals. The Methodist, Roman Catholic and Anglican Churches have widely diverse traditions, beliefs and ritual procedures, and it is because of this that we prefer to adopt the more specific terms 'minister' (Methodist), and 'priest' (Roman Catholic), delimiting the 'clergy' to its Anglican denotation. These terms, used by the Churches themselves, are part of the traditions of each Church and have come to denote distinctively different ways of conceptualising the nature of the full-time religious functionary. They represent, semantically, the different realms of meaning and relationship.

Of course, the extent to which the overall label 'clergy' or 'religious functionary' is a useful one depends largely on the context of description and explanation. This problem will be taken up in more detail later on in the chapter when we deal with the relatively voluminous American literature on religious occupations. Suffice it to say here that a prime aim of the sociology of religion should be to examine critically the empirical bases of its concepts.

An important part of our task, therefore, is to chart such inter-denominational differences, that is to say the degree to which differences do exist between the three denominations in our survey. Thus we shall be looking to discover that which is distinctive about the priests of the Roman Catholic Church, for example (their theological beliefs, their liturgical tradition, their organisational context) which mark them as totally different and separate from the clergy of the Church of England, or the ministers of the Methodist Church.

We are interested, equally, in the variations within each denomination, that is, the important intra-denominational differentiation of belief, age and status. Many theorists contend that the within-Church differences are more important than the between-Church differences; thus Krause (1971) asserts that

> in all organised religions at present there is a split between the activist clergy and the traditionalists. Both groups, but especially the activists, find allies across denominations and are disagreeing radically about the function of the clergyman in a changing scene. At present knowing whether a clergyman is an activist or a conservative is sociologically more important than knowing whether he is a Minister, Rabbi or Priest.

Whether or not the denominational influence is of consequence in deciding the pattern of religious faith and ritual of the functionaries in our survey is thus a persistent theme throughout the book.

A basic task then is to describe, simply to provide information about variations between and within denominations. It is still the case, as David Martin (1967) said, that 'we do not know about religion in Britain'. Who are the ministers, priests and clergy? Are they characterised by distinctively different theological beliefs and styles of ministry? Can we attribute to each denominational group a particular kind of social origin and professional experience which members have in common? Is there a distinctive age range and level of status peculiar to each Church? Is there a characteristic denominational response to the pressing issues of the day?

Much has been written recently within the sociology of religion of the need to go beyond empirical studies of institutional forms and levels of church attendance and focus upon the crucial area of religious belief and symbols. Berger and Luckmann (1963) have been instrumental in encouraging this development even to the point of suggesting that the analysis of religious values should be envisaged as part of a wider study of knowledge and culture. The position is neatly expressed by Roland Robertson (1970) who dedicates his book *The Sociological Interpretation of Religion* to 'the idea of religion as culture. Religious beliefs symbols and values comprise the departure point'. Budd (1973), however, in her study *Sociologists and Religion* exhorts us to

> go beyond this answer, to avoid the phenomenologists' tendency to merely state the role of religion in structuring reality and to provide a few illuminating examples. This can only be done by returning to the classical tradition of sociology; that is by trying to quantify beliefs and symbols, to relate them to groups, to relate them to historical experience.

In our study, therefore, we have attempted to elucidate and quantify the belief systems of the clergy, ministers and priests. We examine the Anglican notion of 'churchmanship' which we have defined elsewhere as 'that theological stance or framework of religious belief, which defines a person's relation to God in specific forms of devotional and ritualistic activities and defines for him how he is to interpret his faith in the secular world' (Bryman *et al.*, 1974). Michael Daniel (1967) has also defined 'churchmanship', more specifically, as referring to 'ideological differences held by individuals or parties within the Church of England, though differences may sometimes come to be expressed as variations of behaviour'. These categories of belief, include 'Anglo-Catholic', 'Central or Broad Church', 'Evangelical' and so on. Do these churchmanship groupings preclude a distinctively Anglican belief system? We look at Methodist ministers and the extent to which they adhere to categories of churchmanship familiar to Anglican clergy, and the extent to which there is a much more singular evangelical/ecumenical strain to Methodist belief. Finally, we look at the theology of Roman Catholic priests and the degree to which it is informed by a cohesive, uniform, traditional belief in ritualism, visually symbolising an ontological hierarchy. Is this conception of a unitary belief system a reality or a contemporary fiction?

When studying religious functionaries the focus lies usually on theological belief while important social characteristics are taken for granted, their delineation omitted. We tend to neglect the age of the typical clergyman, priest or minister and what kind of social experience we can typically ascribe to him: his origin in a particular social class and form of education. Is there a familiar professional orientation which we can typically attribute to each denomination? Given a particular social and educational background and professional orientation, is there a typical occupational experience by which we can characterise each denomination; that is, what positions do they tend to hold and for how long do they usually work, for example, within a parish or diocese.

But a basic aim in this book, following the notion of the clergy as 'a group in crisis' is to consider and describe their response to certain crucial issues, themselves products of social change, as a means of helping us to further characterise and differentiate between religious functionaries. Indeed, it is these responses that form the point of explanation, or dependent variables. Is there uncertainty among religious functionaries about their roles, are ritual practices changing, how far do they feel that restructurings and ecumenical amalgamations are necessary? Thus we will attempt to explore and explain the extent to which clergy, ministers and priests see changes as desirable or not.

We were therefore interested in how they conceive their role or ministry; how they regard the organisation in which they work, whether or not they believe the organisation, the Church, requires reform; the degree of their ecumenism, that is, whether or not they believe their Church should amalgamate or co-operate with other Churches; whether or not they recognise the existence of, or feel the need to develop, self-conscious occupational or professional groups to protect them in a time of upheaval. The religious functionary's conception of ministry is undergoing considerable change. On the one hand, as is well known, many of his traditional functions have been slowly eroded and passed on to secular specialists – social workers, psychiatrists, magistrates and the like (Wilson, 1966). This is one of the chief causes of role-uncertainty among clergy, priests and ministers. They have been divested of many traditional functions and are trying to forge new ones. Consequently, there is some doubt among both functionaries and laymen concerning what the former really are supposed to be doing.

On the other hand, the religious functionary has become increasingly involved in administrative and organisational duties within the context of an ever-growing ecclesiastical bureaucracy (Blizzard, 1956; Paul, 1968). This in fact contributes even further to uncertainty concerning his role. Although his work is generally conceptualised in spiritual terms, he is none the less supposed to maintain a healthy organisation. That he is not seen as an administrator by his laity does not seem to immunise the clergyman, priest or minister from criticism if he is mishandling his organisational work (cf. Lauer, 1973). Consequently we have been particularly interested in how priests, clergy and ministers conceive their ministry; the specific aspects of their role that are given stress – pastor, administrator, counsellor, leader, celebrant or whatever. What are the denominational differences? Are there important variations within each Church?

We shall also be concerned with the amount of support given by each group to issues surrounding reform in their respective Churches. Talk of reform in the Churches was very prevalent in the 1960s and the reverberations of both talk and action are being felt in the 1970s at the same time that new issues are being raised. Cecil Northcott (1971) has noted the centrality of reform issues in the Churches in the 1960s and has written:

Ever since the Vatican Council of the 1960s change and reform have been the dominant note in the Roman Catholic Church, and during the same period the Church of England has also been under the constant scrutiny of commissions and investigations bent on reordering its structure. In the Free Churches too

the dwindling of influence and numbers has been accompanied
by some stringent observations about the future of the churches.

In our research we were concerned with the extent to which clergy,
ministers and priests in the three Churches we investigated were in
favour of a number of important issues regarding reform and change.
In addition, we sought to discern variations in the degree of support
for such reforms within each Church.

Another issue around which much contemporary theological
debate centres and which entails vital consequences for the denominations is the ecumenical movement. There has been considerable
effort invested in unity negotiations between Churches in recent
years. Although the ecumenical movement was described by
Archbishop William Temple in 1942 as 'the great new fact of our
times', little has been done to indicate the extent of support for
unity plans and ventures among religious functionaries. In our
research we drew a distinction between support for co-operation
between Churches, and what clergy, ministers and priests have
actually achieved. We have noted elsewhere that the distinction
between unity and co-operation is a very important one, in that in
a study of Anglican lay and clergy views, we found that laity were
consistently less favourable to unity with other Churches, but were
equally favourable to co-operation between Churches (Bryman and
Hinings, 1973, 1974).

Description searches for an adequate narrative, one which is
complete in detail of event and meaning, but explanation seeks to
illuminate the crucial axes upon which the narrative revolves,
focusing upon the connection of fundamental events, why one
occurrence happens because of another. A central part of our analysis,
therefore, is concerned to go beyond the description of the previous
section and elucidate those factors which are critical in determining
events, crucial in moulding the attitudes and behaviour of our
religious functionaries. Thus our *explicandum* (dependent variables):
concept of ministry, ecumenism, reform, organisational context.
Our explanatory factors (*explicans*, independent variables) lie
basically within three categories. First, those which stress the
denominational setting in accounting for the attitudes and conduct
of priests, clergy and ministers, such as denominational experience,
organisational status, theological college training; second, the
importance of *theological beliefs* and belief systems in moulding
behaviour, a factor which may be completely determined by the
denominational context or be relatively independent of it; and
third, those exogenous factors which emphasise largely *extra-
denominational* influences as crucial for predicting and understanding
the religious functionaries' attitudes and behaviour—such factors

7

may incorporate social class origins, professional allegiance, age and so on.

The first two categories of factors, denominational context and systems of theological belief we suggest are the most crucial. They are often conceived as virtually conflicting explanatory factors but a number of writers (Smith, 1973; Lovell, 1973; Peel, 1973; Allardt, 1973) have recently presented arguments, correctly we believe, which denigrate any simple espousal of either belief or ideas, on the one hand, or structure and institution, on the other, as the primary factors in any explanation, but stress the way in which they interrelate to shape the responses of men to particular situations. Smith criticises the traditional cleavage between 'cultural' and 'structural' theories and the tendency to gravitate to either one or other of these basic models. He says that 'To overcome this confusion and create a more unified framework of explanation, we need a model which includes both cultural and structural elements and seeks to relate exogenous to endogenous factors' (Smith, 1973). The task of this section, therefore, is to discuss the disparate factors and unravel their relative weight or importance, and to discover the nature of their influence. This will be expressed in the form of a model which can be tested empirically in subsequent chapters.

Beliefs first. We have already suggested that any account of religious behaviour must take beliefs as its departure point. Yet in the past many sociologists have avoided incorporating ideas or beliefs or myths in their theoretical frameworks because they were thought to be either ostensibly subjective, amorphous and intangible in nature, or irrelevant (see Gill, 1974). Recently, however, a number of the theoretical formulations of Weber and his generation are being recalled. For Weber beliefs lend meaning and orientation to action: 'the action of each takes account of that of the others and is oriented in these terms'. By linking belief to the notions of 'orientation' and 'relationship' Weber rescued the actor from theoretical isolation and solitude rooting him in specifiable social contexts and forging a link between the individuality, subjectivity, concreteness of action and its more general, social and historical antecedents and consequences.

Beliefs will thus be crucial and uneliminable for any explanation; but exactly what is likely to be the relationship between beliefs and subsequent behaviour, between one belief and another? There are some (Winch, 1958; MacIntyre, 1962, 1971; Allardt, 1973) who suggest that it is sufficient to lay bare the beliefs, ideas, concepts to which men adhere for their activities to be delimited. Beliefs are said not to be independent from, or external to, actions but related internally and conceptually: actions follow logically, syllogistically, from beliefs.

Yet this account envisages and expects a much too precise and specific relationship between belief and behaviour. Beliefs are more general than MacIntyre admits, permitting expression in completely diverse forms of activity. Thus Lovell (1973), for example, describes how the Jansenism of the *noblesse de robe* and the Calvinism of the bourgeoisie both contained exactly the same complex of beliefs and yet the ethical imperatives were completely opposed: one exhorting withdrawal from the world, and the other intense worldly activity. Lovell (1973) wants to suggest that

> the 'fit' between ideas and social situation is never more than imperfect; that ideas, religious beliefs, literary expressions, etc., can be put to uses in social life to which they are intrinsically little adapted. This is especially true of abstract and general ideas, and it is certainly true of all the great 'world religions', whose imperatives for conduct are wide open for interpretation in every case.

Similarly, Vallier (1962) in his study of Mormons and Re-Organites shows how these two groups with identical values, beliefs and missionary outlook arrived at different solutions to missionary manpower imperatives. He shows the need to take account of the immediate social setting as the context in which beliefs are operationalised. Weber too was more aware of this relationship in his later *Religionssoziologie* than in *The Protestant Ethic and Spirit of Capitalism*.

It is not therefore in the nature of beliefs to prescribe in exact detail what is or is not to be done; at best they determine general shape and limits within which action can vary. It is at this point that we need to be more precise about the relationship of one belief to another in order that we can make clear their characteristic relationship to behaviour. Beliefs do not usually exist in isolation but as part of an extended and elaborate web of attitudes, beliefs and values. These structures of belief, these cognitive or theological cosmologies, may not prescribe in detail the required action, but they nevertheless tend to define, map or create what constitutes our reality, shape and sustain our world, interpret it for us and help us to grasp its manifold complexities. A number of writers (Douglas, 1966, 1970, 1973; Jarvie, 1972; Peel, 1973; Budd, 1973) have recently focused upon this characteristic quality of belief systems to provide our cluttered and confused social life with some structure, clarity and consistency. Mary Douglas (1966) has studied this propensity of men to create a 'unity of experience' which eschews ambiguity, contradiction and anomaly. In this way systems of cognitive classification, socially given, 'have as their main function to impose system on an inherently untidy experience', to provide 'a positive pattern in which ideas and values are tidily ordered'. Susan Budd (1973) writing within the context of the sociology of religion emphasises, likewise, that the central question of what is the role of religion in society 'is to be found in that layer of fragmentary, unrealized, emotionally charged symbols and beliefs which structure reality for us and make common understanding possible'. We shall be looking therefore to relate (and by connection thus explain) individual attitudes, expressions, ideas and beliefs to some more total, coherent and comprehensive structure of cognitive classification. Thus we might hope to understand and explain an attitude towards Church reform, or an attitude towards ecumenism, by relating them to some belief-system or churchmanship, 'Anglo-Catholic' or 'Evangelical', for example (cf. chapter 3).

Once more the logic of this argument has a powerful and seductive charm and one should therefore beware. While some of us do possess such all-encompassing avowedly held structures of thought whose rigorous internal logic is lucid and clarifies all, many of us possess beliefs and values which are related in a much more uncritical, unexamined and confused manner. Some of our values may be adopted from socially given general cosmologies, but many attitudes may be learnt in quite specific contests. As Susan Budd (1973) says:

> the research into the operation of reference groups illuminates
> the way in which general concepts such as 'fairness' and
> 'justice' are built up from specific contexts and a standard of
> acceptable behaviour established. It is this which produces
> such widespread inconsistencies between beliefs, between actions
> and between beliefs and actions.

To what extent therefore are the belief systems of clergy, priests and ministers unified or contingent and disjointed? We are interested in the way, therefore, certain attitudes or beliefs stand outside the general pattern; or the way in which religious functionaries may state a general attitude towards the reform of the Church and yet hold specific beliefs about particular reforms which may appear quite contradictory to or inconsistent with the general view; or the way in which there may exist a lacuna or disjunction between precept and practice—for example, between a belief in ecumenical co-operation and a reluctance to preach or celebrate the eucharist in the church of another denomination.

Beliefs and belief systems of religious functionaries may be largely independent of the denominational setting: for example, an Anglican clergyman may claim to be an 'Anglo-Catholic' a theological cosmology which has perhaps more in common with the Roman Catholic Church than the Church of England. Yet such an exogenous belief system is not necessarily typical and in a great

many instances beliefs are completely homologous with the denomination, that is an integral part of the Church's structural and
institutional tradition. What exactly, however, is this 'denominational' influence upon behaviour and belief?

Denominations are simultaneously both cultural institutions and
structural organisations, that is, they embody on the one hand a
shared framework of enduring rules, procedures, values, theological
imperatives which define appropriate and expected conduct—
'institutionalisation involves formalised procedures that perpetrate
organising principles of social life from generation to generation'
(Blau, 1964)—and on the other hand a persisting structural differentiation of social relations, roles, positions and groups: 'It is not
simply, therefore, that the notion of "structure" presupposes
distinguishable elements but that these elements constitute a system
which displays a minimum persistence over time and is in principle
comparable with other similarly identifiable systems' (Runciman,
1969). Denominations will therefore seek to achieve continuity and
endurance in a number of ways, but two are critically important
—first, denominational socialisation and, second, regulating conduct
by clearly defining an hierarchical structure of positions and roles.
We take the latter first. Locating a person within an organisational
hierarchy introduces us overtly to a defined role, incorporating
prescribed behaviour and the kind of sanctions which seek to exact
correct performance. It also introduces us perhaps more significantly
to the crucial experience of subordination or superordination: an
incumbent of a prestigious office is more likely to be imbued with
the appropriate values and to have proved himself competent in
performing necessary liturgical and administrative rituals, whereas,
correspondingly, those in positions of subordination we might
expect to be less bound by denominational conventions or practices
and so prepared to adopt a more detached and radical stance
towards the Church in which they work. Also, organisational roles
entail different contents and degrees of prescription; some organisational members face more uncertainties than others. Payne and
Mansfield (1973), amongst others, have shown the way in which
one's position in the organisation affects the views that one has.

Denominational socialisation is a more subtle and persuasive
process by which the church seeks to exact conformity. Whereas
hierarchical differentiation achieves spatial control, socialisation is
much more of a temporal process in that gradually through time
members are instilled with the approved values, beliefs, sentiments,
thoughts and also the imperative skills, rituals, customary habits;
in short, they constrain members to believe and to act in prescribed
ways. We would expect therefore those clergy, priests and ministers
who have been exposed to the same denominational experiences

over a considerable period of time to have internalised the values and practices of their respective Churches and to adhere to their respective Churches' approaches, if there is such a thing, to the canons of 'ministry', reform, ecumenism and so on. We should also expect the theological colleges, the seminaries to play an important role in moulding acceptable standards and patterns of behaviour. Thus, we are interested in the theological colleges that clergy, ministers and priests attend, the length of time they have been ordained, the amount of time they have spent in particular positions, etc.

Within the denominational context the influences of beliefs and the institutional structure of the Churches themselves will be the crucial explanatory factors in accounting for, and predicting, behaviour. Yet our third category of explanatory factors comprises a number of important influences upon behaviour—age and social and professional experiences. Age is customarily conceived by sociologists as an important factor in explanation, the usual conjecture being that the older a person becomes the more conservative he will inevitably become. The process of ageing is seen to represent incipient decay and an increasing inability to respond with flexibility to new situations and problems. We are interested therefore in the degree to which this piece of 'conventional wisdom' is reflected in our religious functionaries—is it true that the older clergy, priests and ministers are less amenable to 'reform', 'ecumenism' or whatever? Sociologists have traditionally been preoccupied with the influence of social class upon the belief, perceptions and behaviour of particular social strata. Social class has been conceived as the determinant of consciousness, the mould for ways of life and life chances. Yet in our survey what exactly is the influence of social class upon the attitudes and values of clergy, priests and ministers? A further possible factor which has been commonly used for explanatory purposes is that of education. Apart from their theological college education, religious functionaries have a variety of other educational experiences.

III

Before going on to delineate our conceptual scheme in more detail it is important to examine some of the past work that has concentrated on religious functionaries.

Whereas it is true to say that in Britain the treatment given by sociologists to the religious functionary has been relatively impoverished, this has not been the case elsewhere. A literature of considerable size has accumulated which concentrates on various aspects of American clergy. Much of it is solidly empirical. The most frequently encountered problem to which American sociologists have addressed themselves is that of the nature of the 'role problems' of clergy. As has frequently been noted, the clergy in largely secular societies tend to find many of their traditional roles increasingly appropriated by secular specialists like social workers, psychiatrists, counsellors and school teachers. At the same time, new responsibilities have appeared: as ecclesiastical institutions become more and more bureaucratised at both national and local levels, so the minister finds himself confronted with a whole range of administrative and organisational tasks which take up large chunks of his time, yet which seem subsidiary to his more obvious functions. The issues then become: exactly *what* is the role of the minister and how does he respond to these changing circumstances?

Most of the research concerned with the role problems of American clergy takes the work of Blizzard (1956) as its starting point. His research showed that although ministers rated their administrative role as the least important and one of the roles they enjoyed least, it was the responsibility which they spent most time on. Similarly, a study of pastors and ex-pastors in the United Church of Christ discovered that both groups found their organisational and administrative tasks the least enjoyable of their responsibilities. Such is also the case with Roman Catholic priests in the USA. A study by Stewart (1969) of priests in an 'inner-city ministry' found that 'too much time was being invested in administrative functions much against the desires of the respondents'. Hall and Schneider's (1973) study shows that priests attached considerably less importance to administration than to their parochial, community involvement, and personal development tasks. Pastors, however, were much more likely than curates or those in special ministries to confirm the importance of administrative tasks. Hall and Schneider found that pastors spent far more time on administrative tasks than the other two groups of Roman Catholic priests and are therefore more firmly wedded into the bureaucratic work of the diocese, a factor which presumably accounts for their greater inclination to regard such work as important.

The subject of the role problems of the clergy has also been tackled from the viewpoint of parishioners. Here an important contradiction emerges. For while ministers are expected not to spend too much time on administrative and organisational tasks, as the research of Glock and Stark (1965) indicates, they are none the less expected to be good at such tasks, as is suggested by a survey of Protestant congregations by Lauer (1973). This confirms the evidence derived from the study of Springdale by Vidich and Bensman (1958) which drew the conclusion that if a clergyman was lacking in these abilities he was a poor minister.

Another area where there has been a growth of American literature is concerned with the views of ministers on important social and political issues of the day (e.g. support for civil rights, anti-Vietnam demonstrations, Black Power movements and the like) and the factors which condition such views. For example, Stark and his colleagues (1971) examine the ways in which adherence to certain doctrines and orthodoxies 'spills over' onto the extent to which clergy delivered sermons on political issues. Similarly, recent research by Winter (1970) confirms that of Cox (1967) and other writers that

> a societal orientation, such as that of the 'new breed' of clergy, is linked to views on how to fulfil obligations in the secular realm; to beliefs about the role of the church in obstructing change; and to conceptions of the proper tactics of reform efforts.

Theological cosmology has also been of considerable interest. Both Johnson (1967) and Hadden (1969) have found that liberals in a theological sense are also more liberal in views on social and economic affairs than are their conservative and fundamentalist brethren. The research of Jud *et al.* (1970) indicates that pastors in the United Church of Christ show a marked tendency to become theological liberals.

Not all such research has been concerned with employing strictly religious or theological categories to discriminate between clergy of different views. A recent study of Roman Catholic priests by Struzzo (1970) shows the extent to which 'professionalism' affects a priest's views on a variety of issues. Those priests who were categorised as 'professionals' were found to be more likely than 'non-professionals' to dissent from the papal edict over birth control, to experiment with new liturgy, to invite non-Catholics to communion, and to readmit divorced or remarried persons to the sacraments. These findings lead Struzzo to conclude:

> as an ideology, professionalism is not simply related to individual issues, but rather serves as a basic foundation for response to a wide range of pastoral issues . . . the more professional a priest is, the more he tends to deviate from the institutionalised norms of the hierarchy in resolving pastoral issues.

Thus American sociologists of religion have carried out a great deal of research which has examined how clergy view their role, their attitudes on a variety of issues, both endemic to the Church and of a more general nature, and the correlates of these attitudes. In addition, there has been a good deal of sociological work on American clergy which derives more from a sociology of occupations perspective. Fichter's (1961) book on Roman Catholic priests is concerned with problems like: What sorts of people become priests and why? From which social strata do they originate? How are they trained? What does their work entail and to what extent do they constitute a profession? The latter issue has been taken up by a number of people. Some, like Glasse (1968) agreed with Fichter that clergy do indeed constitute a profession, a view which has been further endorsed in Britain by both Leslie Paul (1964) and Dunstan (1967). Others, like Gannon (1971), offer a dissenting view which asserts that clergy are a profession only in certain senses but not in others. It is not our intention to become embroiled in this dispute, although we do believe that an occupation may exhibit a professional attitude in dealings with people and in the work, a view which is in line with Gannon's suggestion that whether clergy constitute a profession or not is an empirical problem.

The little research undertaken by British sociologists such as Towler (1969) and Coxon (1965) on Anglican ordinands, by Morgan (1969) on Anglican diocesan bishops, and by Carlton (1968) on the Baptist minister, has been concerned with recruitment issues like: Who become clergy? From which social strata? Where were they educated? What type of vocation do they have? The Paul Report (Paul, 1964), which still contains about the largest amount of data on the Anglican clergyman, is a largely descriptive study of the nature of the Anglican ministry. It drew on the work of Coxon and Morgan for some of the information on recruitment. Very little research seems to have been carried out on the role problems of the clergy. Opinion poll data has often been a source of information on how the British people view the clergyman. A Gallup Poll survey concluded that the minister of religion is thought to be 'influential in the community, devoted to public service, useful in the parish, sincere, overworked and underpaid'.

The fact that the clergyman not only has status problems such as these but also role problems is thus avoided in the literature, although there is some indication that there are problems. Of the clergy surveyed by Paul, 59 per cent said they would most like to spend more time on reading, and 34 per cent cited parish administration as the activity with which they would like most help.

The research of Daniel (1967) on ninety-six Anglican clergy in Greater London looked at some of the areas which American sociologists have tackled. For example, he found that of the six roles examined in Blizzard's research the pastoral role was regarded as the most important with 53 per cent endorsing it as the most important; 17 per cent the role of priest; 8 per cent preacher; 6 per cent teacher; 0 per cent organiser/administrator. Moreover, those who categorised themselves as Evangelicals were far more likely to enjoy the role of preacher, than 'Catholics' who were more likely to enjoy their pastoral and priestly functions. Daniel's respondents were asked whether they were in favour of a number of reforms suggested by the Paul Report. Evangelicals were found to be more resistant to change than Catholics.

IV

As this brief survey demonstrates, the dominant thrust of this research, particularly in the USA, has been to focus on the clergy as an occupation and the religious functionary as a role player. Both of these approaches operate at a level which misses much of the appropriate context within which most religious functionaries operate, that of the institution.

The occupational model is, in some senses, too general and abstract for the sociology of religion unless one asks the question: Do religious functionaries belonging to different organisations constitute different occupations? For the sociology of religion it is intra-religious variations which are crucial. For occupational sociology it is the comparison between religious and other occupations which has been central. Concepts such as occupation or profession sensitise a level wider than one institution and their considerable use for the sociology of religion is to highlight the way in which members of the religious occupation differ from other occupations in terms of task, background, recruitment, career development etc. Thus the emphasis on the question of professionalism leads to comparison with teachers, psychiatrists, etc. (cf. Naegele, 1956) and to examining generalised occupational beliefs and occupational organisation, treating 'clergy' as a general occupational category.

As already stated our aim is to examine differences within the religious sphere and the question of whether Anglican clergy constitute more of an occupation than Methodist ministers, while interesting to some, is not critical. However, the work on religious roles could be seen as considerably more promising. The concept itself though is a problematic one. We would go a long way towards agreeing with Coulson and Riddell (1970) that role is at best a difficult and possibly misleading concept and at worst an irrelevant one. While we have suggested that the concept of occupation may possibly be too broad for the central concerns of the sociology of religion, role is too limited. The concept of role can lead one away from the organisational and institutional level at which so much that we categorise as religion operates. The religious functionary invariably is an organisational member embedded within an organisational structure, deriving his position from the place of his embedment, trained by that organisation and dependent on it for his future. The concept of role can tend to lead away from such

16

considerations, away from an examination of the experiences that structure belief and position. Role leads to a consideration of the immediate interactive situation in which the role player finds himself.

We have identified a central area in the sociology of religion as the relationship between beliefs on the one hand and historical/ institutional factors on the other. We have also followed others in suggesting that the clergy constitute a group in crisis. This crisis comes in part from the disjunction between the avowed aims of Churches and the organisational means and resources at their disposal for achieving them. Thus one is led to a framework of initially examining the nexus of beliefs and attitudes held by clergy, in general terms, about their position and functions and, in specific terms, about the reforms, developments and changes necessary to move out of crisis, e.g. restructuring the Church, participating in the ecumenical movement.

To explain the pattern of belief among clergy it is no good asking questions concerning occupation and it is not too germane to ask about role in the way in which previous studies within the sociology of religion have handled this. One must examine the kinds of experience that the individual clergyman has had; it is for this reason that the sociologist deals with age, education, class, etc. One must examine the nature of the organisational setting in which he operates and one must discover the wide-ranging encapsulating beliefs that he has developed.

We have so far attempted to isolate the factors which will be crucial for any explanation of our religious functionaries' attitudes towards ministry, reform, ecumenism and so on without yet, except occasionally and tacitly, seeing how they relate to each other in complex ways. This is because the literature itself is not very helpful on the interrelationships between factors such as age, social origins, organisational position and belief, on the one hand, and ecumenicity, reform and organisational orientation on the other. But at least a preliminary model is necessary to guide data collection and analysis and carry it beyond demonstrating that, for example, organisational position is related to support for ecumenism. We wish to go some way towards presenting a total view of the position of the clergyman, the minister and the priest.

To present an initial model two simplifications will be made. First, it will be assumed that the action of the independent variables such as age, position, etc. is the same on all of the dependent variables. While this is a useful starting point, it is, in fact, empirically unlikely that the effect would be the same for ecumenism as for organisational perceptions. However, this can be left for the moment as an empirical question. Second, it will also be assumed that the same model will operate for clergy, ministers and priests. In a sense, our general null hypothesis is that there will be no differences between these three groups. Again, the extent to which our model is applicable to these groups will be subject to empirical test.

A causal model of the kind envisaged entails disentangling two types of relationships: first, between the individual explanatory variables and the different dependent variables; second, between the explanatory variables themselves in order to evaluate their relative impact. The basis of the ordering of the causal variables can be partly chronological. Variables such as social class origins occur before general education which then can be conceptualised as determining Church educational experiences, leading to a particular first denominational position and so on. Other variables, such as age and beliefs are not so clearly chronological but have an important part to play in any causal scheme.

We would suggest that the starting point for constructing any model that attempts to explain the way in which religious function-aries see ecumenism, reform, their ministry and the organisations in which they work, is their belief systems. Religious organisations have their basis in belief systems and their full-time members tend to get a rigorous training in the theological systems and values of their Church. Such theological beliefs systems have direct impact on more specific ideas such as the nature of the Church as an organisation, the relationship of one Church to another and so on. Hinings and Foster (1973) have suggested with regard to Church organisation that theologies can be seen as having a direct impact. A theology that emphasises the transmission of beliefs through a priestly hierarchy will produce different attitudes about, for example, priestly roles from that of a theology that stresses individual 'soul competency'. Harris (1969) showed that the variety of theological positions found among clergy in a diocese of the Anglican Church in Wales had implications for attitudes towards reform.

However, for us, beliefs go beyond the theological to include the occupational conception that a minister, clergyman or priest has of himself, of who the community of the faith are and of how their affairs should be ordered and governed. The extent to which they define themselves as professionals has implications for role definition in a variety of situations, for their views of the organisation in which they work and so on. The work of Struzzo (1970) suggests that priests who espouse the belief systems of professionalism (such as autonomy in work, colleagues as reference, etc.) are more likely to be radical in outlook and thus one would expect them to be more reform-orientated.

Although we are arguing for beliefs to occupy a central position in the model we also wish to show the causal paths relating to such

18

beliefs and to suggest that other variables will have direct effects on our dependent variables. Beliefs of both kinds, i.e. theological and occupational, are formed by previous experience and modified or reinforced by current experiences. So we would hypothesise that the age of a religious functionary is indicative of a particular time of socialisation into a set of beliefs and also reflects the possible process of increasing conservatism with ageing. But, as well as expecting age to be related to belief, because it is a rough and ready index of a whole range of personal experiences we would also hypothesise a direct relationship between age and reform, ecumenism, etc.

Turning to aspects of the denominational setting we would, as with age, hypothesise both indirect and direct effects on our dependent variables. Denominational variables are made up of both past experiences and current influences. The former consist of such things as the theological college or seminary attended, the age at which a person was ordained, the number of posts he has held. We would expect all of these to affect beliefs, particularly the theological college attended, where the initial patterns are laid down. Other aspects of past denominational experiences we would suggest also have direct effects. For example, the numbers and kinds of posts an individual has held could be expected to have an effect on his perceptions about organisations or his feelings about the need for reform.

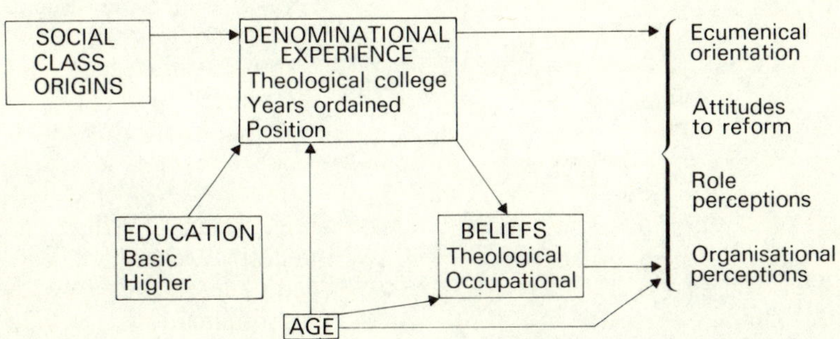

FIGURE 1.1   *A model of religious orientations*

The current denominational influences are the position that one of our religious functionary holds and the context of the ministry in which he serves. While these will be related to belief, either modifying or reinforcing, they are probably more likely to have direct effects. Hall and Schneider (1973) have demonstrated that the position a priest holds is related to his activity in the organisation and the rating that he gives to an administrative role. In a wider context, Payne and Mansfield (1973) have demonstrated the impact that one's organisational position has on one's conception of aspects of the organisation's structure.

To round out the model we would further suggest that the theological college attended and the kinds of denominational experience that a religious functionary can expect will be at least partly determined by education received and social class background. The overall model is then as shown in Figure 1.1.

Thus our aim in this book is to delineate the general beliefs and attitudes of religious functionaries in the three Churches to their organisations and role, to examine their attitudes to the specific issues of reform and ecumenism which are so often seen as the answers to their 'crisis', and to relate these to the general and organisational experiences that they have had.

In the next two chapters we will deal with the first half of the model, namely delineating the origins and current characteristics of clergy, ministers and priests and then detailing their beliefs. This will be followed by four chapters dealing one by one with each of the dependent variables, leaving the drawing together and general testing of the model to the final chapter.

2 Positions, experience, origins

Any survey of a social collectivity must of necessity focus upon certain descriptive social and demographic characteristics of that group, however mundane some of the information may appear, if it is to achieve a well-rounded understanding. We are interested, therefore, in what positions the religious functionaries hold within their Church organisation; how old they are and what kind of experience they have had; from what social class they originate and what form of education they have received.

This kind of information is crucial in two respects: in the first place, no description or classification of the group, religious functionaries, can be complete without it; but a second and more important consideration is that descriptive vignettes are a preliminary exercise preparatory to the more essential task of explanation, that is, the position members hold, their age and experience and their social origins are all central factors which can help us to explain and account for behaviour, beliefs and attitudes by providing crucial antecedent ('initial') conditions. As we have suggested earlier these factors and conditions may not be the only explanatory variables but they are likely to be significant and must be taken into account amongst others. This is because in describing such things as a person's age, his education, his career development, we are summarising his experiences. The behaviour and attitudes exhibited by an individual are an admixture of his current situation and other situations through which he has passed which lead him to expect certain kinds of reactions, which in turn lead him to explain events in particular ways. The so-called socio-demographic variables so common to sociological analysis, such as age, sex, social class, are used as secondary indicators of complex social processes. Our initial aim, then, is to spell out the characteristics of our samples along such dimensions. From now on the various chapters in the book will be presenting material collected by means of a mail questionnaire from samples of Anglican clergy, Methodist ministers and Roman Catholic priests. The numbers concerned are 564 clergy, 251 ministers and 412 priests. Full details of the sampling and methodology are given in Appendix 1 and the questionnaire is contained in Appendix 2.

I Positions

One of the most important defining characteristics of the member of a social group is the position he holds within its social hierarchy. Locating a person within an organisational hierarchy introduces us to the kind of behaviour which is prescribed and expected; but a more important consequence of such a location is the chance to discover the very important effect that the experience of subordination or superordination has upon beliefs and attitudes: that is, those in a position of subordination, emancipated from the contricting ties of formal office—managerial, financial, administrative —might be expected to hold more radical attitudes towards the organisation within which they work. The notion of position summarises both the kinds of organisational experiences that a respondent is likely to have had and also the nature of his role. In the context of the Roman Catholic Church Hall and Schneider (1973)

TABLE 2.1   *Positions*

		Church of England	*Roman Catholic*	*Methodist*
		%	%	%
Were you an				
Incumbent/Parish Priest?	Yes	72.9	45	
	No	27.1	55	
If not, were you				
Curate/assistant priest		65.4	53.8	
Chaplain		15.1	27.0	
Rural dean/dean		17.5	12.8	
Hierarchy (bishop/archdeacon, etc.)		2.0	3.2	
Other		0	3.2	
Probationer minister				2.1
Supernumerary minister (still working)				4.2
Sector minister				7.1
Minister				56.5
Circuit superintendent				29.7
Chairman				0.4

have demonstrated the way in which position relates to attitudes. In a wider context, Payne and Mansfield (1973) have shown how it relates to perceptions about the nature of the organisation.

What therefore were the positions of clergy, priests and ministers? The great majority of clergy were incumbents, responsible for a parish. A substantial proportion of the remainder were curates, chaplains or deans as Table 2.1 shows. Within the Roman Catholic Church, priests who responded tended to represent a rather different position within the hierarchical spectrum. Only 45 per cent of priests were parish priests as such and the greatest proportion of those who were not incumbents were assistant priests and chaplains, that is, those priests not as yet fully established within the Roman Catholic Church. In the Methodist Church, half of our respondents were ministers as such while a solid proportion represented 'supervisory' levels: 30 per cent held the position of circuit superintendent.

This shows differences between the Churches which could result in attitudinal variation. The Methodist Church has no curacy system; the probationary minister serves his term (in charge of a church) and quickly becomes a fully fledged minister. Similarly, Methodism lays little stress on ministry outside the normal pattern of serving a geographically based congregation, so there are few chaplains (sector ministers). The basic experience that every Methodist minister has is that of working with a congregation (shown by 84 per cent being in this category). The episcopal Churches on the other hand have extensive curacies, specialist chaplains and a relatively well-developed hierarchy. The Anglican and Roman Catholic Churches provide the possibility of differences in outlook developing from the different tasks that members undertake. The Methodist Church is liable to present a unified set of experiences whereas there is the possibility of different patterns in the other Churches.

II Age and experience

Having defined the clergy, priests and ministers who compose our survey we can proceed to describe some of their demographic characteristics: how old they were, the number of years they had been ordained, the number of positions or incumbencies they had held, the years they had spent in their present position, and the amount of time they had worked in their present dioceses or districts.

It has long been a part of 'conventional wisdom' that the older a person becomes so the more conservative he becomes as an inevitable corollary; this proposition as such might be arguable and require empirical confirmation, yet the notion of one's age as constituting a crucially significant factor in shaping behaviour and precept remains sound. Ageing reflects two processes. One is that the basic processes of acquiring values took place in the past thus leading to a more conservative belief structure. The other is that ageing itself is a process of decay which makes change more difficult. Age represents exposure to more experiences which often cumulatively show the difficulties of change.

Table 2.2 gives details of the age structure of the three Churches. Even though a greater proportion of our Anglican sample were established incumbents it is interesting to note that clergy as a whole were relatively younger than the priests or ministers in our survey. Thirty-four per cent of the clergy were under the age of 39 which compares with 26 per cent priests and 25 per cent of ministers. If we focus upon the priests, however, we discover that 50 per cent of them were over the age of 50, as against 47 per cent of ministers and 43 per cent of clergy. This is particularly interesting when we remember that many priests were in relatively junior positions within the Roman Catholic hierarchy—in general where relatively elderly people have been kept in positions of inferiority and sub-ordination for long periods one might seriously expect to discover attitudes of dissent, resentment or disenchantment. When we subsequently focus upon the attitudes of priests we shall need to discover to what extent this generalisation is true or not.

TABLE 2.2   *Age*

Age	Church of England	Roman Catholic	Methodist
	%	%	%
−30	6.9 ⎱ 34.3	4.7 ⎱ 26.5	2.9 ⎱ 25.2
30–39	27.4 ⎰	21.8 ⎰	22.3 ⎰
40–44	12.6 ⎱ 22.6	10.7 ⎱ 24.9	14.7 ⎱ 27.3
45–49	10.0 ⎰	14.2 ⎰	12.6 ⎰
50–54	10.7	14.2	15.1
55–59	13.7	13.3	13.9
60–64	9.8 ⎭ 43.1	12.4 ⎭ 48.6	12.2 ⎭ 47.5
65–69	6.8	5.7	5.5
70 +	2.1	3.0	0.8

In the Methodist Church most ministers, that is 53.8 per cent lay within the age categories 45–64, something which is also true for priests (54 per cent), but not for clergy (44 per cent).

Of course, as a general point one has to note something which has often been commented upon, that is, the age structure of all three

Churches is very much skewed towards 'old' age This fits in with the difficulties that the established religious groupings have experienced in recruitment. Indeed, many of the projected reforms in Churches have been at least partly in response to manpower problems and an ageing 'workforce' (cf. Paul, 1964).

Age has traditionally been accredited as an important category which can help us to explain beliefs and attitudes. But the notion of a man's experience as being a crucial antecedent condition quite independent of age is less fashionable. This is probably because age is seen as summing experience. But the length of time a man has spent within a profession—what we might call 'career experience'—and the time spent within a particular role or within a particular physical and social environment—what we might call 'local experience'—can reveal the degree to which a person is likely to have internalised the values or follows prescribed procedures of his profession, role or local organisational unit. Experience as such, therefore, can be qualitatively different from age in determining behaviour and attitudes. Age sums a very wide range of experiences (all those of one's life to date!), whereas we may often need to summarise and indicate more particular experiences.

A religious functionary might be middle-aged yet have only recently been ordained into his chosen Church; the years that the clergy, priests and ministers have been ordained, therefore, is a crucial statistic informing us of the degree of experience they have of their chosen vocation.

TABLE 2.3   *Years ordained*

Years	Church of England	Roman Catholic	Methodist
	%	%	%
0–9	33.4	20.8	19.0
10–19	26.8	21.2	33.2
20 +	39.8	58.0	47.8

Statistics on ordination generally reinforce those for age, particularly for Roman Catholic priests, in that a significant number of clergy have been ordained relatively recently while the great majority of priests and ministers have been ordained for a considerable number of years; we must note especially that 58 per cent of priests have been ordained for over 20 years (see Table 2.3).

The number of positions and incumbencies that clergy, priests and ministers have held provide further evidence of experience, of the length and depth of careers. The clergy appear to represent a reasonably conventional career pattern: a few years in positions of subordination prior to being granted a position of responsibility. Under a quarter of clergy were not incumbents, while a large number were undertaking their first or second incumbency, as Table 2.4 demonstrates.

TABLE 2.4   *Numbers of positions and incumbencies*

| | Church of England | | Roman Catholic | | Methodist |
	Positions	Incumbencies	Positions	Incumbencies	Positions
	%	%	%	%	%
0	0	24.0	0	43.9	0
1–2	29.0	58.3	21.6	41.9	19.4
3–5	54.1	17.1	52.6	13.7	43.3
6 +	16.9	0.6	25.8	0.5	37.3

Within the Catholic Church, however, 44 per cent of priests have been parish priests, while nearly 80 per cent of the sample of priests as a whole have held three or more positions. This suggests that a good many priests have been in the Church for a substantial period of time as assistant priests, and can expect to be moved around in positions of subordination, far more so than those within the Church of England.

The Methodist Church, we must remember, is in a rather different position on this subject as it is the practice of the Church to move ministers regularly, both within a district and between districts.

TABLE 2.5   *Years in present position*

Years: Anglican/Catholic	Methodist	Church of England	Roman Catholic	Methodist
		%	%	%
0–4	− 1–1	50.7	39.2	22.4
5–9	2–4	27.5	29.8	51.8
10 +	5 +	21.7	30.0	25.8

We have considered the amount of experience, 'career experience', that the clergy, priests or ministers have had as religious functionaries. But the amount of experience, the length of time spent within a particular position or locality can be crucially important factors in shaping attitudes and beliefs: someone who has lived and worked within an organisation for a considerable period of time is more likely to have internalised prevailing values and to generally follow prescribed rules and procedures. Staying in a particular diocese or district over a long period of time allows the functionary to routinise his work, to establish more certainty about his relations with others, to become used to the established ways of doing things.

In general the Roman Catholic priest can expect to spend longer in each position than the Anglican clergyman. Table 2.5 gives details. It is necessary to point out here that the 'scale' of years is different for Methodist ministers, covering much less time because of the practice of regular movement in that Church. Indeed, as many as 74 per cent have only been in their present position for up to 4 years.

The second statistic of local experience constitutes the number of years clergy, priests and ministers have spent within their diocese or district; we are interested in discovering the degree to which religious functionaries have become moulded and shaped by the social organisation within which they work. The figures are given in Table 2.6. Again the Roman Catholic priest can expect to have spent far more of his working life in fewer dioceses than his Anglican counterpart. This, of course, reflects the way in which a priest is attached to a diocese with relatively little subsequent expectation of moving from that diocese. Again the 'scale' is different for Methodists because of their much greater movement.

TABLE 2.6 *Years in diocese/district*

Years: Anglican/Catholic	Methodist	Church of England	Roman Catholic	Methodist
		%	%	%
0–9	— 1–1	61.3	23.2	16.9
10–19	2–3	24.7	21.5	28.4
20–29	4–5	8.4	25.1	24.1
30 +	6 +	5.5	30.3	30.6

We can then say that the Anglican clergyman is generally younger than his equivalent within the Roman Catholic or Methodist Church; his career within the Church has tended to be shorter in that he has been ordained more recently and has held fewer positions and incumbencies; he has also tended to have had less local experience in that he has occupied his present position and has worked within his present diocese for a shorter period of time than priests in the Catholic Church.

Certain facets of the priestly career need emphasising: the priest can perhaps expect to spend a far greater proportion of his career as an assistant priest, assuming two, three or more positions in a subordinate role, than the Anglican clergyman or Methodist minister. He can also expect to spend far more time in each position, whether as an assistant or a parish priest, than clergy and minister, and to be located within fewer dioceses than clergy throughout his career.

III Social class and education

It is a universal feature of all societies that they are hierarchically divided into social strata. Sociologists have thus long been pre-occupied, often myopically, with the overarching influence of social class upon its members' beliefs and behaviour. Social class is purported to be the determinant of consciousness, the formulator of life chances and the conditioner of the styles of life and behaviour of its members.

Social class and education are intimately interrelated. Much research has focused upon the manner in which education merely seems to reflect or reinforce the influence of social class. Taken together, therefore, both provide crucial indicators of the effect, if any, that social origins have.

TABLE 2.7   *Social class. (When you were 18 years old what was your father's occupation?)*

	Church of England		Roman Catholic		Methodist	
	%		%		%	
I Employer/manager	12.0		9.2		3.8	
		49.1		28.6		29.3
Professional	37.1		19.4		25.5	
II Intermediate and junior non-manual	16.7		19.1		17.3	
		42.9		42.5		60.5
Personal service	6.3		6.6		19.2	
Foreman/supervisor	19.9		16.8		24.0	
III Unskilled manual	1.6		7.2		2.4	
Agricultural worker	0.5	5.5	19.7	28.9	1.9	5.3
Armed forces	3.4		2.0		1.0	
Other	2.5	2.5	0	0	4.8	4.8

No description of clergy, priests and ministers would be complete therefore without some account of the kind of background in which they grew up and Table 2.7 gives details. Clergy tend to originate from the middle and upper echelons of the social hierarchy: on the one hand, the fathers of many clergymen (49 per cent) were professional men, employers or managers; on the other hand, their fathers tended to have been supervisors or to have worked in personal service or in intermediate and junior non-manual jobs.

The social class origins of ministers and priests are distincty different in kind from clergy. Most ministers have grown up in lower-middle-class homes although a substantial number have come from backgrounds which are professional or managerial. The social class membership of priests' fathers is more evenly distributed between the three classes: the significant category, however, is that of farm workers (20 per cent); one of the Catholic urban dioceses reported that 35 per cent of their elder generation were farm workers.

The evidence we have accumulated on the education of clergy, priests and ministers does indeed suggest that the religious functionaries have received an education which both reflects and reinforces the disparate social class origins, as Table 2.8 shows. Clergy, for instance, have predominantly been to grammar or public school (35 per cent went to public school). Following secondary education, as many as 73.4 per cent went to university, where they tended to study humanities and theology. Most, that is 85 per cent, received a bachelor's degree, half of whom proceeded to qualify for a master's degree.

It can be seen again that the experience of priests and ministers has been qualitatively different. Far fewer ministers went to public school (12.6 per cent) while a substantial proportion went to the less esteemed elementary, technical or comprehensive schools. Following this secondary education far fewer proceeded to university

TABLE 2.8 *Secondary education*

	Church of England	Roman Catholic	Methodist
	%	%	%
Elementary	7.0	11.8	26.8
Technical	4.1	1.2	5.9
Comprehensive	1.4	1.2	0.4
Grammar	50.1	58.3	54.0
Public	34.9	22.8	12.6
Other	2.5	4.8	0.4

—only 23 per cent. Of those who did reach university the educational pattern was, however, similar to that of clergymen: ministers studied humanities and theology, 81 per cent receiving a bachelor's degree (34 per cent a master's degree).

The secondary education of priests is a little more complicated. Fifty per cent went to a grammar school and 25 per cent to a public school—but it is quite probable that a great many of this category went to a Roman Catholic public school rather than the conventional secularly financed public school. Like the Methodist ministers, very few priests received a university education (22 per cent). Of those who did study at university the usual pattern was followed—studying humanities and theology—72 per cent being awarded a bachelor's degree. It is at this point that a rather interesting feature of Roman Catholic education arises; for, even though a small proportion of priests have received a university education, a relatively large proportion of those with such an education are highly qualified—44 per cent have a higher degree (30 per cent a master's degree and 14 per cent a doctorate). This evidence might suggest that some attention is given by the Church to selecting only those pupils/students who are clearly likely to benefit from a university education. In both the Anglican and Methodist Churches, particularly the former, university education is liable to occur before theological college and as a choice of the individual. In the Roman Catholic Church it is much more likely that it will be part of the whole process of guiding the would-be priest.

The theological education of religious functionaries appears at the very close of their formative years yet is perhaps one of the most important stages in shaping values and framing attitudes. We are able to classify the colleges which clergy attended according to the churchmanship to which they ascribe. In doing this we use general labels espoused by the Anglican Church, which will be explicated in more detail in chapter 3. Most of the clergy attended a college which pursues an essentially 'Catholic' or 'Central' and 'Broad Church' theological style (see Table 2.9).

TABLE 2.9   *Anglican theological college*

College	*Percentage*
Anglo-Catholic	13.2
Prayer-Book Catholic	31.5
Central or Broad Church	22.3
Modernist	6.7
Liberal Evangelical	16.4
Conservative Evangelical	9.9

It is not possible to adopt the same form of classification when studying the theological colleges of the Roman Catholic Church and the Methodist Church. As far as the latter is concerned, the Methodist Church is said to attempt to ensure that their theological colleges do not develop individual theological stances; as we shall see in later chapters this claim is largely upheld in that there is generally no very clear association between the theological college a minister has been to and the beliefs and attitudes he has towards particular issues. Our sample was spread over Handsworth, Hartley Victoria, Richmond, Headingley, Wesley Hall and Didsbury colleges mainly. These six accounted for 91 per cent of the sample, with the largest group (26 per cent) coming from Handsworth.

In the Roman Catholic Church with its process of a priest 'belonging' to a diocese one sees a clear pattern of priests attending the local seminary. The would-be priest is directed to a particular seminary by his bishop. As Appendix 1 shows, our sample of priests come from three dioceses, two of which had a local seminary. In those two 83 per cent and 52 per cent of the priests respectively attended the local seminary. The other most striking thing about the priests is the extent to which their theological training took place outside England, in particular in Eire (22.0 per cent) and in Italy (14.0 per cent). The former statistic illustrates the place of Eire as a recruiting ground for Roman Catholic priests.

Our data show then that in terms of positions, experience and origins, clergy, priests and ministers are different groups. Clergy are likely to be incumbents, whereas priests are more likely to be assistants and ministers will be the equivalent of incumbents or in the 'hierarchy' as circuit superintendents.

In terms of experiences, the clergyman will be younger than the priest or minister, as a result of which he will have been ordained more recently and so held fewer positions within the Church. Not only has he held fewer positions *in toto* but he has worked at the local level within a particular diocese less than priests or ministers. In this context it is important to emphasise the special position of the priest; he can expect to spend a far greater time as an assistant than a clergyman or a minister, spending more time in each position and most of his career within one diocese.

Again, the origins and pre-work experiences of these three groups are different. Clergy are from the middle and upper strata of society; ministers are solidly from the middle; priests are predominantly middle, but are the only group with a substantial manual element. These differences in social class background are further reflected in educational differences. All three groups have strong grammar school components, but a substantial number of clergy went to public school; ministers, on the other hand have a large minority with only elementary education; priests are intermediate. Clergy are largely a university educated body, whereas priests and ministers have, in the main, no higher education.

Thus, the three Churches are recruiting different kinds of people and putting them through different kinds of experience. Our next task in this chapter is to examine the ways in which these aspects of experience and origin go together within each denominational context to form a coherent pattern.

The Church of England

We have shown that the Church of England recruits its clergy from distinctively different strata from the Methodist and Roman Catholic Churches, that they have a different age structure and go through different sets of experiences. But to what extent do these experiences, such as the length of time one spends in a particular position or a particular diocese, the number of posts that one has held, the length of time that one has been ordained, etc. go together to form a distinctive set of experiences? Are there patterns internal to the Church of England which mean that clergy with particular educational backgrounds are likely to hold certain positions rather than others? For example, Morgan (1969) has shown that bishops are liable to be highly educated and to come from public schools and Oxbridge. Coxon (1967) has suggested that there are two differing groups for recruitment into the Anglican Church and it is possible that as they move through the structure of the Church they have distinctively different experiences.

The best initial way of approaching this is to use the distinction made in chapter 1 between the extra-denominational influences and the denominational setting. Beliefs, because of their hypothesised importance will not be dealt with in this chapter, but will be left until chapter 3 for special treatment. First we will examine the relationships between the indicators of extra-denominational influences, then between those of denominational setting, ending with the relationship between the two groups of indicators.

There are four measures of extra-denominational influences, namely the age of the clergyman, his social class origin (that is the occupation of his father), the basic education that he received and the higher education if any, that he received. The pattern found confirms what we know from general sociology. There are strong relationships between social class background, type of secondary education received, and higher education. The higher a clergyman's social class origins, the more likely he is to have attended a public school. Essentially, the ex-public school boys come from the highest professional and managerial groups, the ex-grammar school boys are distributed across higher and lower professional groups and also the lower non-manual. Those who did not receive either grammar or public school education mainly come from the lower non-manual group. These relationships are then reflected, as one would expect, in the fact that those with an elementary education rarely have a higher education at a university, grammar school boys have a fair chance and the public school attenders are highly likely to have received a university education. The social class relationships with higher education reflect those with basic education. The higher a clergyman's social class origin the more likely he is to have received a university education. This, then, confirms the general pattern that is now part of the conventional wisdom of sociology. The age of a clergyman is not related to any of these three indicators.

Turning to the denominational setting in which the clergyman operates, we have seven indicators. These are the type of ministry he is currently working in, such as an incumbent, a chaplain, etc.; the situation of that ministry, whether it is group or team, one with assistants; the number of posts the clergyman has held; the number of incumbencies held; the number of years he has been in his present position; the number of years he has been in the diocese; and the number of years he has been ordained. Our data show that all of these measures are highly interrelated, and basically in a linear way. Taking the five measures of past experience we can say that those who have been clergymen for the longest period of time (that is, ordained the longest), will have been in the diocese longer, have held their present position longest, have held the most posts and the most incumbencies. This is a coherent and understandable pattern.

The other three denominational setting indicators are all indicative of the clergyman's current position. Again they are highly inter-related. By definition curates are not currently incumbents; members of the hierarchy (i.e. rural dean upwards) often are. In terms of ministry situation, incumbents either work on their own or are assisted. Chaplains tend to work on their own whereas those in the hierarchy are assisted. These aspects of current situation are related in an entirely predictable way to past denominational experiences. Those clergy who hold incumbencies are more experienced than their assistants and the members of the hierarchy are more experienced still.

The picture, then, is one of a stable 'career' system based on experience and seniority. The relationships are all very strong indeed with p at 0.001. The newly ordained clergyman takes up a curacy, stays in it a few years, then probably moves to another curacy, after which he takes up an incumbency. Once at this point his time in each position and diocese begins to lengthen considerably. In this situation he may well have an assistant, and become a rural dean, and for the few a move to becoming an archdeacon. However, as Bryman (1974) has shown it is unlikely that this stable, well-established route will lead to a bishopric. The archdeacons are products of parish and organisational work; bishops are products of educational work in public schools, theological colleges and universities.

As one would expect all of these indicators of the denominational setting are strongly (and linearly) related to the age of the clergyman. A system of career movement based on such a clear pattern of graduated movement produces a pyramidal organisation which approximates a gerontocracy. This is reflected by bishops in their late forties and early fifties being regarded as 'young'.

However, the relationships with the other extra-denominational influences are not so overwhelming. First, the social class background of the clergyman is not related to the career experiences that he has within the organisation. Nor does our data show any clear evidence for any change in the social class origins of clergy. Similarly, there are no relationships between the basic education received by a clergyman and his denominational experiences. But our data does show that whether or not a clergyman has received a university education is of some importance. University educated clergy are likely to have been ordained longer, to have held more posts and more incumbencies than those who did not attend university. Also they are more likely to currently be incumbents or members of the hierarchy and also have curates working for them.

This pattern represents the effects of two processes. First it reflects the changing nature of entry into the clerical profession. While there might not be any great change in the social class origins and basic education of entrants to the clergy, less of them are entering by way of a university education. Second, it reflects the fact that having a university degree is no doubt a factor in determining the promotion prospects of a clergyman.

Thus we have an overall picture which shows movement within the Church of England being mainly based on seniority and experience. There is also evidence that having a university education is a further feature which underpins this situation.

The Roman Catholic Church

Taking the same approach with Roman Catholic priests, the initial pattern is very similar to that for Anglican clergy, particularly with regard to denominational factors.

With extra-denominational factors things are slightly different. As one would expect, basic education and higher education are very strongly related; it is those priests educated at grammar or public schools who go on to university. But there is no relationship between social class origins and education at any level for Roman Catholic priests, something which is very unusual. Of course, it is a reflection of the Roman Catholic education system and the way in which possible candidates for the priesthood are chosen at an early age and then guided through the appropriate educational channels. Again, as with Anglican clergy, age is unrelated to either social class background or education.

The same seven indicators of denominational setting are used for Roman Catholic priests as for Anglican clergy. As with the latter group our data show a very high degree of interrelationships between these aspects of denominational setting for priests. Those priests who have been ordained longest will be those who have been in their particular diocese longest, have held their present position longest, have held the most posts and the greatest number of posts as a parish priest. Again this is a standard, predictable pattern.

Similarly the relationships between aspects of their current situation are the same for priests as for clergy. Parish priests work on their own or are assisted; members of the hierarchy have assistants. By definition, assistant priests work for others. Members of the hierarchy are the most experienced priests having been ordained longest, been in the diocese longest and so on. Parish priests are also fairly experienced and assistant priests the least. Again, age is linearly related to denominational experience and to the degree of seniority of a priest's current position.

Thus there is the stable system based on experience and seniority. The priest moves slowly through a number of positions, usually spending all of his time in one diocese and gradually spending more time in each position.

On examining the relationships between extra-denominational factors and denominational setting it is basic education that is most strongly related. There is some evidence of a changing social class background of priests as those who have been ordained longest are likely to be from manual and lower non-manual groups whereas those more recently ordained have a greater likelihood of being from managerial and professional groups. Our data also suggest a tendency for members of the hierarchy to have received a university education. However, neither of these relationships are particularly strong ($p = 0.05$). But the basic education received by a priest is related to his current situation and past experiences, although not necessarily in the same way.

Those priests who attended a public school are liable to have been in their current position longer than those who attended a different kind of school. In line with this, these same priests are much more liable to have held a number of posts as a parish priest.

But, as one would expect, consequent upon the indicated change in social class origins, assistant priests are more likely to have received more education at grammar and public schools than parish priests; the latter have a fair sprinkling of priests who only have an elementary education. What this represents is a twofold process. On the one hand, those priests who some time ago received a Roman Catholic public school education are likely to have achieved the status of parish priest faster than those who did not and consequently to have held more of such posts. On the other hand, as more recent recruits to the Roman Catholic ministry are likely to be from non-manual social groups, so we find that assistant priests are increasingly likely to have received more than an elementary education.

Thus, while stability of career pattern would seem to be an essential element in the Roman Catholic Church we see the impact of education both in terms of its effect on moving an individual through the system a little faster, and as a reflection of a small change in the social class origins of priests.

The Methodist Church

In examining the situation of ministers in the Methodist Church, the variables are the same as for clergy and priests with two exceptions. With regard to denominational setting there is no distinction between incumbents and non-incumbents and consequently there is no variable of incumbency status or of the number of incumbencies held.

Looking at extra-denominational factors first, there is the same relationship between social class origins, basic education and higher education as for clergy. That is, those who attended only elementary school tend to come from a lower social class than those who went to grammar or public school. The relationship with social class is even stronger for higher education; university attenders originate from professional and managerial groups whereas those who 'missed' university are from skilled manual and clerical backgrounds. As one would expect, those who attended public schools are the most likely to have received a university education, followed by those with a grammar school education. Those with only an elementary education are unlikely to have been to a university. In contrast to the case of priests and clergy, age does have a relationship with one of these variables, namely education. There is clear evidence that the younger ministers have received a grammar school education; older ministers are more likely to have attended either a public school or an elementary school.

Turning to the indicators of denominational experience and current position there is not quite the same overall pattern as for clergy and priests. The various aspects of experience tend to go together. That is, the longer a man has been ordained, the more posts he has held, the longer he has been in the circuit, and the longer he has been in his current position. All these four aspects are strongly and linearly related to each other.

Also, the two indicators of current situation are strongly related. Circuit superintendents tend to work in smaller circuits; sector ministers are likely to be in the bigger circuits, with ministers spread over all sizes of circuit.

Where the pattern differs markedly from that for clergy and priests is in the connection between past experience and current situation. There is no relationship between any of the indicators of past experience and current ministry situation (i.e. the kind of circuit in which a minister works). The type of ministry being performed by a minister is connected with the length of time that he has been a minister and the number of posts he has held. Circuit superintendents and chairmen have been ordained longest and held more posts than others. But this ministerial situation is not related to the length of time that the minister has been in the district or to his current position. Thus, while there is a stable seniority system it is not contained within a limited geographical situation. The Methodist system of 'stationing' ensures a volume of movement which tends not to occur in other denominations.

As a result there are not the same relationships between extra-denominational and denominational factors. While age is related to type of ministry, in that circuit superintendents are older than others, and linearly to the number of posts held and the number of years ordained, it is not related to years in the circuit, years in one's current position or the kind of circuit worked in. Social class background and basic education are unrelated to any aspects of experience and position. The acquisition of a university education is strongly related to being a sector minister.

Thus while the career pattern of a minister in terms of organisational movement is as stable as for clergy and priests, moving like them through a series of posts into more organisationally important posts, it does not have the same geographical stability. The basic underpinning to this pattern is seniority, reflected by the relationships with age.

Summary and conclusions

The information analysed here demonstrates the initial basis for suggesting that clergy, ministers and priests do in fact constitute distinct groups. These three groups show clear differences in origins, past experiences inside and outside the denomination and the distribution of current positions. They have differing social class origins, different basic and higher education experiences. There are further differences in age distributions between the three groups, in the numbers of positions held and in the current positions of members.

These are not haphazard differences but they reflect the fabric of the respective denominations and the ways in which they handle their 'employees'. Although the Church of England, Roman Catholic Church and Methodist Church all have a stable pattern in which seniority plays an overwhelming part, there are further differences. Although the two episcopal Churches appear somewhat similar, with a geographical as well as an organisational stability, the clergyman is liable to move through his system a little faster than the priest. Nor is the impact of extra-denominational factors the same in both. For the Methodist ministers the focus is national rather than local with a large amount of geographical mobility creating disjunctions which do not occur for clergy and priests. Indeed the organisationally prescribed 'career' system overrides the extra-denominational attributes of the minister.

With these three backgrounds, enveloping as they do considerable variation, there is strong prima facie evidence for predicting differences in attitudes towards such things as reform, ecumenism, role and the organisation. After examining beliefs in the next chapter the rest of the book will be devoted to examining how far and in what way these predicted differences do occur.

3　Beliefs

In this chapter we take up the issue of the way in which a religious functionary's beliefs define and orientate his activities. Obviously there are a number of ways in which it would be possible to approach this. But the nature of Churches together with existing literature clearly point to two major areas, namely theological cosmology, or churchmanship, and professionalism. As we suggested in the opening chapter the position of beliefs can be regarded as a crucial starting point in the analysis of Churches and their members.

Unlike many occupations, the full-time religious functionary has many models of his role and position on which to draw. These models emanate from his views on a number of complex issues such as the role of the Church in the world, the nature of the priesthood, the nature of God, etc. (for a summary of these and their organisational consequences see Rudge (1968)). However, because of the strong intellectual base in theology these questions are answered by recourse to systematic systems of belief which in many Churches are summarised by labels such as 'Evangelical', 'Modernist', 'Sacramentalist', etc. Our aim has been to explore these on the assumption that such general conceptions have important implications for a wide variety of more specific beliefs and actions.

But the religious functionary conceives of himself not only as representing a particular stream of theological ideas, but also as a member of an occupational group. Here the most common self-assigned and imputed label has been that of a professional. Many texts in the sociology of occupations seem to start from the position that the three base professions which have served as models over the past century are medicine, law and the clergy (cf. Krause, 1971). Clearly, defining oneself as a professional has implications for the way in which particular problems are approached. This should be especially true for problems of an organisational kind and those over the nature of authority. Our aim in this chapter, then, is to explore these two areas of churchmanship and professionalism in more detail.

1 Theological cosmology

In recent years there has been an accelerating interest in types of theological classification and how different categories of theological belief operate to condition and affect other beliefs and attitudes. Most of this research has been confined to religion in the USA, and so the categories employed are those which have particular relevance to the American experience. For example, Stark and his colleagues (1971) were able to describe Protestant ministers as either Fundamentalist, Conservative, Neo-Orthodox, Liberal or 'Other'. They found that such theological classifications seemed to be part of an internally coherent belief system. To take two examples they present, 85 per cent of those ministers who emerged as very 'high' on a scale of religious orthodoxy were Fundamentalists or Conservatives; whilst 61 per cent who emerged as very 'low' were Liberals. And again, to take two extremes, 95 per cent of Southern Baptists and 87 per cent of Missouri Lutheran ministers classified themselves as Fundamentalist or Conservative, as opposed to 8 per cent of United Church of Christ and 9 per cent of Methodist ministers.

Similarly, but employing different theological classifications, Kent Spaulding (1972) has employed the terms Liberal and Evangelical to characterise Christian congregations. Moberg (1970) has also attempted to characterise congregations along a Conservative–Liberal axis. His findings are interesting in that he finds the institutional age of Conservative congregations to be lower than Liberal ones, the former have a smaller number of paid staff members and they have more Sunday-school classes. Conservative congregations have higher rates of church and Sunday-school attendance and higher per capita budgets. Among other things, Liberal congregations were larger and more likely to be active in local Councils of Churches. These studies indicate that the examination of theological cosmologies is a neglected area and that the few studies which have been carried out point to their potentiality in discriminating between different sets of attitudes and forms of behaviour.

In this chapter, therefore, we shall consider a number of inter-related things: we shall focus upon the theological cosmologies of religious functionaries as such, and we shall consider a number of secondary factors which help to illuminate religious beliefs—how clergy, priests and ministers conceive of the relationship of their Church to others, and how priests regard the relationship of their Church in Britain to the centre of Rome.

We are also particularly interested in noting the way in which functionaries' beliefs are related to their social origins, educational experiences and organisational career patterns. To what extent, therefore, do beliefs exist independently of the institutions in which they are located? Or are the beliefs radically shaped and moulded by their institutional context?

In Britain a number of theological positions are often referred to which have different titles and different meanings from those categories adopted in the American context. We shall consider in more detail those theological cosmologies related to our chosen Churches.

The Church of England

A feature of the Church of England is that Anglicanism has been capable of embracing a variety of frequently diverse theological standpoints. In the mid-nineteenth century W. J. Coneybeare (1853) distinguished between Anglican clergy of 'High', 'Low', and 'Broad' Church inclinations. High Churchmen were mainly those of a Catholic persuasion, Low Churchmen were generally Evangelicals, and those of the centre were a mixture of both wings. The Catholic and Evangelical stances were, and still are, in many ways, polar opposites in theological and doctrinal inclination, and there has tended to be a tension between them (Molland, 1959).

On the basis of a sample of 500 from the Clergy List of his day, Coneybeare (1853) calculated that 41 per cent of clergy were High Churchmen of various hues, 38 per cent were Low Churchmen, and 21 per cent of Broad Church inclination. Of the 28 bishops and archbishops 13 were High Church, 5 were Low Church and 10 were Broad Church. These figures suggest an under-representation of Low Churchmen among the episcopate of that era. This can be partly accounted for by reference to the social background of the Low Church tradition, which as Coneybeare (1853) pointed out, tended to be lower class. Presumably those elevated to the status of bishop were in need of the respectability of an upper-class background or of well-to-do parishioners.

These theological dispositions have by no means disappeared and have persisted with considerable force. They now tend to be called forms of 'churchmanship' by both clergy and laity alike. Their strength over the years has been documented by Thompson (1970). We have defined churchmanship as a 'theological stance, or framework of religious belief, which defines a person's relation to God in specific forms of devotional and ritualistic activities, and defines for him how he is to interpret his faith in the secular world' (Bryman, Ranson and Hinings, 1974). The notion of churchmanship has not been examined to any considerable extent by sociologists of religion, which is surprising in view of the importance of belief systems to this area of sociology.

The categories of churchmanship derive to a considerable extent from the theological positions which Coneybeare (1853) adumbrated over a century ago. At one end of the main axis which differentiates forms of churchmanship is the 'Catholic' position. Still largely synonymous with a 'High Church' conception of the Church as a 'divine mystery' (Irving, 1966), there is a stress in this tradition on ritualism (frequently with Roman emphases such as celebrations in Latin and the use of incense) and on visual symbolism to heighten the senses to the unique supernatural quality of the mysterious. These preoccupations are prominent in Catholicism because, as Pittenger (1966) writes, it

> suggests a view of Christianity which lays strong emphasis on the *structures* which have appeared historically in the Christian body. . . . [It] implies a conception of the Christian religion in which there is an emphasis upon the community, the Church as integral to the whole message, life and purpose of the fellowship of Christian believers. This articulates itself into forms of structures—sacraments, creeds, ministry, etc.—which are regarded as not only highly important and valuable, but as in some way necessary to the persistence of Christianity as an identifiable reality through historical change.

This quotation brings out the importance of the conception of hierarchy in the Church as a divine gift to Christianity which is not merely expedient but also necessary. Among many Anglican clergy of the Catholic persuasion there is a high respect for, and in some cases a practice of, the Catholic conception of the priest as the incumbent of a divine office within the hierarchical Church and as a man above other men. This embraces an ontological view of the priesthood.

At the other end of the axis is the Evangelical form of churchmanship with its stress on what David Martin (1967) has called 'a stereotyped scheme of psychological dynamics'. The three main tenets of the Evangelical tradition were enunciated by Coneybeare (1853) as 'the universal necessity of "conversion"', 'justification by faith', and 'the sole authority of Scripture as "the rule of faith"'. There has been an emphasis on oratory and simplicity of worship. It has been identified with Low Church 'because it ministered to people *where they were*: literally at first in the open air, and only later in meeting halls which were not intended to be rival churches, but also where they were psychologically and socially' (Irving, 1966; his emphasis). In the middle of the Catholic–Evangelical continuum can be found a branch of churchmanship which has been called the 'Central' or 'Broad' Church tradition. This is a highly adaptable, liberal tradition which contains a good deal of the Catholic and Evangelical traditions, whilst being attacked by extreme members of the two wings. According to Molland (1959) it 'has been associated with a special concern for a close connection between the Church and cultural life' and has strong humanistic tendencies.

Not all forms of churchmanship can be located on the Catholic–Evangelical axis. In addition to the three types discussed, some people have pointed to two fairly closely related theological dispositions called 'Modernist' and 'New Theology'. Modernism is a 'progressive' form of theology in its beliefs surrounding the Church and its ministry in the world. This 'progressivism' consists of making the Church and the world relevant to and consistent with the experiences and the knowledge possessed by twentieth-century man. The 'miraculous' side of Christianity is played down in an attempt to come to terms with and utilise current scientific understanding of man and his world (Barbour, 1966; Williams, 1966). The 'New Theology' school, which we have also been able to identify, bears a considerable resemblance to 'modernism' but, in its embrace of radical and secular theology, it is frequently very extreme on certain issues regarding doctrine or organisation. Its main intellectual previsers are Bultmann, Bonhoeffer and Tillich, and the tradition continues, particularly in the work of John Robinson.

Our research reveals that Anglican clergy do indeed strongly adhere to and identify with particular types of churchmanship. Table 3.1 shows the proportion of clergy who identified with each of a number of religious stances. The large proportion of 'Catholics' reminds us that the Oxford Movement did much to revive the spirit of Catholicism in the Church of England and that this high proportion is a testament to its impact and subsequent survival. The proportions of Evangelicals (whether Liberal or Conservative) and radicals (whether Modernist or New Theology) are relatively

TABLE 3.1 *Clergy identifying with different forms of churchmanship*

	%	
Anglo-Catholic	12.1	} 40.3
Prayer-Book Catholic	28.2	
Central/Broad Church	25.0	
Modernist	1.7	} 7.2
New Theology	5.5	
Liberal Evangelical	11.1	} 19.0
Conservative Evangelical	7.9	
Other	8.5	

small, although there is, as would be expected, a sizeable proportion of those clergymen who regard themselves as Central or Broad Church. It is interesting to compare these figures with those of Coneybeare collected more than 100 years ago. It shows the stability of the High Churchmen and those of a Broad Church persuasion.

We must now consider the extent to which Anglican clergymen have come to identify with their churchmanship cosmologies independently of their association with any particular institution or whether in fact their churchmanship is a product of earlier theological socialisation.

In chapter 2 we have reviewed various aspects of the origins and experiences of clergy; it will be instructive to examine how far theological beliefs are related to such factors. Our data do indicate strongly that the early training and theological experiences to which clergy are exposed at theological college are crucial in determining which churchmanship class they come to identify with. That is to say, if a clergyman has been to an Anglo-Catholic college, or a Liberal Evangelical college then he is most likely to become an Anglo-Catholic or a Liberal Evangelical, respectively. Indeed the relationship is an extremely strong one. However, it is possible that theological colleges recruit from particular strata. It is also possible that attendance at particular colleges and the development of specific theological positions will lead to a clergyman espousing one career pattern rather than another. For example, bishops may not only come from higher education, but also be of a Catholic persuasion.

Our data show some modest relationships between origins and experience on the one hand, and theological beliefs on the other. The relationships found suggest a changing theological pattern. First, the group identified in the previous chapter as the 'traditional' recruiting ground for Anglican clergy, i.e. those from professional backgrounds and with a university education, are more likely to be of a Catholic persuasion (and have attended a 'Catholic' orientated theological college). However, these relationships are not all that strong ($p = 0.05$). Second, and more strongly, there are relationships between theological beliefs and age, organisational experience and current position. As one would expect, it shows that younger clergy, who have held less posts and are non-incumbents, working as subordinates, are more likely to class themselves as Modernists and as Evangelicals. Interestingly, those who find it impossible to use any of the labels offered and thus indicated 'other', are the youngest group of all. The older incumbents, working on their own are much more likely to be either Catholic or Broad Church.

We would suggest that a clergyman is unlikely to change his basic theological beliefs during his life; this is particularly so as the

Anglican church makes it possible for him to find a position which is compatible with his beliefs. The relationships described are more suggestive of, on the one hand, a small change in the origins of recruits to the Anglican Church and, on the other, a growing reorientation of younger clergy. As Ritti *et al.* (1974) and Hall and Schneider (1973) have pointed out this can lead to considerable problems in finding meaning in day-to-day church work.

The Methodist Church

It is not customary to use the term 'churchmanship' in the context of the Methodist Church. This may be because the Church is believed to contain few theological strands since it is so patently a component of the eighteenth-century Evangelical Revival. However, we asked our respondents to locate themselves theologically—the actual categories were left open. Table 3.2 presents the proportions of ministers that mentioned each of a number of categories. (It is important to realise that unlike the Anglican question we did not specify the theological categories, and ministers frequently employed more than one category.) The majority of ministers identify themselves as either Evangelical or Ecumenical in theological disposition, whilst 10.6 per cent identified with both positions. These proportions are indicative of the persistence of the Evangelical position in Methodism and also of the commitment of the Church to the ecumenical movement. The terms liberal, radical and conservative tended to be used as adjectival qualifications of positions like Evangelical or Ecumenical; only 9.7 per cent identified themselves in terms like Catholic, Ritualist or Sacramentalist. There appears then to be a 'theological core' in Methodism which dictates that the majority of clergy are Evangelicals or Ecumenicals or both,

TABLE 3.2 *Methodist ministers identifying with various theological positions*

	%
Evangelical	53.7
Ecumenical	55.5
Liberal	37.9
Middle-of-the-road	6.6
Radical	22.0
Conservative	3.5
Catholic (including 'Ritualist' and 'Sacramentalist')	15.9
Other	8.8

Note: As it was possible for Methodist ministers to indicate more than one category, the percentages do not add up to 100.

and that there are various hues (e.g. liberal, radical) of these three basic positions.

As with Anglican clergy we must consider finally the extent to which ministers' beliefs have been conditioned by earlier theological training and by origins. Also we examine the extent to which it is related to experiences. At the interview stage of our survey we were repeatedly assured and given to understand that the Methodist Church imposed strict precautions to ensure that colleges did not develop distinct theological strands as had occurred in the Church of England. Our data uphold this contention: Methodist theological colleges do not possess any separate and distinct theological cosmology which is systematically taught to (trainee) ministers. Each college educates its members in a similar manner, each inculcating, socialising, potential ministers in the one central and relatively unitary Methodist theological tradition. We find no relationship between the college attended and current self-reported theological position.

However, as with the Anglicans, there are relationships between theological position and aspects of origin and experience. In terms of pre-ordination experience, social class background, basic and higher education are all related in the same direction to the espousal of Evangelism. Those from lower social class backgrounds, with an elementary education and no university attendance are much more likely to classify themselves as Evangelicals. We have pointed out that this is one of the central Methodist traditions and our data show that its current proponents come from a longstanding recruiting ground.

It is not this Evangelical dimension, though, which is related to experience in the Church, but Ecumenism and Radicalness. Again, as with clergymen, Radical ministers will be young, have held few posts and work in circuits longer. The latter is probably related to younger clergy having a preference for working in urban areas. Radicals are also more likely to be sector ministers. Ecumenicals are liable to have been ordained longest and also to be circuit superintendents.

Thus we find that beliefs are systematically related to other aspects of a minister's experience. Once again an important distinction is between young and old, experienced and inexperienced (in organisational terms). The younger recruits to the ministry, as with their Anglican counterparts, are more likely to espouse a theological position which is possibly at odds with that of their superiors.

The Roman Catholic Church

The data that we have collected on the Roman Catholic Church do not contain any information on theological positions as such.

46

This Church has tended to identify with a very clear branch of Christianity. The distinctiveness of the Roman Catholic conception of the Church and the priesthood has already been articulated. What is important about this position is that the basic tenets of the Roman Catholic Church remain stable and constant in the face of changes in the Church. As Fogarty (1963, p. 8) has pointed out, although the Roman Catholic Church has become more flexible at the edges 'the need has increasingly been felt for a firm centre of authority to confirm, establish and guard the principles emerging from the Church's experience and tradition and to serve as a point of reference and a focus for loyalty'. Change does take place, and indeed has taken place on a grand scale, since Fogarty was writing, in the form of Vatican II. But change is steered along the path of Roman Catholic central tendency. Moreover, once reinterpretation and change take place, they take the form that Roman Catholic faith and creed has traditionally imposed from above on the parish priests of all countries. The very nature and characteristic forms of procedure in this Church make it extremely difficult to establish theological schools. In a sense, there is only one theological stance— the 'Catholic' position. This does not mean that all Roman Catholic priests passively receive papal edicts. However, the vast majority do seem to adhere to the basic theological position of the Church. Those that do not are likely to defect—and in the USA the number of defectors is rapidly growing (Illich, 1971)—or they can find themselves in considerable difficulty with the Vatican hierarchy, e.g. Ivan Illich. In such a climate, the Roman Catholic priest is unlikely to stray far at all from the central position of his Church.

The information we do have upon Roman Catholic priests' belief does tend to confirm this concept of them as adhering to a

TABLE 3.3 *Conception of Church in relation to others*

	Church of England	Roman Catholic	Methodist
	%	%	%
I think of my Church as one denomination among many	10.7	7.5	31.4
I think of my Church as having a special responsibility to the whole population of an area regardless of people's religious or other affiliations	69.2	63.0	25.5
Other	20.0	29.1	43.1

unitary, cohesive theological cosmology. The uniformity of belief can be illustrated in a number of ways: by considering how they view the relationship of their Church to others; by considering how they view the relationship of their Church in Britain to the papal authority in Rome; by focusing upon their conception of ministry; and, finally, by looking at their theological training.

When we focus upon the way priests conceive of their Church in relation to others, inter-denominational comparison is particularly illuminating, as Table 3.3 shows. Methodist ministers for example, clearly view their Church as one denomination among others: a substantial proportion of the 43.1 per cent who classified themselves as 'other' were merely elaborating the overriding denominational sentiment, as can be seen from (some examples of) the way in which they annotated their questionnaires:

> 'sharing with other denominations in responsibility to the whole population of an area',
> 'part of the Christian Church to serve the community . . .',
> 'part of the Church Universal, sharing in the responsibility of mission to the whole community'.

Anglican clergy on the other hand tend to conceive of their Church 'as having a special responsibility to the whole population of an area regardless of people's religious or other affiliations'. This is very much a product of the secular 'establishment' of the Church of England rather than theological creed: that is to say, because theirs is the national Church, clergy see themselves as having a responsibility to all the members of their parish whatever their religious belief.

Now although Roman Catholic priests conceive of the relationship of their Church to others in exactly the same manner as Church of England clergy, that is, a general non-denominational responsibility, an important distinction has to be made. For, whereas there is a substantial secular element to the Anglican commitment, the Roman Catholic conception is completely theological: that is, the Roman Catholic Church is the one true Christian Church and therefore possesses a theological right, a divine duty, to care for its ordained charge. This proposition is validated by the way in which priests annotated their questionnaires. The weight and uniformity of their written comments was quite astonishing. Forty-one per cent of priests annotated their questionnaires in a similar style and theological vein, thinking of the Roman Catholic Church as:

> 'the one true church founded by Christ',
> 'the true Church established by Christ which expects all men to follow . . .',

'holding a unique position amongst Christian denominations
as being substantially the one true Church founded by Christ',
'the standard or norm for Christianity',
'the One True Church, the pillar and ground of Truth',
'the one true Church founded by Christ and containing and
preserving all the essential Christian truths',
'the only authentic Church which continues the work of Christ',
'the only true Apostolic and Catholic Church',
'the centre of unity and true Authority',
'the authentic embodiment of Christ . . .',
'the people of God'.

The quality of certainty of knowing in these statements is unequivocal. The degree of theological unanimity in tone and word
is unparalleled in either the Church of England or the Methodist
Church.

TABLE 3.4   *Relationship between Rome and national Churches*

	%
The national Church should wait for Rome to make important initiatives	7.1
The national Church should consult Rome before adopting any new initiatives and only act with their approval	26.5
The national Church should be free to adopt its own policies except on major issues of faith and morals	60.1
The national Church should be completely free to adopt its own policies	6.3

The uniformity of Roman Catholic belief and its rather traditionalist nature can also be appreciated by focusing upon how they
consider the relationship of their Church in Britain to the Mother
Church in Rome (Table 3.4). Although priests tend not to believe
that Rome should be able to dictate the minutiae of their working
lives they do adhere to the belief that Rome should determine the
basis of their theological framework.

The way in which priests define their role and ministry will be
outlined in more detail in chapter 4. But a note here will help to
illuminate our general point that Roman Catholicism is a unified
belief system within which theological nuances are relatively few.
Priests uniformly (88 per cent) define their role in a manner which
we regard as central to the Roman Catholic theological tradition
laying considerable emphasis upon the celebration of sacraments.

What importance can we attribute to the theological seminaries when we consider this uniformity of theological belief and practice? Like the Methodist Church and unlike the Church of England we have discovered no theological pattern whereby particular colleges identify with distinct theological positions. We have discovered the surprising degree to which dioceses prefer to recruit priests from their local seminary: thus 85 per cent of priests from one large urban diocese were trained at the local theological college (see chapter 2). This indicates perhaps a considerable effort to achieve a consensus and uniformity in the theological socialisation of priests.

However, while there are no clearly defined theological schools in the Roman Catholic Church and our sample show a remarkable uniformity of view, there are two items which we propose to use as surrogates for direct statements of theological belief. One of these is the item on the relationship of the national Church to Rome, already detailed in Table 3.4. The second item we take from a series of questions on attitudes towards reform which are dealt with in chapter 5. This particular item asked priests about the amount of reform thought necessary over liturgy and forms of worship. Given the centrality of liturgical matters to Roman Catholicism we feel that this is a useful indicator of belief. Our data show that 11 per cent of priests feel that reform of the liturgy is most important; 12 per cent think it is quite important; 48 per cent not very important; and 29 per cent not necessary.

In a sense, both of these items are concerned with radicalness, with challenge to the existing order and beliefs. It has been suggested by Krause (1971) generally, and by Ritti *et al.* (1974) with regard to Roman Catholic priests, that this is the most important element in beliefs. The two items outlined will be used as indicators of belief for priests in the rest of this book.

When we further examine the relationships between belief and aspects of origins and experiences it is the statement on relations with Rome that stands out. Those who feel that the national Church should be completely free from Rome, or at least free on all matters except those concerned with major matters of morals and faith, are the younger priests. We have the same picture as for Methodist ministers and Anglican clergy. Those priests who are younger in age, who have been ordained for less time, who have spent less time in the diocese and their present position, are more likely to stress separation from Rome. Along with this, these priests are also unlikely to be parish priests, or have held only a few such posts. While the item concerned with liturgical reform is significantly related to only two aspects, the relationships are in the same direction as for freedom from Rome. Those priests who favour reform are unlikely to be parish priests or to have spent much time in the diocese.

Thus, as one would expect, the major finding concerns age and experience, on the one hand, and radicalness. It is those who are younger, with the least organisational experience, who are more likely to be radical in terms of the indicators of belief used here.

Summary and conclusions

We have, therefore, described the way in which clergy, priests and ministers each adhere to distinctly different kinds of theological cosmology. Anglicanism as such incorporates a variety of diverse theological positions or 'churchmanship' from Catholic 'High' Churchmen through Central or Broad Church to 'Low' or Evangelical churchmanship. Some clergy also embrace the more modern and radical 'new' theologies. Each strand of churchmanship, however ostensibly incompatible, is accommodated in the Church of England.

The situation in the Methodist and Roman Catholic Churches is somewhat different in that both ministers and priests adhere to far more unitary and coherent theological belief systems than clergy in the church of England. The majority of ministers identify themselves as either Evangelical or Ecumenical in theology and usually adopt other labels 'catholic' or 'radical' or 'liberal' to qualify their position around the central Evangelical axis—the central theological core which seems to have altered little since the eighteenth-century Evangelical Revival.

Roman Catholic priests equally tend to adhere to a central and singular theological tradition with its stress upon divine mystery, visual symbolism, ritualism and the importance of Rome and religious hierarchy as necessary to the persistence of Christianity. We found considerable uniformity in the manner in which priests expressed their theological cosmology, a uniformity of style and tone unparalleled in the other Churches: the certainty of 'knowing' their Church to be the one, true, authentic Church as founded by Christ.

As well as portraying a detailed description of the religious functionaries' theological cosmologies, we were also particularly interested in locating the historical and social origins of these beliefs for the clergy, priests and ministers as individuals. We discovered a very powerful association between the identification with a belief and an earlier theological training for Anglican clergy so that, whatever part autonomous choice or revelation may have played for them, their theological beliefs were considerably reinforced and given formal shape during their period of theological socialisation. The clergyman who went to an Anglo-Catholic college for example was most likely to adhere to an Anglo-Catholic churchmanship. On the other hand, the Methodist and Roman Catholic Churches strictly control to ensure a much greater uniformity in theological socialisation.

Overall, our findings on the three groups point in the direction suggested by Krause (1971) and by many current commentators on the Church. The important distinction seems to be between young and old, with the younger recruits, who have less experience of the institutional life of the Church, likely to hold beliefs which are out of line with the mainstreams of Church thought.

II Professionalism

A further aspect of the way in which the clergyman, minister or priest defines himself is in occupational terms. In the sociological literature clergy have often been defined as one of the basic professions. While their exact status as a profession has come into question recently (cf. Towler, 1969) this questioning shows the importance of ascertaining how individual religious functionaries perceive themselves occupationally. Apart from the interest of sociologists in the extent to which clergy fit the model of a professional occupation, clergy themselves are increasingly unsure of their general occupational position.

Essentially two processes have been at work which lead to unsureness and possible subsequent variation in a clergyman's occupational conception. First, the general position and status of the clergy has changed. No longer does the clergyman have a close relationship with a particular geographical area and membership, providing a variety of services. Many of the functions he performed in the past have been taken over by other agencies (Wilson, 1966). The clergyman has been subject to the general processes of differentiation and specialisation in society. This in itself leads to a changing occupational position and subsequent questioning.

Second, and partly as a result of this, there has been and is continuing specialisation within Churches. The basic role in the Anglican, Catholic and Methodist Churches is still that of the religious functionary in his geographical area with a responsibility for the members of his Church in that area. But other clergy roles have been developing and growing. The hierarchy has developed with more archdeacons, suffragan and auxiliary bishops, etc., who have administrative cum pastoral roles. Also, more specialist chaplains have been introduced whose responsibilities are for particular groups such as youth, immigrants, industry, students, rather than a geographically defined population. Furthermore, 'sector' ministries in the Methodist Church have grown with religious functionaries retaining their ordained status but carrying out non-priestly jobs. While it has always been common for ordained clergy to be teachers and academics, some now operate as social workers, doctors and personnel managers. Finally, the nature of the parish ministry itself has changed with the development of group and team ministries.

All of these developments and changes mean that one can no longer view clergy, priests and ministers as belonging to an homogeneous occupation, even within the context of their own Churches. External and internal pressures have led, and continue to lead to a more heterogeneous situation and occupation. It is this growing differentiation which has meant questioning the basic nature of the religious functionary's occupation.

However, it seems clear to us, following Fichter (1961) that the starting point for an analysis of occupational self-conception of the clergy is the idea of professionalism. This is partly because the available evidence points to this (professionalism) as being the way clergy think of themselves and partly because the three groups dealt with here exhibit a number of the structural characteristics of a profession. Harrison (1970) has even suggested that the notion of a profession has priestly origins. Struzzo (1970) suggests professionalism serves as a basic formulation for responding to a wide range of pastoral issues.

When discussing professions, sociologists of occupations usually distinguish between structural and attitudinal aspects (cf. Hall, 1968). The structural characteristics which are part of the reason for conceptualising the religious occupation in professional terms are:

(1) the theoretical knowledge base, in theology,
(2) the existence of a formal training period in seminary and theological college,
(3) The development of an individually based relationship with a client.

Thus Paul (1968, p. 73) has written:

> I explored, in the Paul Report, the sense in which the ordained ministry is a profession. It certainly is this. Priests, as it were, decide who shall be priests. They set the conditions of entry, the terms of training. Priests control priests. As professionals in terms of liturgy, doctrine, theology, they are guardians and transmitters of specialised knowledge. In this they resemble lawyers and doctors; in that they service an institution rather than serve a craft or skill, they are more like dons or schoolteachers; as professionals finally responsible to a movement much greater than its officers, or its institutions, they are

turned outwards, towards the movement, to which they must account, rather than inwards towards the autonomous profession.

This statement represents a more extreme view of the professional nature of the ordained ministry.

There is some doubt over the extent to which these attitudinal characteristics are in fact applicable or relevant to the religious functionary. Gannon (1971), for example, has argued that the Hall (1968) scheme is problematic when applied to religious functionaries. He shows a lack of 'fit' between these attitudinal professional attributes and the realities of the work of the functionary. However, Hall's scheme *is* an attitudinal one and, although it may be the case that the ordained ministry does not *seem* to endorse some of these attitudinal attributes, it may still be the case that many of its members *do* adopt a set of attitudes which may be termed 'professionalism'. Thus when Gannon (1971, p. 70) writes: '*whether in fact the clergy has become a profession is itself an empirical question*' (his italics) we are in total agreement. Precisely because this is an empirical question we are not assuming that the ordained ministry does constitute a profession; but we are using a professional model to discern *whether* it is one.

The main area in which the religious occupation is not a profession is the non-existence of professional associations in the sense of a body which controls the membership, protects standards and defines more clearly the nature of the professional task. There are bodies though which attempt to do this, e.g. the Parochial Clergy Association.

However, the attitudinal aspects of professionalism are concerned with the way in which the practitioners view their work. To the extent that professionalism is an attitudinal matter, part of one's occupational self-conception, it can be thought of as analytically separate from the structural characteristics. (This is notwithstanding the fact that one would expect a correlation between the extent to which an occupation can be classed as a profession structurally and how far the occupational members view themselves as professionals.)

In dealing with the attitudinal characteristics of a profession we follow Hall (1968). This involves five main ideas, namely:

(1) The use of the profession as a major reference. This involves the individual professional using the formal professional organisation and informal colleague groupings as the major source of ideas.

(2) A service orientation involving the ideas of benefits to the public from professional performance and also the indispensability of that performance.

(3) Colleague control, meaning that the regulation of behaviour
    should be in the hands of fellow professionals, they being
    best qualified to judge performance.
(4) The idea of vocation, reflecting the dedication of the
    professional to his occupation.
(5) Autonomy, of the professional from the pressures of
    clients, employers and non-professionals generally.

Given the changing role demands of the clergyman, priest and
minister it is entirely likely that they will differ in terms of their
self-conceptions as professionals. It is also possible that there will
be significant differences between our three groups, based on their
different traditions and different periods and patterns of organisational socialisation.

Each of the five attitudinal characteristics was measured by means
of a set of items in a Likert scale, with four items for each characteristic. Each respondent was asked how far each item corresponded
to his own attitude. For the five characteristics the possible score
range is from 4 to 20. Further details can be found in Appendix 1.

Between-Church differences

Table 3.5 shows the mean scores for clergy, ministers and priests on
each of the five scales of professionalism. There is no strong, overall
pattern (although there is some patterning). Overall, all three
groups come out as above average in terms of their professional
attitudes. They are particularly high on feelings of vocation and
autonomy. The former idea has, of course, been injected into
concepts of professionalism from ideas about the clerical occupation.
The Anglicans and Roman Catholics both score lowest on colleague
control, and for the Methodists this is also a low score.

TABLE 3.5 *Professionalism*

	Church of England	*Roman Catholic*	*Methodist*
Professional reference	13.04	14.20	14.61
Service orientation	13.42	14.96	13.15
Colleague control	12.43	13.52	13.88
Vocation	15.28	16.65	15.67
Autonomy	15.92	14.62	16.24

When we examine the way in which each group orders these five
aspects of professionalism some patterning occurs, but it is not the
same over all three groups. While vocation and autonomy are high
scoring for all three, the Roman Catholic priests score much less

on autonomy than the other two groups. This reflects the way in which the ordering of the three groups changes from dimension to dimension. In particular, service orientation is the one that moves around the most. Priests are considerably higher on this than either clergy or ministers and they rank it second to vocation. For clergy it is ranked third, while it is the dimension which ministers rank lowest.

Basically, the Methodist ministers appear to have the most highly professional attitudes, as measured by these five dimensions. They have the highest scores of the three groups on professional reference, colleague control and autonomy and the second highest on vocation. They are closely followed by the Roman Catholic priests who are the most professional in terms of vocation and service orientation and second on professional reference and colleague control. The Anglican clergy quite clearly have the least professional attitudes.

In many ways these findings do not square with what might have been predicted. Anglican clergy, as we have already demonstrated, are the most highly educated group, with university backgrounds, from upper-middle-class social origins, operating in relatively autonomous situations. This training and experience should be conducive to the production of a professional ideology. While our data show that they score above average they are low relative to the Methodists and Roman Catholics. These latter groups come from lower-class origins and are less educated. Roman Catholic priests operate in a more restricted environment; Methodists, of course, have much more autonomy, at the level of day-to-day activities, than do Roman Catholics.

However, the development of a professional ideology is not purely, or even mainly, dependent on class origins, education or work situation. More important is the training period and its control by the professional association. As we have shown earlier in this chapter, when discussing theological perspectives, there is less diversity in the training of Methodist ministers and Roman Catholic priests when compared with Anglican clergy. With the many different conceptions of ministry that exist among the Anglicans, reinforced by the strong differences between theological colleges, it is unlikely that a clear professional/occupational ideology will develop. The more cohesive situation of ministers and priests helps to engender a clearer occupational identity, which, given the nature of the occupation, is likely to be a professional one.

Within-Church differences

Turning to the extent to which there are differences in professional orientation with each of our denominational groups, and attempting to explain any differences that do occur, the picture built up in the preceding section is confirmed. Essentially, there are very strong differences amongst Anglican clergy, some differences amongst Methodist ministers, and almost no differences amongst Roman Catholic priests.

A number of things can be thought of as having an effect on the extent to which an individual develops a professional ideology. Obviously there are indicators of the type and time of socialisation, that is, churchmanship or theological orientation, the age of a cleric and the number of years that he has been ordained. For example, one would hypothesise that older clerics, ordained in a period when the role of the Church in the world was more certain and when, consequently, the occupational self-definition had more clarity, would have a more professional self-image. Following from this one would also expect that those espousing more traditional and less questioning theological conceptions would have a more definite professional orientation. Traditionally, the occupation of religious functionary has been defined as professional in sociology (cf. Marshall, 1938; Parsons, 1939; Krause, 1971). It is in the past two decades that there has been increasing questioning of this definition (cf. Glasse, 1968).

However, any individual socialised in a particular way faces the inevitable stresses and tensions of maintaining his values, norms and behaviour patterns in a variety of situations. Some situations may be supportive, whereas others are hostile. Much of the work on professions has concerned the supposedly inevitable conflict between the demands of autonomy and colleague reference by the professional, and those of control and hierarchy imposed by employing organisations (see Hall (1968) for a good summary). Hastings and Hinings (1970) have shown the patterns of accommodation to organisational demands that occur among accountants. Thus, there is good evidence for hypothesising that the position an individual occupies in an organisational hierarchy will affect his occupational self-image.

The Church of England Within the Church of England we find that all of these factors have some effect, and that nearly all of them are related to every dimension of professionalism. In fact, taking our indicators of age and experience, we find that they are all related in exactly the same way to four dimensions of professionalism, namely vocation, service orientation, the use of the profession as a major reference, and a belief in control by colleagues. Essentially, it is the clergyman who is older, who has been ordained longer, who has spent the longest amount of time in both his present position and the diocese, and who is towards the top of the diocesan hierarchy who is the most professional. All the indicators point to increasing professional orientations the more senior one is in the occupation. Certainly one important element in this will be the changing definition of the occupation, away from traditional concerns which produce relative certainty, towards an occupation 'in flux'.

This is borne out when we examine the relationship of church-manship to these four aspects of professionalism. One consistency is that those of a Catholic persuasion (Anglo-Catholics and Prayer-Book Catholics) score high on all four dimensions, whereas those who label themselves as being of a 'New Theology' position are always low scorers. Professional self-definition is to be found amongst those whose theology stresses traditional beliefs, leading to clear task definition rooted in socialisation at the theological college. On the two dimensions where the differences between churchman-ship are statistically very strong, namely service and colleague control, those who define themselves as 'Conservative Evangelicals' are also high scorers, again underpinning the relationship between a professional orientation and traditional concerns.

It is with regard to the dimension of professional autonomy that the picture changes somewhat. None of the relationships are linear. It is those in the middle of the hierarchy who have the strongest feelings of autonomy, with curates being the least professional in this sense and archdeacons and bishops the next least. This is reflected in the relationships with number of years ordained and the number of years a clergyman had occupied his present post. It is the longer-serving clergy who perceive least autonomy, followed by those with least experience. The middle groups perceive the most.

This pattern reflects a negative relationship between autonomy and the other aspects of professionalism. This, we think, is largely for methodological reasons. In the actual items used in the attitude scale, the other aspects of professionalism continuously refer to one's occupation (see Appendix 1 for details). This is not so for autonomy, where the item references are to the job or the position of the respondent. Thus it is open to doubt whether autonomy is measuring professionalism or an aspect of the job which the re-spondent fills. If we take the latter to be the case, our results are immediately explicable. It is those in the middle positions in the Anglican Church, namely incumbents, rural deans and chaplains, whose jobs give them the most leeway. Those at the foot of the organisation, directly controlled by superiors, are likely to feel much less autonomy. Similarly, in an organisation which is subject to forms of control from encompassing organisations, those right at the top are liable to perceive a brake on their own freedom of action.

The Methodist Church We have already said that there are less differences amongst Methodists than amongst Anglicans. Indeed, none of the indicators of organisational experience, are related to any aspects of professionalism. Conversely, feelings of autonomy are unrelated to any aspects of organisational position, age, organisational experience or churchmanship. This leaves us with possible relationships between position, age and churchmanship on the one hand, and service, colleague control, vocation and professional reference on the other. Essentially the same relationships hold across all four aspects. Position is the only variable which is associated with all four dimensions in a statistically significant way. The association is a linear one with those higher in the organisational hierarchy having the strongest professional orientation. While age is statistically associated only with service and colleague control, the same relationship holds true for vocation and professional reference. This relationship backs up that with position; the older a minister is the more likely he is to define himself as a professional.

These findings are further strengthened by the association between churchmanship and professionalism. Again, while the relationships are not always statistically significant (although they mainly are), they are, without exception, in the same direction. They show that those who classify themselves as Evangelicals or Ecumenicals are always more professionally orientated than those who do not, and that ministers who claim to be Radicals in theological outlook are consistently less professional than others. As with Anglican clergy, this suggests that Methodist ministers espousing the traditional concerns, based as they are in clear role prescriptions, are liable to be much stronger in defining their occupation in traditional terms, namely as a professional. And it is the older, organisationally senior ministers who espouse these theological positions.

The Roman Catholic Church Looking at the Roman Catholic priest, it is only the dimension of professional reference on which there are any differences. As far as vocation, service, colleague control and autonomy are concerned, Roman Catholics present a relatively even face. On professional reference we find that the older a priest is, and the longer he has been ordained, the more likely it is that he will see his profession as a major reference, giving it an extremely high valuation. As one would expect, it is those at the top of the hierarchy who have a similarly high score on this aspect of professionalism.

Summary and conclusions

Initially we showed that there are clear differences between the three groups, both in terms of level of score and also in the ways in which the five dimensions of professionalism were ordered. We suggest that Methodist ministers have the most professional attitudes, especially with regard to professional reference, colleague control and autonomy. They are closely followed by Roman Catholic priests who are particularly professionally orientated with regard to vocation and service orientation. Anglican clergy are the least professionally orientated. We suggest that these differences arise from the relative degrees of cohesiveness in training and work situation between ministers, priests and clergy.

When we examine the extent to which each group shows internal differences, there are more amongst Anglicans than Methodists and very few among Roman Catholic priests. The differences within the Anglican and Methodist groups seem broadly explainable by means of the same argument. In particular, the existence of a professional self-identification as represented by vocation, service, colleague control and professional reference is related in both Churches to age, position and churchmanship. It is those who represent enduring strands of theology, and who are likely to be older and more senior organisationally, who will have a stronger professional definition of their occupation. Amongst Anglican clergy this is underpinned and reinforced by other indicators of organisational experience. The only real difference between Anglicans and Methodists is that amongst the former, clergy more subject to direct control by superiors or indirect control by outside organisations are likely to be lower on autonomy.

Amongst Roman Catholic priests differences occur only on the dimension of professional reference; the finding parallels those among Anglicans and Methodists.

4　Definitions of role

The question of how clergy, ministers and priests view their ministry is particularly pertinent during a time of theological controversy. Religious functionaries have been subjected to considerable pressure from radicals within the Churches, from intellectuals outside, and from many lay people, to make the content of their beliefs, their daily activities and their forms of worship relevant to the complexities and exigencies of modern society. Many clergy have responded to this demand by giving far more expression to the counselling aspect of their ministry; for example, Diana Leat (1973) has recently pointed to the significant proportion of ordained ministers who have turned to counselling as a means to 'putting God over'. This does not involve a leap of faith for them as Halmos (1965) has pointed out, there is a high degree of congruity between counselling and many aspects of the Christian faith.

Other non-theological changes have put religious functionaries under pressure to reallocate their responsibilities; for example, the growth of diocesan bureaucracy has forced them to become far more conscious of their administrative responsibilities. With the Churches finding it difficult to maintain current levels of finance and manpower, pressures are put on individuals to emphasise administrative efficiency.

At the same time members of the ordained ministry have shed many of the roles which were once their prerogative. For example, Dean Church (quoted in Drewett, 1966) has written of the ordained minister in the early nineteenth century that he was 'often the patriarch of his parish, its ruler, its doctor, its lawyer, its magistrate, as well as its teacher, before whom vice trembled and rebellion dared not shew itself'. Although this central position was not enjoyed by all ministers, it is clear that many roles which clergy once played have been lost. The emergence of 'caring' professions (e.g. social workers) has done much to exacerbate this process.

As a result, religious functionaries have had perforce to re-think the nature of their ministry. This naturally involves reflecting upon the components of what is entailed in being an ordained minister in an increasingly secular world. This is not to say that all agree that re-thinking is necessary; nor that all those who do believe it necessary agree on the end-product. As Leslie Paul (1973, p. 226) has put it: 'There is no doubt that there is much confusion in the minds at any rate of Church of England clergy about the roles they should play (the plural is necessary).' There is not just an issue of 'which roles?', but also of the relative importance of each role.

It was with such interests in mind that we sought to gain an understanding of how religious functionaries view the relative importance of their roles. In the first chapter it was pointed out that there is a growing American literature on this issue, but a dearth of such information in Britain, with the exception of the work of Michael Daniel (1967). Consequently, we were concerned in our research to articulate the clergyman's view of how he assesses the relative importance of some of his functions. To this end, we asked the following question of our respondents:

> For certain purposes, the main tasks of the ministry can be summed up under seven general headings: the ordained minister as *administrator* (of church affairs); as *celebrant* (of sacraments and services); as *leader* (of the local community); as *preacher* (of the word); as *official* (of the Church); as *pastor* (and father of the congregation); and as *counsellor* (adviser and confessor).
>
> Will you now please rank these seven responsibilities in terms of the order of priorities in which you believe they *ought* to be placed. (Please number them from 1 to 7, i.e. 1 = first priority.)
>
> administrator ....
>
> celebrant ....
>
> leader ....
>
> preacher ....
>
> official ....
>
> pastor ....
>
> counsellor ....

The term 'official' was used in the case of our Anglican and Roman Catholic respondents, whereas 'representative' was used for Methodists. Otherwise the question was identical for each Church.

According to this scheme, then, the lower the number ascribed to each 'responsibility', the greater its relative importance. It can always be argued that a limitation of this approach is that it pre-selects the options available to respondents. For example, many would have included the responsibility of 'teacher', although we would argue that an ordained minister's teaching role is nowadays barely distinguishable from his role of preacher. However, we feel that this scheme selects some of the most significant aspects of the ordained ministry from both an historical and a contemporary perspective, and that its fruits are evident from the findings we discuss.

A further important reason for examining role definitions is because of its possible status as an intervening variable between aspects of origins, experience and beliefs, on the one hand, and attitudes towards ecumenism, reform and the organisation, on the other. Through this question we are getting at the operation of the religious functionary in his job. This will be a resultant of his overall definition of the nature of the Church and his sense of mission. But from this and the day-to-day experiences of his role will spring certain attitudes.

I Between-Church differences

Table 4.1 presents the mean rank order and the ranking of each role by the religious functionaries of each Church. The table reveals both differences and similarities in the way in which clergy, priests and ministers ascribe priorities to their disparate responsibilities. The functionaries of all three Churches ascribe to the role of pastor a high position, indicating that whatever the differences between the Churches the role of the ordained minister as the shepherd of his flock is fairly central to the Christian ministry.

TABLE 4.1   *Ranking of roles*

	Church of England		Methodist		Roman Catholic	
Pastor	1	1.895	1	1.843	2	2.474
Celebrant	2	2.667	5	4.480	1	1.963
Preacher	3	3.117	2	2.509	3	2.928
Counsellor	4	3.392	3	3.623	4	3.817
Leader	5	4.640	4	4.159	5	4.490
Administrator	6	5.232	6	5.575	6	5.541
Official/representative	7	6.542	7	5.581	7	6.444

Clergy, priests and ministers are also alike in their indifference to and antipathy towards their more organisational tasks. In this respect our data are similar to those deriving from American sources, such as those of Blizzard (1956), Jud *et al.* (1970), and Lauer (1973), which also point to the low priority American ministers ascribe administrative and organisational roles. Religious functionaries seem to rank of low importance those tasks which derive from their possession of an office in a bureaucracy, even though these activities take up a good deal of their time: such tasks are perceived as mere drudgery which detract from their central vocational tasks, rather than as means for the accomplishment of these religious ends. Methodist ministers, however, display a slight tendency towards being more favourable to the representative role than were clergy and priests to their 'official' role. The structure of the Methodist Church with its stress on travelling lends itself directly to a greater emphasis upon representation.

There seems to be a much more basic similarity in the conception of ministry which adheres in the Anglican and Roman Catholic Churches, than between the Methodist and either of the other two Churches. The major exception is that the Roman Catholic priests ascribe greater priority to the celebrant role than do the Anglicans. This is largely consonant with the emphasis on ritualism and the celebration of the sacraments which are much more basic to the Roman Catholic tradition. In the Church of England, by contrast, ritualism and sacramentalism, along with the whole aura of mystery in the Roman Catholic Church, have been bones of contention rather than key tenets.

As we have pointed out in a previous chapter the Roman Catholic priest is more likely to have an ontological view of his ministry and his separateness and uniqueness is enshrined in the sacraments.

In the Church of England, where the whole land is caught up in the parochial system, the clergyman ascribes top priority to his task of pastor—of shepherd of his flock. The pastoral area is also the top priority for the Methodist minister. It would appear that Methodism has retained this distinctively Anglican element. In fact, a fairly considerable emphasis on pastoral work can be discerned in all three Churches which would suggest that it is a fairly central aspect of Christian ministry, in spite of the latter's diversification.

The area of celebration, so completely embraced by Roman Catholics and, to some extent by Anglicans, is relegated to the low position of fifth by Methodist ministers. Ritual, and particularly the aura of mystery, have frequently been anathema to Methodists who are firmly situated in the Evangelical tradition, with its emphasis on simple worship. Biblical literalism and sacramentalism do not

come together too easily, and the great emphasis on the former led
to a mistrust of the latter. Within this Evangelical tradition in which
Methodism is rooted, oratory has been deemed to be of considerable
importance; hence the greater priority given to the responsibility of
being a preacher than among Anglican and Roman Catholic clergy.

The three Churches are moderately similar in their evaluation of
their counselling and leadership responsibilities. These two areas are
ranked somewhat higher by the Methodists, in line with their
evangelical and congregation-orientated view of the ministry. The
Methodist minister has a more clearly defined membership to
whom he has functional responsibilities.

These data point to some of the problems which firm adherents of
the ecumenical movement will have to overcome before organic
unity will be possible. Anglicanism, Methodism and Roman
Catholicism entail different conceptions of ministry, which would
indicate that if two of the three come together, it may well prejudice
unity with the third. However, the considerable emphasis by all
three Churches on pastoralia could be a unifying principle which
would override the divergences.

But, above all, our data point to the problem of talking about
the role of the clergy or *the* functions of the ministry. Such a perspective only serves to hide from the observer the reality of the
situation in all its diversity. But does diversity end here? With the
exception of the Roman Catholic Church until recent times, clergy
of even a single Church have not been famous for their unanimity.
In the next section we shall explore this whole area further with
reference to differences within each of the three Churches.

II   Within-Church differences

The Church of England

We know from the previous chapter that in many ways religious
functionaries within a single Church do not adhere to a single,
unitary belief system, but pursue diverse and often divergent theological cosmologies. It was suggested that these cosmologies may
well have an impact on a number of issues. Our discussion of the
way clergy, ministers and priests perceive the relative importance of
their roles affords us an opportunity to discover the extent to which,
and the ways in which, this is in fact so: how far do differences in
theological cosmologies affect ministerial self-conception?

It is quite common at such a juncture for the social scientist to
look to socio-demographic variables in providing the axes along
which differences within each group may be discerned. But almost
without exception one would expect religious functionaries to

rationalise their roles in terms of their beliefs. To anticipate our findings slightly, we find that in the case of Church of England clergy theological cosmology is a much more profound discriminator of how clergy rank their roles than traditional socio-demographic variables. This is highly congruent with our findings regarding a sample of Anglican laity, in which we found that churchmanship was of considerably greater importance than such traditional variables in helping us locate differences in degrees of support for ecumenism (Bryman, Ranson and Hinings, 1974).

When we divide the sample of Anglican clergy into those who are incumbents and those who are not, we find that it is not a particularly potent discriminatory variable. Non-incumbents are considerably less likely than incumbents to stress their pastoral role. In particular it is chaplains and curates who give this role less prominence. Similarly, it is those who are young in age and experience (who will be the curates and chaplains) who regard the pastoral role as of less importance. At the other side of the coin, those young in experience, having spent less time in the diocese and their present position, are more likely to stress the role of preacher. This is not entirely congruent with Coxon's (1965) research which indicated that the role definition of prospective ordinands is changing from a theological to a pastoral perspective.

Beliefs in the nature of the clergyman's occupation are much more systematically related to his ranking of roles. While there are no clear differences with regard to the role of official, all of the others show consistent relationships with the extent to which a clergyman views himself as a professional or not. We have already suggested in chapter 3 that to define himself as being in a professional occupation is essentially traditional for a clergyman. Our results bear this out. Those clergy who score high on the professionalism dimensions of service, professional reference, colleague control and vocation, will be consistently high raters of the celebrant role, the preacher role and the pastor role. Those who see themselves in a less professional occupation will give a lower rating to those three aspects of their role and conversely, give a higher ranking to acting as a leader, administrator and counsellor. The traditional professional definition of a clergyman has been in terms of the former roles; it is the 'new breed' who will stress roles which are of a kind that are liable to facilitate the link between Church and society, clergyman and congregation.

As we have indicated, churchmanship is a far more potent and interesting variable in delineating differences in perception, as can be seen from Table 4.2. The data point to the huge differences in the conception of ministry within the Anglican tradition. The roles on which there is anything approximating unanimity between the strands of churchmanship are those of official and counsellor. Even here there is a marked divergence between the Modernists, on the one hand, and the Catholics, on the other.

TABLE 4.2 *Churchmanship and differences in perception of the role of the clergyman*

	Catholic	Central Broad	Modernist New Theology	Evang-elical	Other	F	p
Pastor	2 1.955	1 1.730	1 2.611	1 1.608	1 2.44	6.2039	0.001
Celebrant	1 1.900	2 2.722	4 3.528	4 3.784	2 2.585	24.2814	0.001
Preacher	3 3.360	3 3.373	3 3.167	2 2.351	3 2.875	8.3663	0.001
Counsellor	4 3.545	4 3.480	2 2.889	3 3.247	4 3.500	2.6092	0.05
Leader	5 4.929	5 4.480	5 3.588	5 4.698	5 4.650	5.5639	0.001
Administrator	6 5.457	6 5.048	6 4.639	6 5.411	6 4.878	4.4507	0.01
Official	7 6.702	7 6.400	7 6.250	7 6.490	7 6.525	2.6769	0.05

The pastoral role is ranked as the top priority by all the churchmanship groups, except for the Catholics among whom celebration is rated the most important responsibility. However, the means indicate that Catholics are far more likely to rate the pastoral role high on their list than are the Modernists. Celebration is less valued, however, in the Evangelical and Modernist traditions. These findings show the way in which ritual is central to Catholicism and is relegated in the Evangelical tradition which, as we have said, emphasises simplicity of worship and therefore plays down an elaborately ritual life. The stress on oratory in this tradition accounts for the importance ascribed to the clergyman's role as preacher among Evangelical clergy. The Evangelicals, and the Modernists even more so, are inclined to emphasise counselling functions. The leadership role is ranked fifth by all groups but the mean indicates that many Modernists favour it, almost to the extent of its being more valued than celebration. Like the role of official, the importance ascribed to the clergyman's administrative tasks is of low rating, though Modernists again show a marked tendency to see it of quite considerable importance.

What does all this mean? We feel that it indicates that there are not only problems in talking about the roles of *the* clergyman, there are also difficulties in making crude statements about the roles of *the* Anglican clergyman. Within Anglicanism there have persisted differing, and often diverse, theological strands which entail different conceptions of ministry.

When we look at the Catholics, it is indicative of their ministerial self-conception that the ranking of the seven roles is the same as that of Roman Catholic priests. We noted in the previous section that Roman Catholic priests rated celebration as their main responsibility whereas Anglican clergy (as a whole) inverted these first two positions and made the pastoral role their top priority.

The marked similarity between Evangelical Anglicans and Methodist ministers is striking. Both groups seem to rate their roles of preacher and counsellor high and to play down celebration. Methodists and Evangelical Anglicans are both very clearly still following in the wake of the Evangelical Revival of the eighteenth century. This brand of churchmanship still emphasises the clergyman's pastoral functions and the stress on oratory; ritual and sacramentalism are still regarded with suspicion. It would appear that these two strands are still very much alive and in latent opposition.

Equally striking is the centrality of the Central/Broad Church group. 'The Revd Average' would be an unhappy but not inappropriate description of their self-conception. Not only do they rank the seven responsibilities as Anglican clergy as a whole do, but the actual means are very similar too.

The Modernist/New Theology group is very different from the other strands of churchmanship in its ministerial self-conception. It tends to place considerable emphasis on pastoral, counselling and leadership responsibilities—a view which appears to indicate a desire to help people in the world as much as in purely spiritual terms. This group is very different from that described by Harris (1969) in the context of the Anglican Church in Wales: 'Centuries of pastoral activity with very little missionary endeavour has served to create a lower elite whose ideology is predominantly pastoral. The role of the clergy is seen as involving direct dealings with people and devotional activities'. The Modernists are also more likely to rate their administrative role higher than any of the others.

TABLE 4.3 *Ranking of clergy roles by Modernists*

	Incumbent	*Non-incumbent*
Pastor	2.389	2.833
Celebrant	3.556	3.500
Preacher	2.778	3.556
Counsellor	3.556	2.222
Leader	4.412	2.765
Administrator	4.222	5.056
Official	6.333	6.116

We would argue that this is primarily because they see administrative competence as an important means of (and not a burden to) the accomplishment of their task as shepherd. There appears to be a tendency towards a 'radicalism' in ministerial self-conception among Modernists. However, we would argue that this is because there is a radical element *within* the Modernist group, i.e. not *all* Modernists are radical. When we divide this group into incumbents and non-incumbents, as Table 4.3 shows, a fascinating pattern emerges. The radical element is made up of those Modernists who are non-incumbents. The ranking for this group is: counsellor – leader – pastor – celebrant – preacher – administrator – official. This is a highly radical re-conceptualisation of Anglican ministry which is most emphatic in its stress on what we have identified as the Modernist's self-conception as leader and helper in the world. As we have already seen in chapter 3, the non-incumbent Modernist is very likely to be young in terms of age and experience.

These findings are indicative of the potential in delineating theological cosmologies. Equally, they suggest that strands of churchmanship are very real to our Anglican respondents in that they are not just the ideological left-overs from Church party battles in the last century, but important stances to which the clergyman adheres, thereby providing a perspective on the world and his place and job in it.

The Methodist Church

As we have mentioned earlier, there do not appear to be in Methodism the sharp theological divisions that have been discerned among Anglican clergy. The theological cosmology of Methodist ministers revolves around a central core of Evangelicalism and Ecumenicalism.

We found that only 10.1 per cent of ministers identified themselves as just Evangelicals and only 6.6 per cent as just Ecumenicals. However, 53.7 per cent of the sample described themselves as Evangelicals or Evangelicals of a certain type (e.g. Evangelical and Ecumenical, Radical Evangelical, and the like); similarly, 55.5 per cent described themselves as Ecumenical or Ecumenical and some other description. This suggests that the overwhelming majority identify themselves within an Evangelical or an Ecumenical tradition, and many identify themselves in terms of both. In other words, there seems to be a tendency for terms like 'liberal', 'radical', 'catholic', and so on to be adjectives for describing oneself as a certain type of Evangelical or Ecumenical or a type of Ecumenical Evangelical – they are ideological hues surrounding an ideological central tendency. Because such a large majority of ministers identifies with one or both of these terms there is very little room for theological cosmology to discriminate between types of ministerial self-conception.

This assumption is largely upheld by our findings. When we look at the difference in role-conception of those who defined themselves as Evangelicals as opposed to those who did not; Ecumenicals as opposed to non-Ecumenicals; Liberals as opposed to non-Liberals; Radicals as opposed to non-Radicals, and Catholics as opposed to non-Catholics, the differences are not as great and profound as is the case with Anglicanism.

Our findings suggest that the division of ministers into Radicals versus non-Radicals and Evangelicals versus non-Evangelicals are of most significance. It is important to realise that there is overlap in all these categories. Largely due to the fact that the question which elicited this information was open-ended, the majority of ministers placed themselves in two or more theological categories.

Radicals tend to stress their leadership responsibility whilst playing down their pastoral and preaching responsibilities. This has little effect on the actual ranking of the seven responsibilities, except in that the leadership role is just ranked above that of counsellor which is the reverse of the way Methodist ministers as a whole rank them. It would appear that the Radicals are 'radical' in a fairly real sense, for they—or at least some of them—appear to have a conception of ministry which is less inclined to emphasise the pastoral and oratorial aspects of Methodist ministry which are central to the Methodist tradition. This would suggest that one would be led to expect that Evangelicals would stress these aspects of their work. Indeed, Evangelicals are far more likely to stress the role of preacher than those who do not identify with this tradition. They are also more inclined to stress their pastoral role though this is not statistically significant. Evangelicals also play down their celebrant and representative roles. It is important to note that the differences between Evangelicals and non-Evangelicals do not alter the ranking of the seven roles as compared with the Methodists *in toto*.

We also found that those who described themselves as Ecumenicals tend to ascribe greater priority to the celebrant role and lower priority to the preacher role than do non-Ecumenicals, though only the first difference is statistically significant. Predictably, Catholics ascribed greater priority to the role of celebrant than did non-Catholics. This difference was not statistically significant though it did result in the celebrant role being ranked fourth, and the role of leader fifth, by Catholics.

The identification of a Methodist minister's theological self-classification, then, is relevant to some extent to the way in which he views the relative importance of his roles. It does not appear to be quite so deep in explaining differences in ministerial self-conception.

This is also borne out by the rather weaker relationship between professional and role orientation among ministers compared with clergy. The only strong finding is that those who are self-defined as professionals are much more likely to give a high rating to the preacher role. As with the Church of England there is some evidence that ministers who are less likely to see themselves as belonging to a profession are more likely to stress the role of leader. Again professionalism is the traditional orientation to the ministerial occupation, a fact which is reflected in role rankings.

However, our findings suggest that other factors are more important in conditioning the way in which the Methodist minister sees the relative importance of the various aspects of his work. Tables 4.4 and 4.5 indicate that the work in which the minister is engaged and his age affect the ways in which he perceives his work.

TABLE 4.4　*Ranking of roles by type of work*

	Ministers, Wesley Deaconesses, Probationer and Supernumerary ministers	Sector ministers	Chairmen circuit superintendents	F	p
Pastor	1.674	2.562	2.000	5.0153	0.01
Preacher	2.632	3.125	2.103	5.4253	0.01
Counsellor	3.514	3.687	3.838	1.2533	NS
Leader	4.098	3.250	4.500	3.6613	0.05
Celebrant	4.490	5.062	4.324	1.2179	NS
Administrator	5.764	5.312	5.235	3.6213	0.05
Representative	5.646	4.250	5.761	5.9275	0.01

The sector minister is a man whose work is marginally connected to the overall work of Methodist districts and circuits. He may have to preach on Sundays but his actual involvement in the Church need be little more than that. It is not surprising therefore that he has a different ministerial self-conception from his colleagues. Thus sector ministers are much less likely to see the roles of pastor, preacher and celebrant as of great importance. These three roles are very specifically of a ministerial nature, and his connection with such roles is less intense than that of his Methodist colleagues. On the other hand, he is much more likely to rank the roles of leader and representative high. This suggests that sector ministers have a considerably different orientation to their work and see their mission as that of ministering to people in a secular context. The roles of leader and representative are less inherently religious and are thus more easily applicable in a non-religious context.

Ministers stress their preaching and administrative roles less than chairmen and circuit superintendents, and their leadership and pastoral roles slightly more. Both chairmen and circuit superintendents are much closer to the bureaucratic machinery of Methodist districts, and are consequently more likely to see their administrative tasks as important.

TABLE 4.5 *Ranking of roles by age*

	−39	40–49	50–59	60+	F	p
Pastor	1.915	1.857	1.698	1.905	0.4066	NS
Preacher	3.186	2.571	2.190	1.952	9.2375	0.001
Counsellor	3.356	3.444	4.032	5.595	2.9285	0.05
Leader	3.328	4.381	4.238	4.833	7.4709	0.001
Celebrant	4.610	4.258	4.270	4.952	1.8616	NS
Administrator	6.169	4.476	5.444	5.143	5.4412	0.001
Representative	5.153	5.635	5.968	5.488	2.5821	NS

Table 4.5 suggests that some of these relationships are closely linked to the age of the minister. Younger ministers are less likely to emphasise their roles of preacher and administrator, whilst tending to emphasise their counselling and leadership responsibilities. There is a suggestion here that younger ministers display a greater tendency towards a role of pastor–counsellor–leader, whilst older ministers are more firmly entrenched in the Evangelical tradition with its stress on the role of the preacher and also in the organisational work of the Church. This picture is upheld by the relationships with other aspects of experience, such as the number of years a minister has been ordained, and the number of posts he has held. It is the young, then, who are liable to redefine their roles.

These findings suggest that there is considerably less theological diversity within Methodism than Anglicanism. Differences in 'churchmanship' do not have nearly the same impact among Methodist ministers. Differences in type of work and age seem to be much more discriminative in regard to ministerial self-conception.

The Roman Catholic Church

Even more than our findings on Methodist ministers, the data on the Roman Catholic priesthood suggest that differences in experience and age have a considerable impact on how priests allocate priorities among their seven roles; whereas beliefs are unimportant. Indeed, there are relationships between some aspect of age and experience and every one of the seven roles. However, the differences are very much centred on four roles, namely, preacher, leader, administrator and pastor. It is the three roles of celebrant, counsellor and official on which there is most consensus.

Belief is related to two of these roles, administrator and leader. It is orientation to Rome which is the belief item of relevance. Those who believe that the national Church should be free from Rome are more likely to regard the leader role as important; conversely they will regard the role of administrator as of rather less importance than those who hold a more traditional belief in relations with Rome.

This relative unimportance of beliefs is also reflected in the lack of relationships between occupational orientation and role rankings. There is a slight tendency for those who show professional beliefs, as we have defined them, to consistently rank the role of celebrant higher than those who see themselves as less professional. The converse occurs with the role of leader. While this fits generally with the findings on Anglicans and Methodists, most of the results do not reach statistical significance, pointing to the effect of other variables.

TABLE 4.6   *Ranking of roles by number of years ordained*

	0–9	*10–19*	*20–29*	*30+*	*F*	*p*
Celebrant	2.047	2.071	1.981	1.831	0.7669	NS
Pastor	3.000	2.494	2.303	2.255	4.8812	0.001
Preacher	2.882	2.471	3.020	3.178	4.8812	0.01
Counsellor	3.767	3.765	3.755	3.926	0.5529	NS
Leader	3.767	4.612	4.684	4.733	8.5947	0.001
Administrator	6.036	5.941	5.235	5.201	11.4322	0.001
Official	6.235	6.165	6.583	6.652	6.6082	0.001

The pastoral role seems to be less highly esteemed by those who are not parish priests, which is related to the fact that the younger and less experienced the priest is, the less likely he is to rank the pastoral role high. It would appear that this aspect of the priest's work is no longer as universally esteemed as it once was. Conversely, the preaching role is more highly esteemed among young, less experienced assistant priests. In fact, priests who are under forty and who have been in the priesthood for less than ten years rank the role of preacher well above that of pastor. There is also a very evident tendency for these very same groups, most of whom are the same people, of course, to lay considerable stress on the leadership role. It may be that their stress on the role of preacher is related to

73

this tendency in that oratory is seen as a means of leading people. Similarly, the greater esteem in which they tend to hold their role as official may also be seen as an instrumental factor in their stress on leadership.

By contrast, the parish priest is much more likely to ascribe considerable priority to their administrative role. Table 4.6 uses number of years ordained as an example of typical relationships for the variables which describe age and experience.

These findings are remarkably similar to those of Hall and Schneider (1973) on American priests. They found that pastors stressed their administrative responsibilities more than curates, who laid greater emphasis on community involvement and personal development. Both groups lay more- or- less equal stress on their parochial duties. Hall and Schneider (1973, p. 60) then concluded:

> These data summarise one of the central issues in the pastor–curate 'generation gap': pastors stress the importance of maintaining and expanding church structures, meeting financial obligations, and administering the parish effectively, while curates want to devote more time and energy to community development and their own personal growth.

The greater emphasis put on leadership and preaching among our equivalent group to the American curates may also be seen in terms of community development.

III Conclusions

Our research points to the differences in ministerial self-conception between clergy in the three Churches, and within each group of clergy. In Anglicanism we stressed the role of theological stances in conditioning differences in role-perception; among Methodists we found that a minister's theological position has considerable import, but so did other factors; and among Roman Catholic priests we find that it is the factors concerned with age and experience that are of importance.

In the Anglican Church, as we have seen, there are differences in the importance ascribed to all seven roles and these differences are attributable to theological stances. There is remarkable diversity. The same is not true for Methodist ministers and Roman Catholic priests. For the former group there is little divergence over the roles of celebrant, official and pastor; for the latter, the agreement is with regard to the roles of celebrant, official and counsellor. In both cases there is agreement over the highest- and lowest-ranked roles.

However, the actual ways in which the factors of belief, age and

74

experience are related to each role differ, because of the ways in which the significance of the roles changes between the three Churches. One similarity is that the younger, less well firmly entrenched members in all three Churches tend to stress their leadership role more than their older, experienced colleagues. But while it is the young curates and assistant priests, not very far into their careers, who give a higher ranking to the role of preacher in the Anglican and Roman Catholic Churches, it is the reverse among Methodist ministers. With regard to the role of pastor it is the young among the Methodists who rate it more highly than the older Anglican clergy and Roman Catholic priests.

What this represents is, in both cases, a challenge to the established order. There is a greater tendency among younger clergy towards the Church's involvement in the world, and the perceived importance of the clergyman as mediator of the ongoing relationship between the Church and the world. It is the younger, less experienced, clergyman who is more likely to approve of the 'new breed' (Cox, 1967) type of clergyman who sees the Church, not as a passive respondent to social change, but as promoter of social action and values.

5 Ecumenism

The Christian Church is founded upon an endemic paradox which has become a central issue. Its doctrine is intrinsically one of the essential unity of mankind and spiritual identity of believers. The self-conscious purpose of Christ's ministry was, ostensibly, to join, to link, to pacify conflict and antagonisms with a spiritual anodyne. Yet the Christian Church has been divided theologically, and as a corollary organisationally, for most of its long history: the Church has been split particularly by two major schisms and a plethora of minor ones.

This history of division and conflict is briefly and cogently summarised by Till in his book *The Churches' Search for Unity* (1972):

> much of the energy of the early church was devoted to evolving
> ways and means of expressing and maintaining unity in the
> face of threats to disrupt it. It was not until the fifth century
> that these efforts broke down permanently for the first time
> and divisions appeared in the Church which have remained
> unhealed to this day. This was in the eastern church; thereafter
> a worsening rift grew up between the eastern church based on
> Constantinople and the western based on Rome, a rift which
> became open and permanent in the eleventh century and which
> is in fact to this day still the greatest schism in Christendom.
> The divisions of the Reformation within the western church are,
> both numerically and ideologically, less serious than those of
> the Rome/Constantinople breach—though most western
> Christians fail to realise this.

Although attempts had been made in the seventeenth and eighteenth centuries to achieve peace between the discordant factions in the western Church, it was not until the nineteenth century that reunion, as such, was contemplated and a movement begun by the Protestant

Churches. They called their movement 'ecumenical', a word derived from the Greek, 'oikoumene' ('whole inhabited world') which was used by the early Christians to mean 'the Church of the whole world'. This was very close to the Greek word 'Catholic' ('the universal Church'). Again, to quote Till (1972), 'When the enthusiasts for the reunion of the Church applied the word "ecumenical" to their movement they were therefore historically justified in claiming that when the church recovered its ecumenicity it would at the same time recover its lost catholicity.'

The word ecumenical properly entered Christian language after the First World Missionary Council held at Edinburgh in 1910, when Christians of all theological shades from all parts of the world met for the first time with the professed aim of 'the evangelisation of the world in our time'. Since that first breakthrough the Churches have moved with deliberation but rather slowly and tentatively towards reunion. The initial work of the ecumenical movement prior to the outbreak of the Second World War was predominantly one of discussion in conferences and committees, little of which was translated into action. The Roman Catholic Church did not yet acknowledge the movement and the Orthodox Church, although recognising the value of ecumenicity, was intractable in its negotiations. In Britain, during this pre-war period, there was generally a manifest divide between a few Church leaders enthusiastically giving support to ecumenicalism and an indifferent or overtly antagonistic clergy and laity. Yet active progress was made, even though it was within one confession. This was the foundation of the United British Methodist Church in 1932, which brought together the United Methodist Church, the Primitive Methodist Church and the Wesleyan Methodist Church.

Following the Second World War the ecumenical movement has seen the foundation of the World Council of Churches (1948) and an accelerated interest in unity negotiations and ecumenicalism as such. The Roman Catholic Church began to take more official interest in the movement towards ecumenical unity, a movement which was facilitated greatly by other related movements: the biblical theology movement whose more open-minded discoveries influenced many denominations; the liturgical movement which afforded greater opportunity for lay members to play a contributory part in Church services; and the Week of Prayer for Christian Unity. The ecumenical movement has been progressively gaining theological credence and organisational impetus as we move into the later part of the twentieth century. The inauguration of the Church of South India in 1947 had a great psychological impact, demonstrating what could be achieved, and encouraged radical unions and discussions elsewhere. In England for example, the Congregational and

Presbyterian Churches have moved from agreement on inter-communion to organic union: they finally formed the United Reformed Church in 1972. While a commission of Roman Catholic and Anglican theologians, appointed respectively by the Vatican and the Archbishop of Canterbury, has produced a Statement on the Eucharist (1971) and a Statement on the Ministry and Ordination (1973).

In spite of these undoubted successes, the progress of the ecumenical movement still has the appearance of being tentative and provisional. The Roman Catholic Church and some extreme Protestant Churches are conspicuously still not affiliated to the World Council of Churches and, in Britain, the anticipated reunion of the Anglican and Methodist Churches has not materialised owing to the breakdown of negotiations. Central articles of faith, such as baptism, ministry, sacraments, celibacy, prelacy, episcopacy and so on, still divide the Churches.

Till (1972) argues that the ecumenical movement has unearthed two incipient and disturbing trends: first, a rift between radicals and conservatives:

> on the one hand there were the western theologians faced with
> a 'post-Christian' situation and the secularisation of society
> and willing to respond if need be with the most radical solutions,
> such as the so-called 'death of God' theology and the questioning
> of the very need of a visible institutional church; on the other
> hand there were the conservatives, mainly the Orthodox, some
> of whom could at least claim to be the world's experts at being
> Christians in a secular society.

And, second, the ecumenical debate has once more illuminated the fact that 'in the greatest basic theological questions the divisions of opinion are not between churches but within the churches', a fact which can be interpreted as either complicating the ecumenical movement or providing hope for possible reunions.

The ecumenical movement, because of its inherent difficulties and contradictions, has prompted intellectuals and theologians to ask probing questions and search for necessary explanations. How do we explain, for example, on the one hand the fact that it has taken the Christian Church many centuries to come to appreciate the paradox—that is to say the lacuna between principle and practice—which lies at the core of its faith and organisation and, on the other hand, the fact that although the movement towards unity has begun and has provided a challenging theological ambience it has not yet conceived the radical organisational changes which the movement's enthusiasts had hoped and looked for.

Sociologists (Wilson, 1966; Currie, 1968) have not been slow to proffer explanations. Bryan Wilson in his book, *Religion in Secular*

Society: A Sociological Comment, argues cogently and plausibly that the ecumenical phenomenon is the institutional response of the Christian Churches to radical social and cultural changes which have threatened the basis of religion in industrial society. In the tradition of Weber, Wilson emphasises that as society has become progressively rational in its beliefs, as its institutions have become secular in form and function, so religious institutions have become increasingly weakened:

> Men act less and less in response to religious motivation:
> they assess the world in empirical and rational terms, and find
> themselves involved in rational organisations and rationally
> determined roles which allow small scope for such religious
> predilections as they might privately entertain.

Where a group is threatened by external forces this may help to establish unity or re-establish unity and cohesion among the members who prefer to subordinate internal disagreements and hostility to the common end of maintaining corporate identity. Wilson suggests that ecumenicalism, or the movement towards Church unity, is the response of religious functionaries to the external secular threat:

> In general we are seeking confirmation of the hypothesis that
> organisations amalgamate when they are weak rather than when
> they are strong, since alliance means compromise and
> amendment of commitment. . . . The ecumenical tendency
> illustrates then the extreme weakness of religious commitment
> and belief, since, much more markedly than for organisations
> which have purely instrumental ends, amalgamation implies
> surrender of principles, or their alteration.

Wilson substantiates his point with formidable arguments: religious functionaries, envisaging the possibility that their professional status might be devalued, work through the ecumenical movement to reassert their common clerical authority and privilege as against the incipient control of laity, stressing their legitimate professional role, qualification and status; many denominations which originated in the form of protest have lost, through secularisation, the social basis of such protestation and such specialised theology as existed no longer suffices to command allegiance; 'there is increasing conformity to the expectations of the wider society. In the Mass Society conformity grows and moral rigour diminishes'; and, finally, Churches find it increasingly difficult to withstand the argument for economic rationalism, 'the wastes of competition': where many Churches of different confessions live in close proximity they will tend to duplicate buildings, services, fund-raising, administration, missionary work and so on. When this is so 'there is a new pressure for ecumenicalism from the argument for the better use of facilities'.

Wilson's arguments are powerful but their weakness lies in the fact that they do not help us to explain the fluctuations in the ecumenical movement during this century and they certainly do not account for the rather languid, sluggish progress that has been made towards the ecumenical ideal, particularly in the face of rapid secularisation. Wilson's notion that there has been 'something like a mass conversion of the clergy' does not square with available evidence, while his theory is too dismissive of the importance of beliefs and does not consider their deep-seated nature and significance. It is, therefore, those explanations which work from the notions of belief or theology and sociological propositions such as status, socialisation and the influence of socio-demographic variables, which will enable us to account for both the origin of ecumenicalism and the leisurely pace of its progress.

It has been argued by some (Latourette, 1954), that the ecumenical movement had its origin in the missionary movement. It was there that contradictions became manifest and the spiritual zeal developed to evangelise the world with a united Church. Till (1972) points out that, although Wilson's arguments prove more valid applied to the Church in the late twentieth century when it feels peculiarly vulnerable before 'the cold winds of secularisation', the arguments do not apply at the turn of the century:

> for the movement in 1910 the mood was one of optimism . . .
> in short, the period at the beginning of the century which
> saw the beginning of the ecumenical movement was in many
> ways the high-water mark of the activity of the Churches. It
> would be more true to say that the movement was born of
> 'optimism in perspicacity' than of 'hope in adversity'.

The mainspring of the movement was therefore theological and spiritual rather than structural adaptation.

When we begin to consider the problems of accounting for the rather slow progress of the ecumenical movement, the explanations will have to take account of those sociological variables which Wilson fails to consider. We should need to consider the deep-seated quality of beliefs, particularly the profoundly conservative or fundamentalist nature of many theological cosmologies or forms of churchmanship; we should need to consider the unwillingness or inability of religious functionaries to detach themselves from ingrained denominational socialisation; the reluctance to endanger ascribed status or authority; the distrust of fashionable ecumenistic jargon; the difficulty of altering the form of monolithic organisations.

It is the purpose of this chapter not to re-open an historical debate but to consider exactly to what extent Anglican clergy, Roman Catholic priests and Methodist ministers are in support of the ecumenical movement. We are interested in noting the attitudes of religious functionaries in the three denominations towards forms of organic union with individual Churches, and towards forms of ecumenical co-operation with other Churches, such as jointly organised services with other Churches, joint missionary work and so on. We are also especially interested in the degree to which clergy, priests and ministers actually have been involved in ventures of co-operation, such as preaching in the church of another denomination and their *actual* membership of ecumenic societies. In this way we will be able to capture any discrepancy between ecumenical belief and practice.

We then seek to focus in more detail upon variations in response and explain them in terms of theological belief, denominational affiliation, organisational status and socio-demographic variables such as age and experience. Such a descriptive and explanatory account should enable us to form a much clearer picture of the current position of ecumenicalism among religious functionaries in Britain today.

I   Church differences

We have suggested in the early part of this chapter that there are liable to be substantial differences between our three groups with regard to ecumenism. Anglicans, Methodists and Roman Catholics have different traditions, different belief systems which lay differential emphases on relationships with other Churches. Roman Catholics, in particular, emphasise their uniqueness as carriers of the Christian tradition. Methodists, seeing themselves as part of a wider Free Church evangelical movement are more likely to attempt to develop ecumenical relationships.

However, there are a number of ways in which it is possible to approach the notion of ecumenism ranging from a situation of organic union to co-operation over specific measures. Similarly it is possible to distinguish between the extent to which a member of a Church perceives ecumenism as something to strive for and how far he actually takes part in a given possible range of ecumenical activity. These distinctions give rise to four areas that we examined, two perceptual and two behavioural, namely:

(1) *Organic ecumenism*, dealing with the extent to which religious functionaries are in favour of eventual union with a range of other Churches.

(2) *Ecumenical co-operation*, dealing with possible forms of ecumenical co-operation short of organic union.

(3) *Ecumenical activity*, being the extent to which religious functionaries have been involved in co-operative ventures with other Churches.

(4) *Ecumenical membership*, concerning current memberships of ecumenical groups.

All of these four areas form scales that are internally consistent; thus, as well as examining them as individual items, we can look at overall scores.

Table 5.1 gives details of the question and responses on organic ecumenism. It shows a general picture of the Methodists being slightly more ecumenically orientated than the Anglicans with the Roman Catholics very different. Ministers show that they are eager

TABLE 5.1   *Organic ecumenism*

'Are you in favour of the eventual union of the Church of England (Methodist Church, Roman Catholic Church) with any of the following?'

| | *% in favour* | | |
	Anglicans	*Methodists*	*Roman Catholics*
Roman Catholic Church/Church of England for Roman Catholics	89	67	59
Methodist Church/Church of England for Methodists	92	91	52
Baptist Church	79	85	48
Congregational Church ⎫ United	83	95	45
Presbyterian Church ⎭ Reformed Church	84	95	
Pentecostal Churches	70	75	42
Orthodox Churches	90	72	58
All Christian bodies	60	62	73
Others	63	68	4
Overall organic ecumenism mean score	14.90	15.68	8.27

Note: When the questionnaires were distributed to clergy and ministers the Congregational and Presbyterian Churches had not yet amalgamated.

to unite with Churches whose traditions are similar—such as the Church of England—and with Churches whose structure is familiar—such as the Baptist Church or the United Reformed Church. They tend to regard the more authoritarian structures—the Roman and

Orthodox—as more alien and are rather reluctant to acquiesce to unity with any Christian or any Church as such.

A similar pattern is true of Anglican clergy, that is, a willingness to agree to organic unity with Churches whose structure and theological traditions are close to their own, i.e. the Roman Catholic Church, the Orthodox Churches and the Methodist Church. Clergymen are rather more reluctant to agree to union with Free Churches generally and with the more radical Protestant Churches.

For the Roman Catholic priests the general picture is radically different. The individual percentage responses and the overall mean score are all very low. Priests are generally more cautious and guarded in their ecumenical expression than ministers or clergy. However, as with these latter groups, priests are far more willing for the Roman Catholic Church to unite with Churches of other denominations whose structures or traditions are similar to their own, namely the Church of England and the Orthodox Churches. But priests appear far more willing to countenance union with 'all Christian bodies' than clergy or ministers. This is largely explainable

TABLE 5.2   *Ecumenical co-operation*

'Union apart, at present in what forms of ecumenical co-operation with other Churches would you like to see the Church of England (Methodist Church, Roman Catholic Church) engage?'

	% in favour		
	Church of England	Methodists	Roman Catholic
Clergy preaching in each other's churches	93	96	52
Jointly organised services with other churches	88	95	77
Joint meetings of clergy	97	98	96
Joint meetings of members	94	98	94
Joint study groups	96	98	94
Joint conferences	89	95	88
Joint publications	87	92	70
Joint theological colleges	72	92	29
Joint education, social welfare and community projects	96	99	89
Sharing churches			52
Joint ministries	59	89	30
Joint missionary work	85	98	44
Overall ecumenical co-operation mean score	21.29	23.36	18.87

from comments written on the questionnaire which show that Christian has a highly Catholic denotation. Indeed, many of the remarks take on the connotation of takeover rather than union.

Moving on to the area of ecumenical co-operation the picture remains the same, as is shown in Table 5.2. Methodist ministers show a high uniformity of response across all the items. They are equally willing to engage in those co-operative ventures which are properly preparatory to the clearing of ground by way of meetings and discussion prior to more definitive action—thus the responses on meetings, study groups, conferences and education. Also they eagerly confront the possibility of co-operation—thus the responses not only on joint publications but also on joint theological colleges, the sharing of churches, joint ministries and missionary work, which are seen to impinge more directly than others upon the core of a religious functionary's theological belief. There appears a much greater willingness to redefine central canons of faith.

Clergy, similarly, were willing to approve, with important reservations, of the notion of the Church of England engaging in many forms of ecumenical co-operation with Churches of other denominations.

The weight of assent on the part of Anglican clergy appears impressive, yet the figures disclose an important unwillingness on the part of many to endorse particular and significant forms of co-operation. The initially tentative and provisionally co-operative measures are acceptable to clergy—preaching in the church of another denomination, meetings of clergy and members, study groups, ventures on joint education, social welfare and community projects. That is to say, those measures which contemplate initial discussions and meetings that aim to establish bridges of communication, and those measures which introduce cautious and prudent co-operation—inter-denominational preaching—and such measures as these, are warmly countenanced by Anglican clergy. The more radical measures, such as the union of theological colleges, or the fusing of ministries, are treated more cautiously. The significance of these two measures is that, compared with any of the others, they impinge much more directly upon the theological beliefs of clergy: theological colleges are the nurseries which cultivate spiritual cosmologies, while the concept of ministry is the most intimate expression of that framework of belief. Thus, although clergy appear willing to begin discussion and provisional co-operative measures, they are as yet more reluctant to agree to measures which impinge directly upon the central articles of their faith, the core of their theological belief and custom.

Roman Catholic priests share some similarities with Anglican clergy. The general impression is one of caution, and priests are willing to agree to those ventures of co-operation which are necessarily preparatory to union—discussion and communication in meetings, conferences of religious functionaries and laity. But there is an important difference from clergy: priests are reluctant to acquiesce to inter-denominational preaching and jointly organised services, and, strikingly, they are particularly suspicious of those forms of co-operation which attack the literary or liturgical as well as the theological basis of their faith; thus the distrust of joint publications or joint education as well as the more usual doubt about church sharing, joint ministries and joint missionary work. It is clear therefore that Roman Catholic priests, even more than Anglican clergy, are at present less willing to compromise the central canons of their theological cosmology.

When we turn to ecumenical activity, we see that the pattern that has already been described is maintained, as is demonstrated in Table 5.3. The more radical conception of ecumenical attitude

TABLE 5.3   *Co-operative activity*

'Have you personally initiated or been involved in any of the following co-operative ventures with another Church or Churches?'

	% *in favour*		
	Church of England	*Methodist*	*Roman Catholic*
Preached in a church of another denomination	87	98	55
Invited a minister of another denomination to preach in your church	80	97	40
Celebrated communion in a church of another denomination	20	77	2
Invited a minister of another denomination to celebrate communion in your church	14	76	6
Planned with a minister of another denomination joint activities other than preaching, joint services, communion, etc. (e.g. meetings for members, study groups, community projects, etc.)	81	95	78

among Methodist ministers is maintained, consistently, in their responses to ecumenical ritual. Ministers are vigorous in their efforts to preach in the churches of other confessions and to invite other religious functionaries, while their willingness to share in services of communion is proof enough of the solidity of their ecumenical intent. There is indeed a difference in the weight of response to having preached and having celebrated the sacraments and, although this may be partially explained as a reluctance to compromise core articles of faith, it may equally be explained by the reluctance of religious functionaries of *other* denominations to countenance inter-denominational services of communion. The uniformly high responses of ministers to attitudes and behaviour gives that latter explanation credence.

There is within the Anglican Church a hint of a rift, a lacuna, between ecumenical precept and ecumenical practice. For, whereas clergy appear willing to practise ecumenicalism in the form of preaching in the church of another denomination, or planning other joint activities such as study groups or community projects, they have rarely, if ever, celebrated communion in the church of another confession, which more closely illuminates the intractable nature of the central canons of faith. It is interesting to note that, even though both percentages are high, Anglican clergy do less inviting than being invited. As we would expect, priests are less willing than clergy or ministers to preach in the church of another denomination and particularly to invite religious functionaries of other confessions. They are also less eager to plan inter-denominational activities such as study groups or the meetings of members. That they are unable to compromise central articles of their faith is clearly manifested in their almost unanimous unwillingness to invite or be invited by other denominational religious functionaries to services which celebrate the sacraments. We must point out, however, that it is unclear whether this is the choice of individual priests, or whether it results mainly from edicts forbidding many of these activities.

TABLE 5.4 *Ecumenical membership*

'Are you a member of any ecumenical group?'

	Church of England	% *in favour* Methodist	Roman Catholic
A Council of Christian Churches	26.8	45	12
A local Council of Churches	59.3	69	31
A local Clergy Fraternal	60.8	74	50
Overall ecumenical membership mean score	4.24	5.29	3.17

When we examine the membership of ecumenical groups the same pattern emerges, as shown by Table 5.4. Methodist ministers, in harmony with expressed ecumenical faith, are more likely to be members of an ecumenical group than either clergy or priests. Membership is uniformly higher than for clergy or priests. While a large number of clergy are members of one kind of ecumenical group or another, a substantial minority are not prepared to commit ecumenical attitude to ecumenical practice. The reservations are even greater for Roman Catholic priests.

Thus we find consistent differences between our three groups. The Methodists are always the most ecumenically orientated both in terms of attitude and practice; the Roman Catholic priests are always the least ecumenically orientated; clergy are in a middle position, reflecting links with both of the other groups. The real break between ministers and clergy is in the relationship between attitude and practice, and also between the emphasis given to specific items. Behaviourally clergy are less ecumenically involved than one would expect from their attitudes. This is reflected in their activity over the sacraments, something which has often been the sticking point between Anglicans and the Free Churches. This is also shown by the way in which ecumenical attitudes are less favourable over the more central forms of co-operation such as joint theological colleges and joint ministries.

II Within-Church differences

As with previous chapters, having established that there are, in fact, substantial differences between clergy, ministers and priests, we now turn to the question of the extent to which there is variation within each group. What influence do position, age, experience and belief have in shaping ecumenical attitudes and behaviour?

The Church of England

The position or status of clergy has some bearing upon ecumenical belief and practice, although not a great deal. One's status as an incumbent affects involvement in ecumenical activity. As one would expect, incumbents, because of their position, are far more likely to have either invited, or been invited by, a functionary of another denomination to preach in a service and have engaged in other forms of joint activity.

As we have remarked in other chapters, the distinction between incumbents and non-incumbents masks differences between types of ministry. Our information on type of ministry shows consistent relationships between organic ecumenism, ecumenical co-operation, ecumenical activity and ecumenical membership. In all cases the members of the hierarchy are most ecumenically orientated in terms of both belief and activity, followed by incumbents, chaplains and curates respectively. This is somewhat unexpected as one is normally led to expect, almost *a priori*, that those in positions of subordination, 'the dispossessed', are more radical in their support of change and reform than those who benefit as incumbents in office from the way things are. We might hypothesise that the more favourable ecumenical disposition of incumbents is in fact a product of their involvement in ecumenical practice, the opportunity for which their office has bestowed upon them. That is, ecumenical practice serves to alleviate rather than reinforce latent fears and conservative tendencies.

There is no clear pattern of relationships between indicators of denominational experience, social origins and ecumenical belief and

TABLE 5.5   *Anglican theological belief and ecumenism*

	Catholic	Central/ Broad Church	Modern- ists	Evang- elical	Other	χ^2	p
	% in favour	% in favour	% in favour	% in favour	% in favour		
A Organic ecumenism							
Roman Catholic							
Church	98.1	87.2	86.8	68.7	95.3	60.26	0.001
Baptist Church	98.1	81.2	92.1	83.3	85.4	16.41	0.01
Congregational							
Church	74.5	85.0	92.1	87.5	87.8	14.29	0.01
Presbyterian							
Church	76.9	85.7	92.1	87.5	88.1	10.74	0.05
Pentecostal							
Churches	47.1	34.1	52.6	61.5	54.8	18.32	0.01
Orthodox Churches	73.6	50.4	63.2	46.3	81.4	36.66	0.001
B Ecumenical co-operation							
Theological colleges	59.7	83.6	91.9	71.3	76.7	31.47	0.001
Sharing of churches	81.3	87.2	92.1	69.8	87.8	15.78	0.01
C Co-operative activity							
Preaching in other							
churches	79.6	90.2	94.7	96.0	84.4	20.76	0.001
Communion in other							
churches	6.7	22.1	34.2	34.7	43.63	43.63	0.001
Inviting others to							
celebrate							
communion	7.2	18.2	28.9	16.2	9.1	18.55	0.001

activity. While there is a slight tendency for clergy who are young in age and experience to favour more ecumenical co-operation this is counterbalanced by the opposite relationship with ecumenical activity and membership.

Similarly, when we turn to ideological factors, the extent of professionalism is basically unrelated to ecumenism. It is only in respect of organic ecumenism that we find that those with a service orientation and a stress on colleague control are likely to favour less ecumenism. But the relationship is not marked.

It is when we examine theological cosmology or churchmanship that it becomes possible to explain variations in ecumenical response. This can be seen clearly if we select those significant items from the scales as shown in Table 5.5. The table reveals that the concept of theological belief helps us to uncover crucial variations within Anglicanism. Those clergy who profess to a Catholic churchmanship are shown to be closely aligned to the Roman Catholic Church and particularly favourable to organic union with the Orthodox Churches. 'Catholic' clergy are revealed to be the most conservative of churchmanship cosmologies in respect of ecumenical co-operation and the most reluctant to engage in acts of ecumenical practice. The Central or Broad Church theological grouping display themselves characteristically as the centre of gravity, the axis about which theological variation pivots. The 'Modernists' are notably radical in their ecumenical conception, uniformly so in attitude towards union, co-operation, and in ecumenical activity. The 'Evangelicals' present themselves as surprisingly radical—surprisingly because they are usually characterised as being conservative, owing to their fundamentalist interpretation of the Bible and their emphasis upon conversion experience which causes them to attribute less importance to the visible Church. That the category includes 'Liberal' as well as 'Conservative' Evangelicals enables us to in some degree account for the unusually radical nature of their responses—a fuller explanation may lie in the fact that evangelism has been fairly central to ecumenicalism since its Edinburgh Missionary inception.

Thus, amongst Anglican clergy, theological belief is the most potent predictor of ecumenical belief and activity. This is to be expected as the various schools of churchmanship have direct links with aspects of the ecumenical movement.

The Methodist Church

We have already seen that Methodist ministers present themselves as being the most ecumenically orientated of all the religious functionaries in our survey. Our aim now is to see how far this ecumenical orientation varies between ministers.

Unlike Anglican clergy, the position or status of a Methodist minister has very little impact upon their ecumenicity. Status does not influence ecumenical attitudes in any way at all and has a marginal bearing upon ritual behaviour—sector ministers are less likely than ministers or chairmen and circuit superintendents to belong to ecumenical groups and societies.

Age is seen to influence beliefs and behaviour in a much more direct way than it does for Anglican clergymen. The younger the minister the more likely are his ecumenical attitudes about organic union and co-operative ventures to be radical in conception as Table 5.6 demonstrates (once more the significant responses are selected).

TABLE 5.6 *Methodist Church: Age and ecumenism*

Ecumenism	-39	40-49	50-59	60+	χ^2	p
A Organic ecumenism						
Roman Catholic Church	83.1	68.3	61.2	54.5	11.08	0.02
Baptist Church	96.6	85.7	78.8	79.5	9.45	0.05
Pentecostal Churches	89.7	73.0	70.8	65.1	9.66	0.05
All Christian Churches	76.7	66.7	52.3	52.3	10.45	0.02
B Ecumenical co-operation						
Joint theological colleges	98.3	84.4	94.2	88.6	8.95	0.05
C Ritual ecumenism						
Preached in the church of						
another denomination	93.5	100.0	100.0	100.0	12.07	0.01

Once more, the older the minister the more likely he is to have actually participated in some kind of ecumenical behaviour, which is consistent with our data on status. As one would expect, these findings on age are backed up by those concerning other aspects of denominational experience such as years ordained, posts held, etc.

Theological belief or cosmology, as in the Church of England, is seen to be the most important explanatory variable in helping us to account for variations in ecumenical response. Like clergymen, those ministers who profess a more 'Catholic' Methodism are highly disposed to support union with the Roman Catholic Church, although unlike Anglican Catholics, Catholic Methodists are not more conservative in their ecumenical attitudes and behaviour. 'Evangelicals' within the Methodist Church are more radical than their Anglican counterparts but more conservative than other ministers within the Methodist church who hold to a different theological belief system. 'Ecumenical' ministers successfully emulate their self-ascribed title and are indeed significantly ecumenical in word and deed: 84 per cent of Ecumenical Methodists have either invited, or been invited by, a minister of another denomination to celebrate communion (this compares with 70 per cent of 'Radicals'). 'Radicals', however, are far more ecumenical than other Methodist churchmanship cosmologies in their attitudes toward organic unity— willing to countenance union with many Christian Churches and other religious bodies—and ventures of ecumenical co-operation— virtually unanimously agreeing to joint theological colleges and joint ministries—in other words, the two co-operative measures about which other religious functionaries feel most cautious on theological grounds.

The most interesting result of this analysis of Methodist churchmanship cosmologies and their comparison with Anglican equivalents is the way in which *intra*-denominational relationships are similar while absolute differences still remain in *inter*-denominational comparisons; that is to say a Methodist 'Catholic' is more conservative in ecumenical orientation than a Methodist 'Radical' but is yet more radical than an Anglican 'Catholic', as shown in Table 5.7.

TABLE 5.7 *Inter-denominational comparisons of ecumenism*

Scale	Catholic		Evangelical		Radical	
	Anglican	Methodist	Anglican	Methodist	Anglican	Methodist
Organic ecumenism	14.967	15.556	14.337	15.180	15.711	16.080
Ecumenical co-operation	20.907	23.611	20.970	23.189	21.974	23.940
Ritual co-operation	7.294	9.500	7.960	9.459	8.289	9.320
Group membership	3.327	5.361	3.574	5.311	4.211	5.340

What this table appears to establish is the interesting way in which theological beliefs and denominational affiliation relate to each other: that is, theological cosmologies cross denominational boundaries and retain intrinsic themes but not without being deeply influenced by their new denominational setting. Methodism's more radical conception of theology will sharply colour the disparate spiritual beliefs held beneath its rubric.

The Roman Catholic Church

In their attitudes towards ecumenism and in their ecumenical behaviour Roman Catholic priests are more similar to Anglican clergy than to Methodist ministers. Can we then establish similar explanatory variables to account for variations between priests? Our analytical task will be to unravel and disentangle the various causal relationships and show exactly in what way each influence—status, age, belief and so on—is brought to bear. The status or position of a Catholic priest has the same influence upon ecumenicity as it does for clergymen and is in that sense predictable. That is to say, priests who are not responsible for a parish are more ecumenical in attitude than parish priests while the latter are more ecumenical in behaviour than non-parish priests. But the Catholic non-parish priest is less radical than the Anglican non-incumbent and less so than any of the methodist statuses. Nevertheless 61 per cent of non-parish priests, as compared with 43.0 per cent of parish priests, were eager to institute preaching in the church of another denomination—a similar chasm divided the two groups upon the issues of education, joint ministries and the sharing of churches.

This position of the non-parish priests is a dual one as there are two groups who are most ecumenically orientated in attitudes, namely members of the hierarchy and assistant priests. It is the parish priest working on his own who is the least ecumenical in both attitudes and behaviour.

TABLE 5.8   *Roman Catholic Church: Ecumenism and experience*

Ecumenism	*0–9*	*10–19*	*20–29*	*30+*	χ^2	*p*
A Organic ecumenism						
Methodist Church	96.4	92.2	86.7	79.5	10.03	0.02
Baptist Church	94.6	91.7	81.0	71.8	15.25	0.01
United Reformed						
Church	92.9	91.5	77.4	70.5	14.82	0.01
Orthodox Churches	100.0	96.2	90.3	89.5	8.06	0.05
B Ecumenical co-operation						
Clergy preaching in each						
others' churches	68.7	53.3	40.4	46.8	15.09	0.01
Joint publications	85.5	79.7	60.6	60.2	22.68	0.001
Joint theological						
colleges	45.8	32.5	26.3	19.0	18.02	0.001
Sharing of churches	66.7	61.5	47.9	39.8	18.30	0.001
Joint ministries	45.7	34.6	29.0	18.0	19.14	0.001
Joint missionary work	56.8	49.4	39.6	36.5	9.87	0.02

Our information also shows that the older the priest is, the more conservative he is in ecumenical attitude. As with the other groups, this age effect is also reflected in experience. Age and experience are important and the two are interrelated: the older the priest the more conservative he is, but also, the longer he has lived within the structure and tradition of the Catholic Church (his length of ordination) the more ecumenically conservative he is. What we are saying, therefore, is that it is experience, the length of time which a priest has been exposed to the social and cultural patterns of the Catholic Church, which is the more important factor in influencing ecumenical attitudes. Parish priests, that is, are more conservative ecumenically because they have lived longer in the Church. Not all non-parish priests are radical; those who are older and who have been ordained longer are as equally conservative as their parish priest colleagues. Let us consider the influence of experience, noting the significant variables as demonstrated in Table 5.8.

Turning to beliefs, we again find relationships but mainly with ecumenical co-operation. This is, of course, to be expected given the traditional nature of the Roman Catholic theological cosmology: the wish to maintain relatively close ties with Rome; the inclination to have a responsibility to the Roman Catholic population within a diocese prior to the general population as such; and the disposition of priests to regard the Roman Catholic Church not as one Church among many but as 'the one true Church', 'the centre of unity and true authority', 'the authentic embodiment' . . . and so on.

Thus there is little variation on organic ecumenism by belief. And ecumenical activity is controlled by diocesan rules. It is in that area where neither union nor direct activity is involved that beliefs operate. Hence those who hold more radical beliefs will have attitudes favouring a wider range of ecumenical activity which stops short of union. A substantial number of priests annotated their questionnaires and commented on ecumenicalism as such in a manner consistent with this traditional theological cosmology. The annotated comments tended to indicate that priests were willing to consider unity and co-operation with Churches of other denominations but only on Roman Catholic terms. Representative comments were: 'I am not against union but only on terms clearly in line with essential Catholicism'; 'union is only possible if others accept the authority and doctrines of the Catholic Church'; 'Yes, if you mean union without absorption, each preserving its own tradition'; 'Yes, if there is due submission to the authority of the successor of Peter'; and so on.

These findings are also underlined by the other aspect of beliefs, namely professionalism; the relationships are with ecumenical co-operation. Those who define themselves as professional, thus accepting a more traditional self-conception are more likely to be less in favour of co-operation with other Churches. The attitude of priests towards ecumenicalism therefore is primarily shaped by the way they are socialised over many years in the Roman Catholic Church to conform to its traditions, customs and theological cosmology, each of which tends to be antithetical to the ecumenical concept.

III Conclusions

The aim of this section is to provide a summary and conclusion of the main points contained in the chapter. What, in particular, are the attitudes of our religious functionaries to the ecumenical movement? Ministers, clergy and priests all display caution about the possibility of immediate organic unity: each group of functionaries is happy to endorse union with those Churches similar in structure and tradition but more wary and suspicious about alien Christian or religious bodies.

The differences in attitudes between our functionaries become more apparent when we consider their opinions upon ventures of ecumenical co-operation. Methodist ministers, as such, uniformly agree to co-operative measures, provisional and radical, whereas clergy and priests become progressively more tentative and uncertain. Clergy, and particularly priests, appear willing to acquiesce in measures which begin co-operation by initial and preparatory discussions—such as joint meetings of members and functionaries, and joint study groups—but are very doubtful about the possibility of endorsing radical co-operative ventures, joint theological colleges, joint ministries and missionary work. They find it difficult to countenance these activities because it is these in particular which impinge directly upon the core of their theological belief, the central canons of their faith.

This more profound resistance to radical ecumenical change is manifested more directly in the ecumenical behaviour of clergy and priests, although ministers are far more radical. Ministers not only preach in churches of other confessions and invite functionaries of other denominations to Methodist churches, but are also prepared to engage in services of inter-communion. Clergy, although prepared to participate in inter-faith services, are, however, much more reluctant to engage in inter-communion services, while priests display themselves as reluctant to engage in ritual acts of ecumenism of either kind. It is true, however, that priests are no less ecumenical than clergy in their membership of ecumenical societies.

There is among the Church of England clergy a hint of inconsistency, a rift between their ecumenical attitudes and ecumenical behaviour; but generally the relationship of practice to precept in our religious functionaries shows a remarkable congruence and consistency. This reveals the powerful disposition of beliefs to give coherence and shape to behaviour. But to exactly what extent has belief influenced ecumenical attitude and practice? Can we attribute all to theological cosmology or are there other causal factors at play—status, age or experience, institutional context, for example?

Status has been seen to have very little influence upon the attitudes and behaviour of Methodist ministers but to have influence upon the behaviour of clergy and priests. Incumbents or parish priests are more likely than their subordinate colleagues to invite or be invited by a functionary of another denomination to preach at a service. Yet this is clearly a function of the ability of office to bestow privileges and opportunities. Those in the hierarchy or at the bottom of the structure are more likely to have attitudes favourable to ecumenical co-operation.

Age too has a relatively predictable influence upon ecumenicalism. The younger the religious functionary the more radical his attitudes towards ecumenical unity and co-operation, whereas the older the functionary the more likely he is to have engaged in acts of ritual ecumenism; however, this latter relationship is affected a little by the overall favourable attitudes and behaviour of members of the hierarchy.

Belief or theological cosmology is seen to have a more pervasive influence upon ecumenicalism than age or status. If a religious functionary is a 'Catholic' or 'Evangelical' or 'Radical' his ecumenical attitudes and behaviour will be deeply moulded by the particular theological belief system to which he ascribes: his individual beliefs and acts will tend to be consonant with the prescriptions of the more total and overarching theological framework. If he is a 'Catholic' he will be more conservative and suspicious towards ecumenism whereas if he is a 'Modernist' or a 'Radical' he will be far more challenging in his ecumenical fervour.

Belief is, therefore, perhaps the foremost influential factor in shaping attitudes towards ecumenicalism; yet we have seen in an interesting way the manner in which theological belief is modified by the institutional context of the denomination. That is to say, a 'Catholic' may be more conservative than a 'Radical' but a Methodist 'Catholic' is likely to be more radical than an Anglican 'Radical'. Theological cosmologies cross institutional boundaries, but not without being severely moulded and modified in the process.

What, therefore, is the current position of the ecumenical movement in Britain? Till (1972) is generally very pessimistic:

> returning to England it was difficult not to feel impatient with the conservatism of the churches in this country, not only in matters ecumenical but in many other areas where it seems that ecclesiastical traditionalism is usually the deciding factor,

even when churches are in a state of desperate crisis . . . . All in all at the beginning of the seventies it looks as if the movement for the reunion of the churches as it has developed so far in the twentieth century may have taken so long to come to fruition that in the end it cannot be supported by the rapidly declining churches themselves.

The findings of this particular survey do not help much to alleviate Till's pessimism. Functionaries in the Church of England and the Roman Catholic Church appear to be most reluctant to modify and compromise the traditional tenets of faith that would be necessary to establish a vigorous ecumenical movement.

6 Reform

The 1960s constituted a decade when many of the Christian Churches began to reflect upon the nature of their mission and the shape of their organisations, in particular the need to make their organisations intelligible to an increasingly secular audience in the second half of the twentieth century. This has created an intractable dilemma: on the one hand, the Churches can be conceived of as bureaucracies with the concomitant problems of improving control and co-ordination, while on the other hand, religious functionaries can be conceived of as professionals preoccupied with a theological mission which makes a bureaucratic work context inappropriate. Each Church has sought to resolve this dilemma by meeting the necessary organisational exigencies in a manner which remains true to its theological cosmology. Every major Church has within the past decade established some form of commission or committee to examine its pattern of organisation and the possibility of appropriate reform. The Church of England has commissioned the Paul Report and the Morley Report, and the change to synodal government; the Methodists the reports on the structuring of districts and circuits; and the Roman Catholics have experienced Vatican II followed by laity commissions devising new organisational forms. More recently there has been the introduction of the management consultant into church affairs and the stirrings of a 'new' subject called ecclesiastical administration (Rudge, 1968).

This concern with organisation springs from two sources. First, it is in the nature of organisations based in belief systems that the actual structure and operation of the organisation should reflect those beliefs. In this sense the organisation is an operationalisation or structural expression of the belief system. In an economic organisation the concern is with efficiency. In a religious organisation the concern is with symbolic appropriateness. As Thompson (1973) puts it, 'a religious group is always fundamentally a cultural organisation in the sense that the end is achieved, at least in part, in the *process* of meetings with others, while in a utilitarian or instrumental association it is the *product* that is directly significant'. This view is echoed by Hinings and Bryman (1974) suggesting that economies of scale do not necessarily occur in religious organisations because of their concern with coverage and service.

What one is examining here is the extent of correspondence between a particular religious symbol system and a particular organisational pattern. Our earlier discussions and data suggest that both between and within our three groups there are liable to be different religious symbol systems and thus different ideas as to which models of organisational reform are appropriate.

The second source of a concern with organisation springs from the changing position of Churches over the past few generations. Over time their position has become more problematic (Wilson, 1966). We are not entering into the secularisation debate here as this is concerned with much wider issues of the place of religion in society. We are examining what has happened to Churches, one institutional form of religion among others. Churches have been losing members, finding it increasingly difficult to recruit staff, running into financial problems, closing down buildings, rationalising parishes, closing down theological colleges and so on. This is, of course, especially true of the Anglican and Methodist Churches, dealt with here, and much less so for the Roman Catholic Church. The pressures generated by this position have led to an 'efficiency' concern with organisation, with the effective use of manpower, the conservation of finance and the rational use of buildings, which has to be developed within the framework of a theological justification. In Thompson's terms (1973) this leads to a shift from symbolic appropriateness as the criterion for organisational evaluation to the use of general logico-experimental criteria (*pace* the introduction of management consultants). Given the size and scope of our three Churches, these problems should produce pressures to bureaucratic solutions, including centralisation and the spread of procedures and paperwork.

There exist strong grounds for resisting these bureaucratic pressures, as is evident in a discussion by Till (1972, pp. 393–4) of Vatican II:

Bishop de Smedt of Bruges, one of the great orators of the Council, has described the Church as being dominated by three devils; clericalism, juridicalism and triumphalism. Clericalism may be defined as the domination of the Church and its thinking by its professional hierarchy to the exclusion or detriment of

the work and problems of the laity. Juridicalism is the habit
of mind of thinking of the Church, of its life and membership
in legal terms, imposing rules and regulations rather than
encouraging freedom and organic growth. Triumphalism is the
danger of applying to the Church and its activities the worldly
criteria of power and glory, rather than the Christ-like
pattern, humility and suffering. No one would pretend that the
Roman Church has a monopoly of these particular devils.

Nevertheless whatever the Church's innate resistance to bureaucratic
solutions each of our three denominations has felt it imperative to
consider the necessary demands of organisational reform. But to
what extent have they done so to the exclusion of their theological
belief system? That is, to what extent is Thompson's conjecture
validated—i.e. has the Church's criterion for organisational
evaluation shifted from 'symbolic appropriateness' to 'logico-
experimentality'? What has been the response of our respective
religious functionaries, clergy, priests and ministers to this climate of
reform? What factors have been influential in shaping their attitudes
toward the reform issues? These are some of the problems we shall
be considering in this chapter.

It is in the very nature of the whole reform debate that most of the
precise issues which have been discussed in each Church have been
specific to that Church. For example, the removal of the celibacy
requirement for priests is totally inapposite as a reform issue to
members of the other two Churches. Thus, one complete section of
questions is given over to asking our religious functionaries what they
felt about the various reports and papers which were commissioned
to review the question of reform in each of the three denominations;
that is to say, we asked clergy about the recommendations of the
Paul and Morley reports; we asked ministers about the Report on
the Restructuring of the Methodist Church; and we asked priests
about the Provisional Laity Commission. We shall consider the aims
and focus of the various reports in each subsequent section.

Where it was possible, we attempted to ask clergy, priests and
ministers rather more abstract questions about general issues which
were comparable in form: 'reform of liturgy and forms of worship';
'the role of the laity'; 'reform of the parochial system'. Some items
were comparable only between the Anglican and Methodist Churches:
'the payment of the clergy' and 'deployment of the clergy'.

And, we did ask one very general question of all three groups of
functionary, that is, whether their Church needs 'reform' (as such).
The percentage distribution of answers for each group is given in
Table 6.1. This table is interesting in that, although it shows the
Roman Catholic priests to be rather less reform orientated than

TABLE 6.1 *Reform in general*

Reform	Church of England	Roman Catholic	Methodist
	%	%	%
Greatly needs reform	26.3	15.3	22.5
Certainly needs some reform	65.1	55.0	67.4
Needs a little reform	8.2	25.2	9.3
Needs no reform	0.4	4.5	0.8

clergy or ministers, it does show that 70 per cent of priests do regard reform in some shape or form as necessary. Thus the prevalent conception that the Roman Catholic Church is more resistant to change than the Protestant Churches must be treated with some caution as we proceed through this chapter.

I The Church of England

The Church of England has in some ways been particularly sensitive to the pressure of a secular society: 'in the country as a whole though not everywhere to the same degree, the Church of England is facing a loss of membership and the attrition of its power and influence' (Paul, 1964). The Church has responded to these pressures by appointing academics, committees and commissions to consider what kind of reorganisation might be appropriate to its belief system yet meet the exigencies of modern society.

Leslie Paul was the first appointed to consider whether the ancient ecclesiastical system developed since St Augustine's mission to Canterbury is still well suited to meet the needs of English society late in the twentieth century. His views are contained in his controversial *Deployment and Payment of Clergy* (The Paul Report) (Paul, 1964) and *A Church by Daylight: A Reappraisement of the Church of England and its Future* (Paul, 1973). Paul states emphatically that the traditional parochial system is now completely inappropriate. The parish has provided the location of appointment for clergy and the source of their benefice income. 'The parish [is] the primary form or structure of the church' (Paul, 1973). Paul (1964) comments, however, that

the system was . . . inherently more suitable to a country
where the population was dispersed over the countryside than
to one where, as now, it is concentrated in the towns: the
increasing urbanisation of England has more and more revealed

the inadequacies of deploying clergy territorially irrespective, for the most part, of population concentrations. . . . The inevitable effect of the parochial system of deployment is at present to place most of the parsons in the country while most of the population lives in the towns.

This points to the necessity of change. But the parochial system is also one which is peculiarly resistant to change (Paul, 1973):

once established each church and parish became a self-regarding unit which defended itself against change. Change in adjustment of parish boundaries could be accepted as long as it was not too radical. . . . Abolition affected the 'amour propre' of the parishioners, threatened the security of the parson and the rights of the patron. Vested interests, in fact, of freeholders, patron, parishioner . . . tended to freeze the parochial system . . . the principle of inviolate parish, freehold and patronage has not *yet* been invaded.

Paul thus describes a structure ossified over time, irrational in its deployment of clergy and therefore one which ostensibly entails a burden of isolation, despair and malaise for many of its clergy: 'the ancient parochial system no longer illuminates the personality but maroons him socially and spiritually'.

The inflexibility of the existing parochial system, impeding as it does the exercise of the Church's mission, led Paul to conceive of a blueprint for the reconstruction of the ministry: 'there is no doubt that what the evidence urges upon us is a reform of the ministerial structure, and of the pastoral machinery of the church, or rather not one single reform but a series of interlocking reforms, in fact an operation of the utmost delicacy and complexity'. Paul envisages the critical tasks to be as follows: to regain 'control' of the clergy, in that it is able to direct them to the areas of greatest need ('thus, the central task of the Church of England is how to carry its faith with urgency and meaning into the hearts of the busy and preoccupied urban multitudes whose very pattern of life seems to estrange them from the church' (Paul, 1964)); to strengthen and rejuvenate the clergy by creating for them the right kind of working parish environment; and to bring the laity into a joint ministry with the clergy. In other words, Paul (1964) argues, 'the Church needs the same control over its organisational life as it is beginning to insist it must have over its liturgical life'.

Paul made, therefore, a number of interrelated recommendations. First came deployment. If the root of the Church of England is its consecrated community church then the bastion of the Anglican clergyman's autonomy is his parsonage, his freehold. Redeployment requires the opportunity to prise the clergyman from his freehold; to abolish it, Paul believes, would create much bitterness as well as being costly and 'legally labyrinthine'. Thus modification is called for if the requisite deployment is to be effected. Paul recommended, therefore, (1) that every freehold shall be transformed into a leasehold as it falls vacant or within a term of ten years, whichever first: 'the leasehold would give an incumbent the opportunity to move on and would give his ordinary the power, which he badly needs, to move a man on for his own or his parish's good, or because re-organisation demands it ... the real problem is not the obstinate misfit, but the clergyman who is "sitting down to it", one who has grown old, or tired, or complacent, or inured to failure. He badly needs to move on to fresh ground.' (2) Paul recommended that 'a reasonable tenure would be ten years with the opportunity to renew for not more than half that time. The powers of patrons and P.C.C.s would not necessarily be disturbed by this measure.' Paul wished thus to create the opportunity for more redirection of clergy and also to make the process a far more open and candid one compared with the present archaic 'old boy network'. (3) Paul recommended therefore that ordinands be subject to redirection for five years rather than two, serving their prentice years in the areas of greatest need. (4) He recommended that in his seventh year the incumbent of a leasehold should be interviewed by his bishop in order that his future be planned. If direction is to be effective there must be far more awareness of the kind and quality of clergy. Paul therefore recommended (5) that an open central registry of clergy be kept. The directory should make available to authorised persons lists of vacant parishes and of men about to move.

The second area of recommendations covered the parochial system. A new form of ministry is needed, especially to cope with problem areas: isolated rural areas, 'down town', and the suburban fringes. Paul recommended (1) looser forms of group ministry (several parishes run together by their separate incumbents) and team ministry (one parish run by clergy working as members of a team). But the crucial proposal (2) is for 'a new parochial form ... a *major parish* run by a college of clergy all of whom enjoy "incumbent status". Single incumbent parishes then become minor *parishes*.'

The third area of recommendations concerned the payment of clergy. Paul proposed (1) the pooling of benefice funds to create one stipendiary fund, and (2) one single system of payment for all clergy, with increments for length of service and special responsibilities.

The fourth area of recommendations focused upon the laity. Paul felt the need to encourage a spirit of theological inquiry among the laity and to involve them far more in the parish ministry. He believed this could be achieved by the formation of (1) a lay pastorate with street organisation based on house communions; (2) pastoral advisory committees of teachers, doctors, social workers, etc.; and (3) a lay voluntary service.

The 'Paul Report' produced much discussion and many reports, one of which, 'Issues Raised' (1965) led to the establishment of the Morley Commission. 'The Morley Report', *Partners in Ministry* (Morley, 1967) also proposed measures which were radical in form. Among other things, Morley proposed that the freehold on patronage be abolished and replaced by a new system of staffing: every man upon ordination would be placed on the strength of the diocese and paid and housed, regardless of whether he had a job, until his retirement. This proposal would have the effect of 'dissociating the ministry of incumbent status from the parochial anchor' (Paul, 1973). Morley also endorsed proposals for legal group and team ministries.

These sets of items cover two areas of reform, one being concerned with general issues, such as the parochial system, the laity, liturgy, etc., the other with more specific reforms, such as lay street teams, leaseholds, payments systems, etc. These items do, in fact, form overall scales according to normal scaling criteria (see Appendix 1) thus it is possible to sum them to form two reform scales, namely 'general reform' and 'specific reforms'.

Thus, the criteria which have guided the proposals of reorganisation have been both those of symbolic appropriateness, in that there has been a desire to make Anglican Christianity more responsive to secular changes, and also the 'logico-experimental' search for organisational efficiency. How have the clergy responded to this climate of reform? What are their attitudes towards the various measures and proposals? What has influenced them most in formation of their attitudes? The attitudes of clergy towards deployment as such are rather inconsistent. Table 6.2 reveals that clergy feel strongly about deployment and the pressing need to improve the rational distribution of clergy: 46 per cent believe it to be a most important consideration. Clergy also accept the need to create a far more 'open' ministry. However, Table 6.2 needs to be read in conjunction with Table 6.3, which is concerned with some of the details of reform. It shows that 93 per cent endorse the proposal for an open central registry to bring available men into touch with available posts. Yet, while recommending redeployment, clergy adopt, with equal favour, the ostensibly contradictory attitude that the freehold is inviolate: only 16 per cent believe reforming the freehold to be 'most important', while the substitution of the parson's leasehold for the parson's freehold receives by far the lowest endorsement in Table 6.3. Clergy, clearly, are only prepared to accept redeployment it it does not interfere with their traditional right of security and autonomy: the attitudes suggest that clergy will only accept persuasion and encouragement as valid reasons for moving, and not 'direction'.

TABLE 6.2 *Church of England: Reform—issues*

	Most important %	Quite important %	Not very important %	Not necessary %
1 Liturgy and forms of worship	21.8	59.7	16.0	2.5
2 The payment of the clergy	14.2	58.9	25.0	1.8
3 The role of the laity	47.9	44.0	5.9	2.2
4 The deployment of the clergy	46.0	43.0	7.9	3.1
5 Reform of the freehold	16.1	24.6	38.2	21.0
6 Reform of the parochial system	20.1	35.9	28.4	15.6

This very cautious attitude towards critical reform measures is reflected in the attitudes of clergy towards reform of the parochial system. Table 6.2 shows that clergy are most reluctant to acquiesce to the kind of radical changes—a new form of 'major parish' run by a college of clergy all of whom enjoy equal incumbency status—which Paul proposed. This unwillingness to alter the existing parish system is also reflected in a lower than average acceptance of the major recommendation of the Morley Report: that is, the suggestion that upon ordination men should be placed on the strength of the diocese and paid and housed whether or not they have a job (see Table 6.3). Clergy, however, are more willing to tolerate measures which are less radical in form, but which they feel may facilitate the system as it already stands—the establishment of group and team ministries (a proposal in fact passed by a Pastoral Measure); the stepping up of the co-ordination work of rural deaneries; and the concomitant improvement in the status of rural deans.

Clergy are much more ready to endorse measures which rationalise their system of payment and those which make for far more lay involvement in the Church. To take payment first, clergy do not regard pay as a 'most important' consideration for reform (only 14.2 per cent, see Table 6.2), but 73.1 per cent overall do regard it as 'important'. As Table 6.3 shows, clergy are prepared to accept the recommendations which Paul makes for making the system of payment much more equitable: that is, to establish a common stipendiary fund for all the clergy and to create one single system of payment for all the clergy with increments for length of service and special responsibilities.

104

TABLE 6.3   *Church of England: Reform—detailed proposals*

	Yes	No
	%	%
1 A common stipendiary fund for all the clergy	77.8	22.2
2 One single system of payment for all the clergy with increments for length of service and special responsibilities	86.2	13.8
3 Upon ordination, the placing of a man on the strength of the diocese and payment of him whether or not he has a job	66.2	33.8
4 An open central registry to bring available men in touch with available jobs	93.0	7.0
5 Substitution of parson's leasehold for parson's freehold	50.9	49.1
6 The encouragement of group and team ministries	72.8	27.2
7 The establishment of lay street team and other forms of organised lay activity in the parishes	93.4	6.6
8 Stepping up the co-ordinating work of rural deaneries and the status of rural deans	72.6	27.4

It is quite clear from Tables 6.2 and 6.3 that the clergy feel very strongly about the exclusion of the laity (cf. Bryman and Hinings, 1974) and believe that it is one of the crucial tasks of the Church of England to rejuvenate the laity theologically and extend the range of their activities and participation in the Church. Clergy almost unanimously lend support to Paul's proposals for lay street teams and other forms of lay activity in parishes.

Although 'deployment', 'the parochial system', 'the role of the laity' and so on are central to the current reform debate in the Church of England we were also interested in discovering the attitudes of clergy towards other important issues, such as establishment.

Clergy, generally, adopt a conservative stance towards establishment. Just over one-fifth favour disestablishment, which implies the truncation of a longstanding relationship between Church and State in England and which would remove many of the Church's legal safeguards. Proponents of disestablishment have stressed that it would provide greater flexibility to mission and administration, and would entail greater autonomy for the Church (for example, the role of the Crown in the appointment of bishops would be greatly reduced). However, this view seems to have found little support among the clergy who tend rather to favour slight modifications.

In answer to a question concerning establishment, only 21 per cent thought that the Church of England should be disestablished and an even smaller number, 8 per cent, thought that there should be no change in the position of the Church. However, 44 per cent did think that the Church should remain established with some slight modifications and a further 28 per cent saw the Church of Scotland as a model for the revision of the Anglicans.

We should now consider the influence that beliefs, denominational influences and age have in differentiating the attitudes of clergy towards reform. 'Churchmanship', or theological cosmology, is once more shown to be an important variable in the moulding of the clergy's disposition towards reform (see Table 6.4). The 'Modernist' group, for example, is especially inclined to view the Church as in need of considerable reform. They are much more likely to agree to the radical reform proposals of Paul and Morley which seek to reshape the organisational basis of the Anglican ministry: that is, they want to abolish the freehold and reconstruct the parochial system and they are more likely to agree to the disestablishment of the Church of England.

TABLE 6.4 *Reform and churchmanship: Selections*

(i)	Catholic	Central/ Broad	Modern-ists	Evang-elical	Other	p
	%	%	%	%	%	
A Issues						
Deployment	43.5	48.1	81.6	26.7	53.3	0.001
Freehold	18.1	12.5	39.5	7.1	14.0	0.001
Parochial system	21.2	15.0	51.4	9.0	24.4	0.001
B Detailed proposals						
Placing and payment	68.8	68.0	80.6	49.0	78.0	0.001
Leasehold	48.1	52.3	83.8	48.4	65.1	0.001
Group and team ministries	74.6	69.1	94.7	68.9	87.5	0.001
C General						
Some reform needed	71.1	78.8	31.6	61.4	46.7	0.001
Great reform needed	17.5	14.4	65.8	29.7	44.4	
(ii)						
D Scales						
General reform	22.706	22.602	26.447	22.139	23.800	0.001
Specific reforms	13.271	13.459	14.842	13.020	13.600	0.01

The 'Catholic' and 'Central or Broad Church' churchmanship groupings are similar in that they strike a much more conservative attitude towards reform. It must not be assumed, however, that the 'Catholics' are the more conservative of the two groupings, as we have found, for example, in attitudes towards ecumenism. 'Catholics' show that they are more prepared to consider reforming the freehold, and the parochial system and support the introduction of group and team ministries, thereby suggesting that they are inclined to accept reforms which might push the Anglican structures towards a greater affinity with those that obtain in the Roman Catholic Church. This conjecture is buttressed perhaps when we consider their attitude towards establishment; for 'Catholics' comprise the more radical of clergymen on this issue, second only to 'Modernists'. We may possibly attribute the substantial support for disestablishment among 'Catholics' to their desire for the reunion of the Church of England with, and for the hegemony of, Rome.

The 'Evangelical' churchmanship grouping presents somewhat inconsistent attitudes towards reform, an inconsistency which is interesting in that it requires some theoretical resolution. 'Evangelicals' take quite a radical stance towards the general need for reform as such (Table 6.4). Yet, when we probe and consider the attitudes of 'Evangelicals' towards detailed reform proposals we find them to be quite the most conservative of our churchmanship groupings. They are generally unwilling to recommend the Paul and Morley proposals, particularly for redeployment and the reconstruction of the parochial system. The discrepancy demonstrates the manner in which general beliefs, embodying perhaps a broad intellectual and moral orientation, can develop and exist quite independently of particular beliefs, usually the product of specific and contingency life-experiences.

Whether or not clergy were incumbents or non-incumbents also had an important impact on their proclivity for reform. Incumbents were generally much less reform orientated than non-incumbents. This is to be expected because many incumbents have a great deal to lose: their autonomy and security of tenure are directly affected by the most radical measures. Non-incumbents, a category which includes bishops and chaplains as well as curates, have much less to lose; they are prepared to support the prevalent recommendations, for example, the substitution of leasehold for freehold and the establishment of group and team ministries. Yet an interesting contradiction arises even here: whereas only 27 per cent of non-incumbents are prepared to abolish the freehold; 70 per cent of them are prepared to substitute the leasehold. This can perhaps be understood once more in terms of the bifurcation of general and particular beliefs: the freehold embodies general symbolical over-tones—independence, security—which clergy of all shades are unwilling to challenge. Yet leasehold is a concept uncluttered with these 'collective representations', and is one which is perceived in a more limited, contingent and pragmatic fashion.

The age of clergy has a fairly predictable influence in that the younger the clergyman is the more likely he is to take a radical stance towards reform. Younger clergy, as well as being willing to support fundamental reform proposals, such as deployment, are also concerned to improve the participative activities of the laity and the equity of payment for clergy. But the conservatism of the older clergy, of whom there are a large number (43 per cent over 50), is pronounced. We have noted that the most conservative church-manship grouping is the Evangelical, yet those clergy aged over fifty are even less orientated to reform than the Evangelicals. As we would expect, these relationships are further bolstered when we examine the impact of denominational experience. Those who are least experienced have spent less time in less positions and are more likely to favour reforms in the Church of England.

Again, in line with previous findings, we find some small relationships between self-image and reform. Broadly speaking, those clergy who define themselves as professionals are less likely to be reform orientated. This is particularly true for 'general reform' and for the professional dimensions of service orientation, vocation and colleague control. This is further support for the position of Coxon (1967) that, unlike most occupations the clergy is de-professionalising so that the traditional stance is a professional one.

In conclusion, therefore, clergy appear reluctant to countenance the radical measures of reform which Paul and Morley envisaged as being necessary if the Church of England were to reconstruct its ministry on a sound footing. The bold recommendations for redeployment and a new parish ministry seemingly strike too directly at the interests of most clergy for them to be perceived as symbolically appropriate to *their* belief system. The more tempered proposals, concerning the laity, payment and moderate pastoral change, are greeted more equably. The responses of clergy are at root a recipe for stability with minor modifications, the existing organisational structure being regarded as quite appropriate. Nevertheless variations do exist: the issues debated are likely to find support among 'Modernists', a very small group, and young non-incumbents, mainly curates. Yet it is precisely this younger group which is least in a position to instigate reform and, since it finds least support among older clergy, many of whom are entrenched in positions of influence or access to influence, the possibility of change within the Church of England seems to be considerably reduced. As Paul (1973) pessimistically commented: 'the Morley Report was rejected by Church Assembly in 1970, a funereal act appropriate to the

Assembly's demise. The safeties of freehold and patronage were preferred to the challenge of mission.'

II The Methodist Church

Methodists have traditionally been preoccupied with perfecting the organisation of their societies and circuits; they have been concerned to improve the spiritual efficacy of their Church. Recently they have, like other Churches, come to appreciate that faith and preaching are perhaps no longer adequate alone and that it is even more essential to have an effective Methodist organisation. Changes have been made with this aim in mind: but as Rupert Davies (1963), in his book *Methodism*, comments, 'they are finally justified only if they enable [the organisation of the Church] to make a more effective impact on the world outside'. Once more, the call is for organisational reform to dovetail with theological belief.

The Methodist Conference of 1967 received a report, part of which considered a call for the reconstruction of the Church's organisation. The report was given a mixed response ranging from complete acceptance to complete rejection. The Conference of 1968, therefore, established a new and enlarged committee to consider the reconstruction of the Church and 'to report to the Conference of 1970 with a complete and co-ordinated scheme for the effective renewal of the Church's organisation'. The committee's deliberations produced the 'Report on the Restructuring of the Church in the Districts, the Circuits, and the Societies'.

The report sought to examine critically and to streamline the structures and functions of the Methodist Church at the level of church, circuit and district, in order that 'the resultant structures . . . should express, sustain and facilitate the Church's service of the present age'. For the local church the report considered the problems of control, administration and non-Methodist membership. They contended that the 'dual control' of the local church's policy by Trustees' meeting and Society Committees (Leaders' meeting, Youth Council) should be brought to an end and submitted proposals for the Church to be administered by the Church Council and its committees. Administration, the report contended, 'should be such that members are liberated from the necessity to attend an undue number of councils and committees, thus being able to participate in the direct action of the church in pastoral care, training, community service and social responsibility. Further, the size of a committee should be such that its members participate fully in its discussions and such that its work is done expeditiously.' The report felt also that it was important to make a positive ecumenical advance to non-Methodist Christians:

modern society's mobility and the development of new residential
areas lead to the inclusion of non-Methodist Christians in our
church families and our cooperation with, and support of,
some who hesitate to commit themselves to full church
membership. We believe that local church committees should
be able to find room for people with appropriate qualifications
even though they may not be members of the Methodist Church.
We recommend therefore that members on the community roll
and non-Methodists should be eligible for appointment as
committee members and officers in the local church.

Many Methodists have come to view the circuit as the least effective
unit of their organisation and are beginning to think either 'con-
gregationally', that is, preoccupied with the local church, or 'ecumenically', in that their responsibilities lie with 'all (the Christians) in
one place'. The report does not support this incipient trend, maintaining that the spirit of co-operative teamwork, integral to the
Methodist movement, can be fostered only in the circuit environment and, therefore, that the basic organisational unit to which
ministers are appointed should remain the circuit. The circuit's
function is to combine spiritual leadership—acting as a focal point
for the working fellowship of the churches in the circuit, overseeing
their pastoral, training and evangelistic work—with that of administrative efficiency, competently deploying the resources of the ministry.
To this end, the report suggested that the Circuit Quarterly Meeting
had ceased to achieve its representational potential in that it had
become too large and cumbersome and could more effectively be
replaced, they recommended, by a six-monthly circuit meeting.

The district structure, although having no place in the embryonic
days of Methodism, evolved gradually, initially as the administrative
and financial link between Conference and circuits, adding only
subsequently its role as a pastoral and missionary link. The report
considered that the responsibilities borne by the district could well
be clarified, regularised and extended. They felt, for example, that
a fuller use could be made of the district for communication between
Conference and circuits and they also recommended that District
Synods should have executive authority, subject to appeal to
Conference, regarding circuit boundaries, cessation of service,
closure of premises, and property schemes where the sum involved
is not greater than £500.

The report hoped that these changes at the level of church, circuit
and district would produce the following beneficial results: first,
they would reduce the self-perpetuating element in the present
organisation; second, they would reduce the amount of administrative work for ministers and laymen; and third, they would increase

110

the flexibility of the Methodist Church, enabling it more adequately to adapt to changing circumstances.

We asked, therefore, what the attitudes of ministers were to reform as such, to the 'Report on the Restructuring of the Church', and to the body of more general items common to the three denominations. The great majority of ministers supported the need for the principle of reform as such, although the number of Ministers who advocated that their Church 'greatly needs reform' is marginally less than that in the Church of England, the overall proportion of those recommending reform is much the same (see Table 6.1).

As we discovered with the Church of England clergy, those proposals which focused upon the structure and functioning of the denomination in particular were received rather ambivalently. Ministers were almost unanimously (98 per cent) prepared to advocate a reduction in the number and streamlining of the structure and function of committees for the local church, circuit and district. Similarly, a large proportion of ministers (78 per cent) wished to recommend the idea of extending the executive authority of District Synods and the notion of making a fuller use of district organisation for communication between Conference and circuits (85 per cent). Yet many ministers did not believe that the substitution of a six-monthly meeting for the existing Circuit Quarterly Meeting was an administrative or representational improvement (42.4 per cent rejecting the proposal). While possibly the most surprising response from ministers, in view of their marked ecumenicalism (see chapter 5) is their reluctance to admit non-Methodist Christians as members of the Methodist Church and allow them to be affiliated to the appropriate Church committees (55 per cent rejecting the proposal).

TABLE 6.5 *Restructuring of the Church*

	Yes	No
	%	%
1 Reduction in the number and streamlining of the structure and function of committees	97.9	2.1
2 Members on the community roll and non-Methodists to be eligible for appointment as committee members and officers in the local church	45.1	54.9
3 Replacement of the Circuit Quarterly Meeting with a six-monthly circuit meeting	57.6	42.4
4 District Synods to have executive authority	78.5	21.5
5 Fuller use of district organisation for communication between Conference and circuits	85.1	14.9

This may mean that ministers believe that ecumenism can operate effectively only when grounded in structural union or systematic co-operation between Churches rather than on an *ad hoc* individual basis. Until such a formal foundation is achieved for ecumenical union and co-operation, ministers appear unwilling to open their structures to non-Methodists. Nevertheless, this attempt to account for an ostensible contradiction may be a vain one, in that an inconsistency does exist and is meaningful as such. Table 6.5 summarises these findings.

Ministers were not totally in agreement about the likely outcome of the report's recommendations. Thirty-six per cent did not believe that the proposed changes would make the structures of the Methodist Church more representative and eliminate the self-perpetuating element in the present organisation; while 43 per cent did not agree that the changes would reduce the amount of administrative work for ministers and laymen. Yet 87 per cent did believe that the suggested reforms would increase the flexibility of the Methodist Church, facilitating its adaptability to changing circumstances. Clearly, ministers believed that the structures of the Methodist Church were in danger of becoming somewhat ossified and that the proposed changes will make for much greater communication and openness of organisational operation.

We can now turn to the collection of common issues presented to all three denominations. With the exception of perhaps two items, the role of the laity and the reform of local structures, the Methodist Church appears to regard the issues as less exigent matters for reform than clergy in the Church of England. A smaller proportion of ministers envisage the liturgy as in need of pressing reform, which is consistent with their greater preoccupation with evangelism, in which ritual is not a focal point, and concern for social responsibility. Methodist ministers are much less interested in improving their levels and structures of pay than Anglican clergy. And only 29 per cent of ministers, as compared with 46 per cent of clergy, regard deployment (the stationing and travelling of ministers in the Methodist case) as a 'most important' matter of reform. Yet 91 per cent of ministers do regard the role of the laity as an important subject for reform (clergy 91 per cent); and an equal number of ministers and clergy believe that the local structures could do with reforming, as shown by Table 6.6.

What were the predominant factors which contributed to shaping the attitudes and beliefs of ministers? What part did theological cosmology, age, institutional experience, and status play in influencing beliefs? The theological belief system of ministers once more proved to be important in conditioning attitudes. The position of 'radicals' in this instance, however, is more ambivalent and

TABLE 6.6   *Common areas of reform*

	Most important	*Quite important*	*Not very important*	*Not important*
	%	%	%	%
1 Liturgy and forms of worship	14.0	61.3	20.4	4.3
2 Payment of ministers	7.3	44.0	38.8	9.9
3 Role of lay members	41.9	49.6	5.1	3.4
4 Stationing and travel of ministers	29.4	45.5	21.3	3.8
5 Reform of the circuit system	24.5	34.8	27.9	12.9

problematic. One would expect those who identified themselves as 'Radicals' to be the group most likely to support reform uniformly. Indeed, 46 per cent, as against 16.1 per cent amongst those who did not so identify themselves, believed that the Church greatly needed reform. Moreover, 24 per cent of Radicals as against 11.6 per cent of non-Radicals believed that reform in liturgy and worship was most important, and 57.1 per cent as against 36.4 per cent believed the role of lay members to be an area where reform was most important. However, there was virtually no difference between the two groups with regard to believing payment of ministers (7.6 per cent versus 6.1 per cent) and the circuit system (24.4 per cent versus 26.5 per cent) to be areas where reform is most important; and more non-Radicals (30.6 per cent) than Radicals (24 per cent) believed stationing and travelling to be an important area for reform.

Far more instructive, from the point of view of delineating where support for, and resistance to, change lie, is the division between those who identified as 'Ecumenicals' and those who did not. Ninety-seven per cent of Ecumenicals feel that some degree of overall reform is necessary, as against 80 per cent of non-Ecumenicals. Ecumenicals are consistently more likely to favour reform over laity, stationing, the circuit system, liturgy and payment, in that order. Table 6.7 demonstrates this situation on specific issues.

It would seem that a minister's identification of himself as an 'Ecumenical' is of greater relevance than might be expected at first sight. This theological approach might be taken to be solely indicative of a concern for other Churches. This orientation is particularly evident in the case of item 2, in Table 6.7. This item's concern for the inclusion of non-Methodists in the structures of the local church gains a considerably greater endorsement by Ecumenicals ($p = 0.01$) than among those who did not identify themselves as Ecumenicals.

TABLE 6.7 *Specific reforms*

	Non-Ecumenicals	Ecumenicals	p
	%	%	
1 A reduction in the number and streamlining of the structure and function of committees	98.0	98.4	*NS*
2 Members of the community roll and non-Methodists to be eligible for appointment as committee members and officers in the local church	34.7	55.3	0.01
3 Replacement of the circuit quarterly meeting with a six-monthly circuit meeting	51.5	64.3	*NS*
4 District Synods to have executive authority	72.3	85.6	0.05
5 Fuller use of district organisation for communication between Conference and circuits	78.6	90.5	0.05
Do you agree that such changes will:			
6 Reduce the self-perpetuating element in present organisation	57.1	72.4	0.05
7 Reduce the amount of administrative work for ministers and laymen	50.5	64.7	0.05
8 Increase the flexibility of the Methodist Church to adapt to changing circumstances	81.6	92.0	0.05

However, it is clear that the Ecumenical is considerably more likely to endorse areas of change outside the ecumenical arena than other theological groups. Consequently, when all the reform items were added together, the mean score for non-Ecumenicals was 29.218 and for Ecumenicals was 31.865 ($p = 0.001$), which is a very large aggregate difference. The level of statistical significance for the difference between Radicals and non-Radicals was only $p = 0.05$.

As with Anglican clergy there was a distinct tendency for younger ministers to be more inclined to change than older ministers. For example, 35 per cent of ministers under forty believed the Church greatly needed reform, as opposed to 11.4 per cent of those over sixty. However, the picture is not a completely convincing one, as there is no general association between age and denominational experience on the one hand, and a proclivity towards reform on the other.

Again, as with Anglican clergy, it is the case consistently that those ministers with the most professional orientation are least likely to favour reform. Professionalism is the traditional self-image.

In conclusion, therefore, although the Methodist Church has focused in a most precise way upon the details of necessary reform, it has nevertheless sought to account for the structural recommendations in terms of making its Church a more appropriate vehicle for its theological mission, of making the Church more effective in a modern society.

Ministers were generally disposed to accept the proposed reforms particularly those which sought to improve the structural efficiency and communication between levels within the Church. Support for the various issues and recommendations, however, was not uniform throughout ministers and once more we have found that those ministers who locate themselves around the Ecumenical–Evangelical theological axis grant the most support to reform.

III The Roman Catholic Church

The Second Vatican Council marked a new beginning for the Roman Catholic Church, the attempt to inaugurate a new theological epoch. The themes which pervaded the Council's discussions were those of reform, change, renewal, of deepening the Church's understanding of itself. As Hans Kung (1972) reported, 'it is indisputable that a new spirit—a spirit of renewal and reform, of ecumenical understanding and of dialogue with the modern world—has taken hold of the bishops and theologians of the Council, and together with them, the whole Catholic Church'. Renewal was to be conceived as a process of broadening the basis of frank and caring dialogue between levels within the Church—bishops, priests and laity, drawing the different layers into more active involvement with each other—and between the Church itself and the outside world, the temporal order, so that the Church may better serve the community in which it is embedded. Thus, as with our two other denominations, the Roman Catholic Church envisaged that one of its major tasks would be to make its beliefs and structures appropriate and relevant to an increasingly secular world.

The establishment of the Provisional Laity Commission 1967–71 was an expression of the impact of Vatican II in this country and we selected it from amongst other commissions and reports as a means of discovering the response of priests to the new climate of reform. The Commission's findings were published as a 'Report to the Laity: The Work and Experience of the Provisional Laity Commission 1967–71' (1971).

The Commission considered that its work involved 'trying to come to grips with the Second Vatican Council and to apply that teaching to the life and mission of the Church in England and

Wales today'. Principally, its appointed aim was to review the position of the laity in the mission of the Church and it came to organise its deliberations in two parts:

> The first dealing with the role of the laity in the renewal of the Church and concentrating on such matters as priest/laity relationships, lay formation and the development of structures in the Church such as Parish Pastoral Councils, whilst the second devoted itself to the layman's apostolate in his day-to-day and secular activities.

In considering the former aspect of their work, the Commission stressed the need for Catholics to reconsider the nature of their Church and its mission. Traditionally they had regarded the Church as a static, hierarchical institution, impervious, to be set apart from the sullied conditions of a frequently evil, changing world. The emphasis had been on sustaining the Church rather than developing it, upon the image of remote authoritativeness rather than upon communication, participation and mutual understanding. Now the preoccupation of Catholics must be much more outward-looking and challenging, carrying the Christian mission to the world, willing to embrace such intractable social problems as poverty, racial discrimination, war and disease, rather than to withdraw from them to reflect upon an otherworldly purity:

> Many see the Church as an institution to be maintained—hence the emphasis on efficient administration of material resources— whereas the . . . particular mission of the layman is to make the Church active and present in all circumstances of his daily life— home, school, work, leisure, and community—and it is the task of the Church as an organisation to give him stimulus, encouragement and support so that he can carry out his mission. For most people, it is the parish which should do this, working through its pastoral council and the organisations.

The Commission proceeded to make several structural recommendations which it considered would symbolise and facilitate the new theological intent:

(1) the laity should be present in all structures to ensure direct lay participation in all decision-making;
(2) a suitable agency for adequate co-ordination should be established;
(3) members of all structures should be as representative as possible of the various groupings and shades of opinion within the Church;
(4) everybody should have the services of experts, in number never more than representative membership;

(5) links between diocesan structures and national organisations, on the one hand, and the Bishops' Conference and its commissions, on the other, should be built into the plan;
(6) the setting up of a professional pastoral research unit;
(7) the introduction of Christian Stewardship;
(8) methods by which people are chosen to serve on the various bodies must be made known and their elections publicised.

How have priests responded to this climate of reform and in particular to the proposals of the Laity Commission? Do their replies lead us to believe that they consider the structural recommendations appropriate to the present and what factors have been important in shaping their attitudes?

We have already noted earlier in the chapter that, although priests are rather less orientated to the abstract of reform than either clergy or ministers they are nevertheless substantially concerned to see some kind of reform take place in the Roman Catholic Church. The conventional idea of innate priestly conservatism must therefore be treated with due circumspection. The response of priests to the Laity Commission confirms our initial impression of their preoccupation with improving and reforming the structures of the Roman Catholic Church as shown by Table 6.8. Most of the recommendations of the Commission are strongly supported by priests, particularly those which seek to improve the extent of communication and co-ordination between levels in the Church, i.e. establishment of a suitable agency for adequate co-ordination and the incorporation of links between diocesan structures and national organisations, on the one hand, and the Bishops' Conference and its commissions on the other. Priests are also especially concerned to advocate reforms which make the structures much more representative and open, in that the methods by which people are chosen to serve on the various bodies must be made known and their elections publicised. Thus, by expressing a marked interest in the co-ordination and representativeness of structures we might infer that priests are concerned to develop an organic Church organisation capable of adaptation and flexibility in the face of environmental change and uncertainty, a structure appropriate to the times.

Priests were much more wary of the idea of setting up a professional pastoral research unit. The Commission believed that it 'would encourage a positive response to change, assist in the discernment of trends and provide a basis for development of pastoral strategy'. But priests were probably more prepared to accept the note of reservation expressed in the report: 'to implement such a project

TABLE 6.8 *Response to the Laity Commission Proposals*

	Yes	No
	%	%
1 The laity should be present in all structures	43.4	56.6
2 A suitable agency for adequate co-ordination should be established	90.2	9.8
3 Members of all structures should be as representative as possible	84.2	15.8
4 Services of experts	81.8	18.2
5 Links between structures be built into plan	91.0	9.0
6 Setting up of pastoral research unit	70.0	30.0
7 Introduction of Christian Stewardship	82.0	18.0
8 Elections publicised	87.1	12.9

may imply diverting resources from other forms of pastoral and educational work in the Church'.

The most significant note of caution and reservation from the priests, however, is in relation to the position of the laity in the Church, and it is a voice of doubt which strikes at one of the central principles of the Commission's recommendations. The Commission, following the advice of Vatican II, counselled that the traditional hierarchical conception of authority—the supernatural and divine presence embodied completely at the apex, but a shrunken and distorted reflection at the foot—must give way to one which permits dialogue, mutuality and reciprocity rather than revelation. Following from this principle it was symbolically appropriate to propose a structure which radically altered the position of the laity in the Church by suggesting that laity should be present in all structures to ensure direct lay participation in all decision-making. Clearly, the response of the priests in our survey indicates that the traditional theological cosmology of priests, outlined in chapter 3 and seen at play in the chapter on 'Ecumenism' is not radically different in the context of reform: priests are not yet completely convinced of the wisdom of granting access and influence to the laity.

As with our other two denominations we asked priests about their attitudes to a number of broader issues, some of which permit cross-denominational comparisons. The most striking statistic in Table 6.9, considering the immediate discussion above, is that concerning the issue of the laity: 90 per cent of priests believe the role of the laity to be an important matter for reform. The ostensible discrepancy between this response and the one relating to laity in the Commission's report can be accounted for in terms of the inconsistency between general and particular beliefs that we have noted before. In a general and abstract way, priests believe that much should be done to improve the position of the laity in the Roman Catholic Church, yet when confronted with a highly specific proposal about the laity they are unwilling to countenance its radical connotations.

TABLE 6.9 *Reform issues*

Issue	Most important	Quite important	Not very important	Not necessary
	%	%	%	%
1 Liturgy	29.4	47.9	12.0	10.7
2 Bishops	33.3	32.6	22.4	11.7
3 Laity	47.8	42.2	6.4	3.6
4 Celibacy	20.9	18.1	25.0	36.0
5 Training	61.1	32.8	2.3	3.3
6 Parochial system	31.0	32.1	22.6	14.3

The most interesting issue which gathers the most support from priests is that of training. The Roman Catholic Church has often been criticised for a failure to adapt to a changing social environment. The priest probably feels the brunt of both this criticism and its relevance to his daily parochial experience. He is most likely to believe that he has been inappropriately trained for the social and religious realities of the second half of the twentieth century.

The influence of the liturgical movement can be seen in that the majority of priests (77.3 per cent) see change in liturgy and worship as areas where reform is at least quite important. The highly contentious issue of celibacy was regarded by only one-fifth as an area where reform is most important. This is an issue which is continually being debated but one where traditions are particularly difficult to shed. It is likely to become more hotly debated as a result of the publication of an article in the *Clergy Review* by Fr Michael Richards, the journal's editor, in which he states: 'The sacrament of holy orders should be received by both celibate and married, and ordination itself should not be a bar to marriage' (quoted in the *Guardian*, 29 January 1974, p. 4). The *Clergy Review* is extremely influential and is likely to rekindle an old debate.

Table 6.9, therefore, confirms the willingness of Roman Catholic priests to countenance reform, and confirms occasionally a substantial desire for reform. It is interesting to note that the proportion of priests wishing to reform the parochial system is higher, although only marginally, than that of clergy and ministers.

What factors have been important in moulding the attitudes of priests towards reform? When we examine our surrogate measures of theological belief there are very strong relationships with the reform items. This is not at all surprising on methodological grounds as our belief indicators were taken from the reform items; and as Appendix 1 shows these items do form a scale with a high degree of interrelationship. Thus a belief in the need for national Church autonomy and also in liturgical reform are excellent predictors of similar more radical reforms both in terms of general issues and the specific recommendations of the Laity Commission.

In contrast with the case of the Anglicans and Methodists for Roman Catholics there is a very strong relationship between all dimensions of professionalism and all aspects of reform. The direction, though, is the same as for the other groups: those who define themselves as professionals in terms of service orientation, professional reference, colleague control and vocation are less likely to endorse the need for reform. The relationship is the reverse for autonomy. Again we see a professional self-definition indicating a traditional stance with regard to the Church.

Our findings also indicate that the parish priest is more resistant to change than the non-parish priest (e.g. assistant priest). Whereas 7.5 per cent of the former believed the Church to be greatly in need of reform 24.3 per cent ($p = 0.001$) of non-parish priests claimed this. Non-parish priests regarded each area of reform as 'most important' more frequently than did parish priests—with the exception of the training of the priesthood. The priests, who are generally far more entrenched in and more thoroughly socialised into the workings of the Church, are far more likely to see areas such as the appointment of bishops, the role of the laity and the reform of the parochial system as ones where reform is not particularly necessary. These three areas would greatly upset existing structures and established ways of life in the Church, and it is therefore primarily those priests who are least entrenched in such structures who experience the need for their reform. These suggestions receive unequivocal support from Table 6.10. On each of the recommendations of the Laity Commission, support is at its greatest among non-parish priests. The greater resistance to change in established modes of organisation of parish priests can be seen in the considerably lower levels of support accorded each of the first six items of reform. The last two items would not have such a radical effect upon existing Church structures and consequently the percentage differences in support for them between the two groups is a good deal smaller.

Finally, parish priests are more inclined to want national Churches to maintain close links with Rome. The two extremes—dependency upon and autonomy from Rome—do not elicit large differences

120

TABLE 6.10 *Specific reforms and status*

	Non-parish priest	Parish priest	p
	%	%	
1 The laity should be present in all structures	57.5	31.0	0.02
2 A suitable agency for adequate co-ordination should be established	94.3	86.6	0.001
3 Members of all structures should be as representative as possible	91.5	77.5	0.01
4 Services of experts	88.4	76.5	0.01
5 Links between structures be built into plans	95.3	86.6	0.01
6 Setting up of pastoral research unit	77.2	63.8	0.01
7 Introduction of Christian Stewardship	84.5	79.8	NS
8 Elections publicised	89.4	85.4	NS

between the two groups. However, non-parish priests are considerably more likely to favour a relationship whereby the national Church should be free to adopt its own policies except on major issues of faith and morals (69 per cent, as against 53 per cent of parish priests). This is highly congruent with other findings regarding the relationship between priestly status and reform.

These findings are further underpinned when we examine type of ministry in a little more detail. It is the assistant priests and chaplains who are most reform orientated, with members of the hierarchy wishing for more reform than parish priests.

The idea that those priests who have lived longer within the structure and tradition of the Roman Catholic Church are the more conservative in their attitudes towards reform is confirmed when we focus directly upon the relationship which experience has upon belief. The more experience a priest has of the Roman Catholic Church, i.e. the longer he has been ordained, the longer he has been in the diocese and his present post, and the more posts he has held, the less approval he is likely to grant to the reform 'issues': on the appointment of bishops, the role of the laity, and reform of the parochial system. The greater the degree of experience, the more extensive the conservatism ($p = 0.001$).

The response to the recommendations of the Laity Commission is similar in that those well embedded in the established organisational structures are less willing to advocate change. Yet the conservatism of the 'experienced' is less marked in relation to the proposals of the Commission: clearly they strike at core problems and grievances.

However, as we pointed out with regard to the Anglican incumbent, the category 'parish priest' is extremely heterogeneous. When the sample of priests is broken down by the respondents' ages, some of the relationships we have noted with priestly status become clarified. We found that whereas 28.2 per cent of priests under the age of forty believed the Church to be greatly in need of reform, 5.4 per cent of those over sixty did so, and only 1 per cent of the former believed it needed no reform, as against 12 per cent of those over sixty ($p = 0.001$). The under-forty group is particularly prone to seeing the reform issues as 'most important'. This is especially evident in the areas of the appointment of bishops, the role of the laity, and the parochial system. It would seem that the young priest without a parish of his own is most inclined to see anomalies and difficulties in the workings of the Church. However, some readers may be surprised that there is not a clearer, more systematic relationship between the age of the priest and the view that celibacy is an area where reform is particularly needed. It has often been supposed that the strains and stresses which the celibate priest has to undergo would have its greatest effect on the younger priest who would consequently wish to see its reform. Our data do not provide any support for the suggestion that younger priests are more favourable to reforming the Church's injunctions on celibacy in the direction, for example, of the proposals made by Fr Richards which were quoted earlier (indeed the largest single category seeing this as 'most important' are those aged sixty and over).

A similar set of relationships can be seen in Table 6.11. By and large, the younger priests are more favourable to the Commission's

TABLE 6.11 *Specific reforms and age*

	–39	40–49	50–59	60+	p
	%	%	%	%	
1 The laity should be present in all structures	69.7	41.7	36.1	21.2	0.001
2 A suitable agency for adequate co-ordination be established	98.0	89.5	88.0	84.0	0.02
3 Members of all structures as representative as possible	91.2	89.4	79.2	74.7	0.01
4 Services of experts	89.7	84.0	74.7	77.8	0.05
5 Links between structures in plan	96.0	89.4	88.2	88.3	NS
6 Setting up of pastoral research unit	82.8	70.7	62.0	61.3	0.01
7 Introduction of Christian Stewardship	81.3	87.8	78.3	78.7	NS
8 Elections publicised	90.0	91.8	82.8	83.5	NS

recommendations than older priests. In particular, the latter, once again, seem more resistant to changes which would undermine existing modes of procedure. They are particularly more resistant to items 1 and 3, both of which are concerned with 'representativeness' or with what Bishop de Smedt of Bruges referred to as 'the evil of clericalism'. What some have called 'the rediscovery of the laity' seems to have had less effect on older priests. They are also a good deal less inclined to favour items 1 and 6 which is yet again indicative of their resistance to changes which would inhibit their autonomy.

In similar fashion, younger priests are much more likely to favour looser links between the national Churches and Rome, and a lot less likely to favour strong links. Seventy-nine per cent of those under forty feel that the national Church should have some form of autonomy, compared with 41 per cent of those over sixty. There is a greater inclination for young priests to favour areas of reform which would depart from existing and longstanding traditions in ways of doing things.

In conclusion, therefore, the Roman Catholic Church, like our other two denominations, has proposed ways of making their beliefs and organisational structures more appropriate to a contemporary era: deference to the secular divine gives way to respectful dialogue and exclusion gives way to involvement and participation.

The priests in our survey are much more prepared to tolerate and stimulate reform than conventional wisdom would lead us to believe, although it is true that they are rather more conservative than clergy or ministers. Priests are particularly concerned to improve the co-ordination and representativeness of their organisational structures, and are clearly vociferous in their demand for an improvement of training in order that they may be more fitted to the demands of a rapidly changing environment.

Although the clamour for reform is rather more uniform across the priesthood than in attitudes expressed towards other issues, for example, ecumenism, there is, however, much the same inclination for those priests who have been embedded in the Roman Catholic Church for a considerable period of time to be more conservative in their attitude towards reform.

IV Conclusions

We began this chapter by introducing a theoretical conjecture, suggested by Thompson, that religious organisations evolve from an initial preoccupation with 'symbolic appropriateness' attempting to make the organisational structure of the Church correspond to its particular religious symbol system, to a stage where, because of accumulating financial, manpower and administrative pressures, the preoccupation shifts to the criterion of efficiency and the general adoption of 'logico-experimental' standards.

Our review of Anglican, Methodist and Roman Catholic proposals for the reform and reorganisation of their organisations suggests that Thompson's proposition is only partially validated. Each denomination's proposals for reform and reorganisation do indeed encompass criteria which take account of the pressing need to improve efficiency: to deploy manpower more effectively, as in the case of the Anglican Church, or to streamline the structure and function of committees, as in the case of the Methodist Church, or to improve organisational co-ordination and communication, as in the case of the Roman Catholic Church. But it is also true that each denomination has sought to reason the changes in a manner which remains faithful to its theological cosmology. That is, they have attempted to keep the changes symbolically appropriate: the structural recommendations in the Roman Catholic Church, for example, symbolise an attempt by the Church to redirect its theology from deference towards dialogue and involvement. (Although this example may well suggest that the values which shape the reforms are those specific Christian values amongst others which happen to match most happily with those esteemed standards prevalent in modern society—such as equality, participation, caring—i.e. the organisational reforms more appropriately represent the contemporary *Weltanschauung* than does the theological belief system of the denomination in question.)

The response of the religious functionaries in our survey suggests that they generally believe that their denominations are in need of reform and that there is much support for the notion of making the Churches more appropriate or relevant to the changed social conditions of modernity. There is much concern in all three of our denominations to improve the position of the laity within the organisation—to extend their role, to incorporate them more fully within the day-to-day life of the Church—and likewise, there is much common interest in the idea of reforming the local parochial or circuit system. There is, however, a tendency for functionaries to define which specific measures are seemingly appropriate according to the kind of churchmanship/belief system they subscribe to, or to their age and experience, rather than to what is denominationally considered correctly appropriate. For example, Anglican clergy resisted the notion of imposing reforms which they considered inappropriate to their symbol system of autonomy, while Roman Catholic priests well socialised and embedded in the traditional theological belief system did not regard the new emphasis and the concomitant reforms as appropriate to their symbol system.

124

Thus, although there is a fairly general inter-denominational desire for reform, and reform which is relevant, there exist intra-denominational tensions, between different churchmanship groupings or between those whose age and organisational experience is markedly different, which make for alternative conceptions of what is to be regarded as symbolically appropriate within each Church.

7   The organisational context

Clergy, ministers and priests carry out their responsibilities within an organisational context. This context has long been an issue within the sociology of religion through the vehicle of Church/sect theory. Churches are, by definition, hierarchically organised, with full-time professionals, developed procedures, articulated belief systems, etc. (cf. Wilson, 1970). Essentially a Church has formalised and routinised the administration of the means of grace. Churches develop routines and procedures to deal with their activities. This tends to produce the hierarchy of authority, differentiation of functions and specification of tasks typical of bureaucratic organisations (Hinings and Foster, 1973).

O'Dea (1963) identified five 'dilemmas' of institutionalisation which are essentially concerned with the bureaucratisation of religious movements. In particular, the dilemmas of administrative order, delimitation and power have clear organisational referents. That of administrative order is concerned with requirements of large-scale management of Churches with the subsequent problem of office-holders having a vested interest in the continued operation of the status quo. Delimitation is the process of translating a religious message into terms related to everyday events, a process of concretisation; this involves a loss of charisma. Finally, the dilemma of power concerns the extent to which voluntary adherence becomes substituted by an institutionalised adherence.

Many studies have suggested that Churches develop greater organisational complexity than other religious movements (cf. Harrison, 1959; Fichter, 1961; Struzzo, 1970; Thompson, 1970; Allen, 1962). Perhaps this is best summarised by Harrison (1959) who points out:

modern social organisation, especially in its Western

manifestations has taken the form of the bureaucratic structure. This is true of the church as well as the state and the business organisation; it is as true of the denominations within a democratic church order as it is of the ecclesiastical hierarchy.

Prima facie, a case has been made out for the bureaucratic nature of church organisation.

On the other hand, we have seen that clergy, ministers and priests may define themselves as professionals, and there is a large literature suggesting that the organisational context within which professionals work should be non-bureaucratic (cf. Abrahamson, 1967). We have previously defined our notion of the attitudinal components of professionalism as feelings of service to the community, a vocational orientation, a desire for autonomy, seeing other professionals as the proper reference group, and accepting these colleagues as the *natural* basis of collective control. Can these attitudes be formed and realised in a bureaucratic structure with its emphasis on a clear division of labour, the existence of rules, a hierarchy of authority? In this chapter we are concerned with the examination of the extent to which clergy, priests and ministers see themselves as operating in a bureaucratic environment, that is, their perceptions of the organisational context in which they work. Arising out of both the literature in the sociology of religion and the sociology of organisations is a concern with the development of bureaucratic structures and the extent to which Churches have developed such structures.

However, there is a further reason for being concerned about the organisational context in which the religious functionary operates, stemming from the changing position of Churches over the past generations. Over time their status and position in society has become more problematical (Wilson, 1966). We do not wish to enter into the debate over secularisation here as it is concerned with much wider issues of the place of religion in society. We are examining what has happened to Churches, one institutional form of religion. By and large, Churches have been losing members, finding it increasingly difficult to recruit clergy, running into financial problems, closing down buildings, rationalising parishes, closing down theological colleges, etc. This is particularly true for the Anglican and Methodist churches, and is beginning to affect the Roman Catholic Church. The pressures generated by this position have led to an 'efficiency' concern with organisation. This concern emphasises the effective use of manpower, the conservation of finance, the rational use of buildings, all of which are dealt with through the application of modern management techniques similar to those used in a wide range of other organisations.

Harrison (1970) has suggested that Churches are in fact gradually accepting the view that ecclesiastical structures are instrumental rather than divinely ordained. We have already looked at the problems facing Churches in structural terms in the previous chapter on reform. There it was suggested that there is a possible tension between symbolic appropriateness as the criterion for organisational evaluation and the use of logico-experimental criteria. In this context we are suggesting that the pressures of Church decline may lead to the application of 'business efficiency' criteria with their roots in instrumentality and logico-experimental argument. This is shown by the use of management consultants. Given the size and scope of operations of our three Churches these problems should produce pressures to bureaucratic solutions. In the Diocese of York, for example, as a response to the organisational problems encountered, consultants were appointed. Amongst other things, their report suggested a functionalised structure with specialists being appointed to deal with particular areas of activity. The bureaucratic solutions will be in terms of increased specialisation of roles, clear definitions of roles, clear systems of authority, etc.

We do not wish to suggest that this is in any sense wrong; indeed it may be argued that the Churches require more clarity in their organisation and operation. We are interested in the extent to which functionaries perceive themselves as operating in a bureaucratic environment. Our argument suggests that Churches are naturally inclined towards a bureaucratic form and that modern pressures on resources may well push them further towards this.

However, the pressures on the three Churches are different, and they operate with different belief systems about the nature of their organisations. These differences should lead to variations in the way in which clergy, ministers and priests view the organisations in which they are located. Priests in the Roman Catholic Church operate within a context of an hierarchically organised episcopate together with an ontological view of the priesthood. By an ontological view we mean that when an individual is ordained, assuming office as a priest, he has divine gifts and qualities conferred upon him which mark him as sacred among men. Yet divinity itself is bestowed hierarchically. The priest is not only separate from the laity by virtue of his special training and a qualitative shift in his position on becoming a priest, he is also subject to the direction of a superior. The bishop has yet greater divine authority. The hierarchical nature of the Roman Catholic Church could well lead to a perception on the part of priests as operating within a relatively centralised organisation. Weber (1947) regarded the Roman Catholic Church as a prototypical bureaucracy.

Also, given the emphasis within the Roman Catholic Church on its worldwide role and importance, and the consequent emphasis on the papacy and the bishops in concert, some form of organisational standardisation may result. The theological statements made are universal and authoritative. Given this, the priest may well find himself operating in an organisational context which gives clear directions in the form of rules and procedures over his responsibilities. In this country, of course, the Roman Catholic Church has been going through a period of expansion. Growth in the size of a Church is liable to lead to an increase in the administrative component (Hinings and Bryman, 1974). Also this Church is dependent on its membership for the financial resources for the provision of church buildings, schools, etc. This is liable to lead to the careful control of such resources and this control is liable to be reflected in the decision-making system and organisational rules. Thus, we are suggesting that the episcopal nature of the Roman Catholic Church, together with the ontological basis of its priesthood, its expansion and its need for careful husbanding of resources should lead to a relatively bureaucratised structure, i.e. compared with the Methodist and Anglican Churches. Following on from this, it is likely that the priests will perceive themselves as located in an organisation which emphasises rules, hierarchy, specification, etc.

The position ought to be somewhat different with regard to ministers. The Methodist Church is within the denominational, Free Church tradition which lays more emphasis on the local congregation. Harrison (1970) has pointed out that in a sacramental Church the priest can maintain a special position. Protestantism emphasises the necessity for an educated and theologically informed laity. *Vis-à-vis* the full-time members of the Church, i.e. the ministers, this means an element of decentralisation. Indeed, the view of the ministry is a functional one. Although individuals are set apart to perform specific religious tasks, all Christians have functions of ministry. It represents an instrumental and satisfactory division of labour to have a full time ministry but in principle confers no special honours. This view, of course, has implications for the development of any hierarchy within the ministry. Organisationally, it becomes necessary for ministers to be grouped together with 'superiors', but these superiors do not have clear theological status, merely greater experience. Pushed to its logical extreme the Free Church tradition has difficulty in setting up national organisations; decision-making, rule-setting, authority is located at the local level.

However, the Methodist Church also lays great emphasis on the uniform and standardised nature of its religious practice. The national organisation is therefore of some considerable importance in this respect. Indeed, it is possible to view the organisational apparatus of the Church as being directed to making sure that allegiances to local congregations are not built up. The aim is to maintain flexibility at national level. To achieve this a complex set of rules and procedures has been developed in 'The Constitutional Practice and Discipline of the Methodist Church'. This leads to a considerable amount of standardisation. On top of this the Methodist Church is in a position of decline. It has a difficult resource base in men and money and this is liable to lead to closer control by both concentrating decision-making and by only allowing action to take place within a context of clearly defined rules. While what we have previously said about growth leading to increasing bureaucratisation may seem to imply that decline should decrease this, we do not think that this is the case. Inkson *et al.* (1970) have suggested that size operates in a ratchet fashion. As organisations increase in size they solve their co-ordination and control problems through an increasing use of rules, and the decentralisation of decision-making. If they then decline in size, their level of proceduralisation will stay the same. We have, in fact, suggested that in a period of decline there is liable to be an increase in centralised bureaucratic control as the problem of resource allocation becomes acute.

We are suggesting, then, that the Methodist minister is liable to perceive himself as operating in a more decentralised organisational context. But due to the importance of the central structures and the problems of decline there is liable to be a clearly defined rule system. This means that the minister will perceive himself as bounded by rules with his tasks specified and his autonomy curtailed.

The position of clergy in the Anglican Church is more difficult to summarise. On the one hand, the definition of the priesthood, while not completely ontological in nature is at the very least representational. That is, the clergyman is seen as a representative of God on earth. But there is a distinct absence of universally applicable, authoritative statements in the Church of England. We have already examined the range of theological cosmologies that operate within the Anglican tradition, suggesting a variety of definitions of the organisational purpose. However, the Anglican Church is episcopal in nature with a hierarchy and authority vested in the bishop.

Also the remarks that we have already made about the effects of decline in the Methodist Church apply to the Church of England. Three other points need making which affect the organisation of this Church. First, there is its established nature. As with the Methodist Church, this leads to an emphasis on the national Church and is thus liable to produce a degree of standardisation of structure. Second, there is the role of the Church Commissioners as the distributors and organisers of many of the resources of the Anglican Church. This could produce both centralisation and standardisation emanating from a pattern of national control and systems for ensuring equity of treatment. Third, though, and arguing against both of these, is the protected position of the Anglican clergyman. The Anglican incumbent has a freehold on his position; this means that it is very difficult for any standard controls to be brought to bear on him. Indeed, many of the reforms that we have previously discussed have been aimed at this freehold with the aim of giving the Church greater flexibility in its use of men and money.

Taken together we would expect the parson's freehold and the wide range of beliefs to have the most important effects. This is liable to lead to an absence of rules and a lack of detailed role prescription. The problems of decline and the links with the Church Commissioners could however lead to a degree of centralisation of decision-making. The Anglican clergyman, then, is likely to perceive himself as operating in an organisational context which is less rule-bound than the Methodists or Roman Catholics, but in between these two Churches in terms of centralisation.

I The measures

There are a number of different ways of measuring the idea of organisational perception. We have suggested certain possible developments in organisation structures and the question here is: How do members of the organisation see these developments? How do they perceive the organisations of which they are members? Do they feel themselves as belonging to organisations which emphasise rules, which are centralised, in which the distribution of influence is lop-sided? The concern is with the way in which clergy, ministers and priests see their organisations and their jobs within them.

One of the basic measures used was an inventory of items developed by Hall (1963) and later refined by Hage and Aiken (1967). This was intended to measure the degree of bureaucratisation of an organisation.

Various analyses were carried out in this research (see Appendix 1), which suggested that the items could be best expressed for religious organisations in terms of four sub-scales. These are:

(1) Hierarchy—the extent to which the locus of authority is at the top of the organisation.
(2) Routine—the existence of clear procedures.
(3) Job autonomy—the extent to which an individual has control over his own task.
(4) Rules—the extent to which rules are enforced.

It is these four scales, developed from the work of Hall and Hage and Aiken which will be used for purposes of analysis in this chapter.

Three further aspects of organisational perception are dealt with, each of which are aspects of the power and authority systems. In examining the way in which organisational members perceive their organisations, this is a crucial dimension. One way is to ask a straightforward question, asking people to rate the relative degree of centralisation/decentralisation and this is one aspect. A rather more complicated way is to get them to rate the amount of influence that various role holders and bodies in the structure have. This was done following Tannenbaum (1968). For example, in the Church of England, each respondent was asked to rank the influence of the bishop, archdeacons, suffragans, deans, rural deans, incumbents, assistant clergy, diocesan and deanery synods, on a five-point scale ranging from 'little influence' to 'a great deal of influence'. From this one can calculate the range from the lowest to the highest rating. In an authoritarian structure the range should be large, the highest-rated individual (e.g. the bishop) having a large amount of influence and the lowest-rated (e.g. the assistant clergy) having very little. Finally each respondent was asked about his participation in a range of organisational decision areas such as hiring people, changing boundaries, etc.

II Between-Church differences

Table 7.1 shows the mean scores on the four scales of organisational perception. This consistent pattern is that predicted above where essentially we suggested that the Roman Catholics would be highest in terms of a bureaucratic climate, the Methodists midway, and the Church of England lowest.

TABLE 7.1 *Organisational perceptions*

	Church of England	Methodist	Roman Catholic	Possible Max.	Min.
Hierarchy	6.83	6.92	7.83	20.00	5.00
Routine	6.99	7.64	8.04	20.00	5.00
Job autonomy	6.57	7.27	7.69	20.00	5.00
Rules	7.63	8.49	8.83	20.00	5.00

As was predicted the Roman Catholic priests see themselves as operating within a bureaucratic climate. That is, they feel that there is a clear hierarchy, procedures exist to routinise tasks, rules are enforced and job autonomy is low. Anglicans, on the other hand, have a less bureaucratic climate, being at the opposite end to the Roman Catholic priests on these scales. The most interesting thing about this is the consistency of direction. The fact that the Methodists are intermediate suggests that in our preliminary hypothesising we were correct in emphasising the centralised nature and national forms of the Methodist Church. While the Methodist minister has considerable autonomy over immediate ritual matters, most other tasks are clearly outlined and codified. As pointed out, the Methodist Church is the only one of the three that has an 'organisational manual', namely, 'The Constitutional Practice and Discipline of the Methodist Church'. This demonstrates the way in which practice is surrounded by rules and standardised nationally. It also emphasises the important role of the annual conference and central departments in decision-making. On the other hand, the significance of the episcopal nature of the Church of England and its adverse resource position are probably less important than the position of the Anglican incumbent with his freehold. This gives him, in his task, ideological and decision-making freedom. Indeed, this independent position has been under attack in, for example, the Paul Report, precisely because it makes rational standardised resource allocation difficult.

However, while this consistency in the ordering of the three groups on all the scales is impressive and good evidence of real differences, we must be careful about taking our interpretation too far. The Likert scale technique allows one to state what the maximum and minimum possible scores are. This is recorded in the last two columns of Table 7.1 and examining it is salutary. Taking the existence of routine, for example, we have the priest, minister, clergy ordering. But if every clergyman had said that he felt his tasks to be completely unroutinised (as defined in this scale) the mean score would be 5. If, on the other hand, every clergyman had perceived his task as being completely routinised the mean score would be 20. Thus average routinisation on this scale would be a score of 12.50. The means of all three groups are significantly below this. In other words, although the Roman Catholic priests see their tasks as more routine than the other two groups, they are still relatively non-routine. Looking at all the scales in this way, while we can describe the priests as seeing themselves as operating in organisations whose climate is more bureaucratic than the ministers, whose climate is more bureaucratic than the clergy, overall, in terms of possible scores, all three groups are operating in relatively non-bureaucratised environments.

Table 7.2 presents the three scales that are not concerned with the notion of bureaucracy as such, but with various aspects of power and influence. In these we find a different picture, that is the priests see themselves as operating in the most centralised Church, with the most influence at the top and participating least in decision-making. The Methodist ministers are in the most decentralised Church, where influence is evenly distributed along the hierarchy

TABLE 7.2 *Perceptions of influence*

	Church of England	Methodist	Roman Catholic	Possible Max.	Min.
Centralisation	2.59	2.39	2.93	4.00	1.00
Influence range	2.66	1.23	2.85	4.00	0.00
Participation	9.11	9.54	7.96	25.00	5.00

and where participation is highest. The clergy are midway, nearest to the Roman Catholics on influence, but to the Methodists on centralisation and participation. It would seem that the episcopal system has its greatest effect on decision-making with the position of the bishop being crucial. Of course, it is not just the bishop, but also the fact that in both the Anglican and Catholic Churches the bishop tends to have his staff in the form of auxiliaries, suffragans, vicars general and archdeacons. This is in great contrast to the Methodist district chairman without even a full-time secretary to help him. Again, examining these scores in relation to the possible maxima and minima we find the opposite of our bureaucratic picture. With the exception of the Methodist ministers on influence, they are all consistently towards the centralised, low participation end. Overall our three groups do not see themselves operating in circumstances of decentralisation, participation and democratic influence systems.

III Within-Church differences

Our results so far show clear differences between the three Churches and in systematic ways. But, of course, there may well be important differences of organisational perception within each Church. For example, past research has shown that one's position in the organisation, particularly one's place in the hierarchical system, may have an important effect on the views that one has about the organisation (Payne and Mansfield, 1973).

The bishop may perceive considerably less hierarchy and fewer rules than the curate. Similarly, in the Anglican and Methodist Churches, where there are some variations in beliefs, these could have some effect. The chain here is a little complicated but to a large extent one's perceptions of a situation are dependent on what one's expectations are. Particular theological stances mean particular expectations about organisational forms. For example, a Modernist or New Theology orientation in the Anglican Church could lead to desires and expectations for an open, decentralised, autonomous organisation, with responsibility resting on the shoulders of the individual clergyman. Any structure which did not produce this is likely to be seen as rule-bound, centralised, etc., whereas to an Anglo-Catholic with his idea of a sacramental Church, the same structures could be seen as less centralised and less rule-bound because of the different starting point in terms of organisational expectations. Thompson (1970) has suggested that there are important differences about the nature and locus of authority in the Church of England.

Also, we have to take account of the extent to which an individual in an organisation defined himself as a professional or not. We have already suggested that the professional will emphasise his autonomy, his relationships with clients and with fellow professionals. Again this is liable to lead to particular perceptions of the way in which the organisation works. In relation to the Roman Catholic Church, Greeley (1973) has characterised the priest as a 'professional caught in a feudal structure'. Struzzo's work (1970) suggests that professionalism serves as a basic foundation for responding to a wide range of pastoral issues and he finds that professional attributes are significantly related to dissent. Much of the literature on the clergy has been concerned with the extent to which they constitute a profession and the ways in which this may affect their perceptions of the nature of the Church, and by extension, the organisational context in which they operate.

Essentially, then, we now proceed to examine the ways in which the organisational position and experience, the beliefs and self-conceptions of religious functionaries act as factors which structure their perceptions of the Church as an organisation. This will be done Church by Church to see whether the patterns are similar or different.

The Church of England

Looking now at the ways in which the characteristics of clergymen relate to their perceptions of the organisation structure we can first of all point out that there are two of our scales on which there is no discrimination (that is, discrimination which is statistically significant). These are job autonomy and routine. Thus, factors concerned with organisational position, experience, beliefs and self-image are not related to the way in which clergymen view the specification of their tasks and the existence of clear procedures. Overall we find that there is, anyway, a perception of limited job specification and routine. Again the existence of the clergyman's freehold gives him a wide discretion in the way in which he carries out his various tasks, and indeed which tasks he will carry out.

We do find, however, that some of our explanatory factors—particularly organisational position, age, denominational experience

—do help us to account for the way in which clergy perceive some organisational characteristics of their Church. Position, for example, is related to perceptions of hierarchy and the amount of participation in the organisation. Taking the latter first, we find a straightforward relationship between position in the hierarchy and participation in decision-making. Those who we have identified as members of the hierarchy (archdeacons, suffragan bishops and bishops) have by far the greatest say in making decisions. Rural deans are the group with the next greatest amount of participation, followed by chaplains, incumbents and curates. Chaplains come before incumbents because of their position in the diocesan structure which is backed up by their involvement in specialist committees. The role of a specialist in any organisation is to give advice and thereby influence decisions. Examining 'type of ministry' it is those who are assisted, i.e. those in superordinate positions, who are most involved in decision-making, and those who assist, i.e. subordinates, who are least involved. Those working on their own are the second most involved group, reflecting their composition in chaplains and some incumbents. Those in group and team ministries are closest to subordinates in rating.

Hierarchy, which is concerned with the extent to which the locus of authority, is prestructured and, at the top of the organisation, is also related to organisational position. While members of the hierarchy perceive the least amount of prestructured decision-making and curates perceive the greatest amount, the relative position of incumbents, chaplains and rural deans changes. Incumbents perceive less hierarchy than chaplains or rural deans, in spite of the fact that they are less involved in decision-making. This is no doubt because hierarchy is seen in relationship to the extent to which there is intervention by superiors in one's task activities. An example of this kind of item is 'a person can make his own decisions in this diocese without checking with anyone else'. Participation is essentially about policy-making decisions with chaplains and rural deans proffering advice and sitting on committees. Hierarchy is about interventions in the day-to-day job. Here the postion changes. The incumbent's freehold, his lack of job definition, geographical distance and lack of direct supervision all contribute to a non-hierarchical position. Rural deans are clear members of the hierarchy and subject to more direct control by archdeacons. Similarly chaplains are subject to the bishop and committees.

A clergyman's organisational position or status is not related to the enforcement of rules. The determining influence of biography or denominational experience upon organisational perceptions is less straightforward. In Chapter 2 we have already demonstrated the close links between the various aspects of experience. This is reflected in the fact that all four measures, age, years in present position, years in the diocese and years ordained, are all related to hierarchy and participation. However, only age and years in position are related to any other aspects of organisational perception, both being associated with the scale of rule enforcement.

When we examine the link between the measures of organisational experience, hierarchy and participation it is a clear one. The older a clergyman is biographically or experientially, the less hierarchy he will perceive and the more he will report himself as participating in decision-making at the diocesan level. This finding also once again shows the fact that older people, experientially, are those people who occupy the more senior, and thus the more participative positions in the organisation.

With regard to other aspects of organisational perception we find that age and years in present position are related to perception of rules (the extent to which rules are enforced). As far as rules are concerned there is a fairly straightforward relationship with age; the older a clergyman is the more likely he is to feel that rules are enforced. The same is true of the years that he has been in his present position. Again, we are coming across a relationship already mentioned under position; older clergy are more likely to be superiors and to feel the need to enforce rules.

Thus, our review of organisational position and experience confirms the effects of the interrelationships between them as far as the perceptions of the organisation are concerned.

What we have looked at so far has shown the strong relationships, in particular between, on the one hand, aspects of position and experience and, on the other, perceptions of hierarchy and reported participation in decision-making. This pattern is repeated for the various aspects of professionalism, one's occupational self-conception, but not for churchmanship. The only relationship for the latter variable is with the perceptions of the existence of rules. The situation here is that Anglo-Catholic Modernists, and Prayer-Book Catholics, perceive the most rules, with those professing a New Theology at the opposite end of the spectrum. But the relationship is not a strong one and, as we have said, overall there seems to be no connection between theological beliefs and organisational perception.

With professionalism the picture is different, as one would expect from the vast literature on professionals in organisations (in particular, see Hall, 1968). We are using the Hall measures (or derivatives) of both professionalism and bureaucratisation and his work has shown a consistent negative relationship between the aspects dealt with here (Hall, 1968). However, while we find relationships between many aspects of structural perception and service orientation, autonomy, colleague control and vocation, only those with autonomy are negative; those with the others are positive. The existence of a professional reference is not related to organisational perception, explainable by the almost complete lack of professional organisations for clergy.

Essentially our results can be summarised as follows: the higher a clergyman's conception of himself as a professional in terms of looking to his colleagues as a control group, a service and vocation orientation, then the more likely he is to perceive himself as working in a bureaucratic environment. If he defines himself as a professional by stressing his autonomy then he will perceive a relatively less bureaucratised organisation. This pattern reflects what has already been reported in chapter 3, the negative relationship between autonomy and other aspects of professionalism. While a full critique of Hall is to be found elsewhere (see Bryman *et al.*, 1974), we feel that the picture we find is more explicable than the expectation of a negative relationship between professionalism and bureaucracy.

It is important to remember that *both* measures are perceptual. The measures Hall uses for organisation structure, we have suggested, measure *perceptions* of that structure. It can be argued that any organisational member who defines himself in the professional terms laid down *is* liable to perceive any organisation as too bureaucratic. The more of a professional one is, the more one has been socialised to reject formal organisation. In a sense, any organisation gets in the way of the professional–client relationship; *ipso facto*, any organisation will be defined as bureaucratic the more professional one is.

Autonomy, again, one would expect to be different for methodological reasons. In the actual items used in the attitude scale the other aspects of professionalism continuously refer to one's occupation. This is not so for autonomy, where the item references are continuously to the job or position of the respondent. Thus autonomy is not really measuring professionalism but an aspect of the job which the respondent fills. The relationship shows that those who see themselves in a job in which 'I make my own decisions in regard to what is to be done in my work' (to quote one of the items) also see themselves in a situation with few rules, little job definition and little hierarchy. This is hardly surprising; indeed it verges on the tautologous and is better used as an instance of the internal consistency of responses.

The Methodist Church

Both measures of organisational position are related to perceptions of organisation structure. However, type of ministry is related over a wider range of structural perceptions, in fact, to all aspects except rules. We find that both type of ministry and numbers of ministers in the circuit are related to perceptions of hierarchy and the amount of participation, also the existence of routine procedures. On hierarchy and participation, sector ministers perceive the least and participate the least; this marks their relative autonomy in relation to the organisation. Then we find that those at the top of the organisation, circuit superintendents, perceive the next least hierarchy and participate the most. In between are ministers and probationers/supernumeraries respectively. With regard to the size of the circuit, one finds that the smallest circuits are perceived as having the most hierarchy, with the largest having the next most. Surprisingly, we find that on participation; the smallest circuits have the most participation and the largest the next most.

With regard to routine, again it is the sector minister who perceives himself as having the least definition in these two senses. Most task and rule specification is perceived by the circuit superintendent, then the circuit minister followed by the probationer/supernumerary. This is something which is very likely related to the centralised nature of the Methodist Church, which leads to those with the closest relationships to central departments perceiving the most control through role and task definition. It is also underpinned by the existence of the 'Constitutional Practice and Discipline of the Methodist Church' and by the society minister. Again the relationship of circuit size to these is somewhat surprising. Essentially it shows that the smaller the circuit, the greater the perception of both the division of labour and routines. One's initial hypothesis would be that larger size would lead a circuit to produce its internal routines and task divisions. This is evidently not the case. It may well be that in the smaller circuit there is a more individual emphasis and a subsequent relying on the 'Constitutional Practice'. In the larger circuit a colleague situation may well arise with a great deal of mutual support leading to less perception of rules.

Turning to other aspects of organisational perception we find that type of ministry is also related to job autonomy. Those at the top of the hierarchy, the circuit superintendents (and chairmen, of whom there are two) see themselves as occupying jobs with the clearest definition, followed by ministers, probationers/supernumeraries and sector ministers, in that order. Here again we have closeness to the administrative apparatus producing clarity of task definition. In nonconformist religious organisations it is the spiritual tasks which remain undefined and the administrative and governmental ones which are codified. Thus, those whose jobs are most involved with the latter (namely circuit superintendents) perceive the most definition, and those concerned primarily with the former perceive least.

On aspects of organisational experience the situation is reasonably straightforward. Two of the variables dealt with under this concept are not related to any aspects of organisational perception, namely the number of years a minister has been in his circuit, and the number of years he has been in the district. Interestingly, it is not 'organisational age' but 'general' and 'ministerial' age which are related to perceptions. Basically, the older a minister and the longer he has been ordained (two strongly related variables) the more likely he is to perceive himself as working in a bureaucracy. That is, as far as he is concerned there will be greater job control, more procedures, more routine, more rules. But, the older minister will not necessarily perceive more hierarchy, and he will participate more in decision-making. We are seeing here the interplay of related variables. We have suggested why those at the top of an hierarchy should see themselves as more surrounded by rules; and, as we know from previous analysis, those in positions of authority are also older and have been ordained longer.

Turning now to self-conceptions of ministers we find that both theological beliefs and professionalism are related to various perceptions of organisation structure. Those who are self-defined as Ecumenicals or Evangelicals are much more likely to perceive themselves as working in a bureaucracy. Again this particularly refers to the rule aspects of bureaucracy, namely, routine and rules rather than the hierarchical aspects. In contrary fashion, those who define themselves as Radicals see themselves in a less bureaucratic situation.

Once again we have the interaction effects of variables at work here. As we suggested in chapter 3, Evangelism and Ecumenicalism represent two central traditions in Methodism. We have shown, also, that the upholders of these traditions are more likely to be in positions of authority. Similarly, the Radicals will be the more junior clergy. Thus, theological position is actually acting as a surrogate for organisational position and experience.

When we turn to the occupational self-conceptions that ministers have, the picture is fairly similar to that for Anglican clergy. The more a minister sees himself as a professional in terms of service orientation, colleague control and professional reference, the more likely he is to see himself working in a bureaucracy. Also, the more he defines himself as 'seeking' or having autonomy the less likely are his surroundings seen as bureaucratic. We would advance exactly the same arguments for these findings as we did for Anglican clergy. The only change from the uniformity of these findings is that on one scale, namely hierarchy, those who are less professionalised

140

in terms of vocation will perceive the organisation as having more hierarchy. While the differences are not statistically significant this relationship is found with most other scales of organisational perception.

The Roman Catholic Church

Both measures of organisational position are related to a variety of aspects of structural perception. Taking the rule aspects first, we find that type of ministry is related to rule enforcement. Those working on their own perceive the most rules, and they are most likely to be chaplains or incumbents. Similarly it is those who are assistants to others, the assistant priests, who perceive the next most rules. Least rules are seen by those who define themselves as working as part of a group.

Both position and type of ministry are related to hierarchy in organisations. The assistant priest, at the bottom of the organisational pyramid, working directly for someone else, perceives the most hierarchy and participates least in decision-making. The parish priest has a similar perception, although it is marginally less hierarchical. It is those working on their own, and further up the hierarchy who perceive the organisation as least hierarchical.

Turning to aspects of experience, all four, namely, age, years ordained, years in the diocese and years in present position, are related to perceptions of hierarchy. The relationship is the same for each one and is linear, that is, the older and more experienced a priest is, the more likely he is to perceive less hierarchy. Once again we are dealing here with the relationship between position and experience. Older people are more likely to be in senior, autonomous positions in the Roman Catholic Church, as is the case in most organisations.

These four aspects of experience are also all related to perceptions of rule enforcement. While the relationship is not entirely linear the general relationship is that the older a priest is, individually and organisationally, the more likely it is that he will perceive the existence of rules and feel that they are enforced. There are exceptions to this general pattern. In particular, the median age groups perceive slightly less rules, something which is related to their position as deans—a group that is at a point in the organisation that possibly has most direct task autonomy.

For priests, there are no relationships between theological cosmology and organisational position.

With regard to professional definition, the results are very similar to those for Anglican clergy and Methodist ministers. Of the five aspects of professionalism, the existence of a professional reference group, and feelings of vocation are hardly related to any aspects of the perception of structure, in a statistically significant way. However, the influence of colleagues as a control group is in the same direction as service orientation. Thus, the higher a priest's conception of himself as a professional, in terms of looking to his colleagues as a control group, having a service and vocational orientation and using a professional reference group, then the more likely he is to perceive himself as working in a bureaucratic environment. If, on the other hand, he defines himself as a professional by stressing his autonomy, then he will perceive a relatively less bureaucratised organisation. We would call upon the same explanation as was given for the Anglican clergy.

IV Conclusions

As with the other chapters, our objective has been initially to establish differences, if any, between Churches, and then to look at within-Church differences. Initially, we demonstrated that Roman Catholic priests see themselves as operating within a bureaucratic structure. Anglican clergy have a lower bureaucratic perception with the Methodist ministers being intermediate. However, it is important to point out that all three groups are operating in relatively non-bureaucratised environments.

This inter-Church picture with regard to bureaucratic perceptions is not repeated with regard to decision-making. Here the episcopal system makes its imprint with the Roman Catholics operating in circumstances of most centralisation, lack of participation and an authoritarian system, followed by the Anglican clergy, with the Methodists most open. But, unlike the perceptions of bureaucracy, the three groups see themselves in relatively centralised and authoritarian bodies.

Our results, then, show clear differences between the three Churches and in systematic ways. But the second question to be asked is whether there are also such systematic differences within each group, and how far similar factors can be used as possible explanations. Looking at these within-Church differences leads to renewed emphasis on the relative uniqueness of each Church in terms of its traditions and central focuses. While the variables chosen as predictors, namely aspects of organisational position, organisational experience and self-conception, all work to some extent in each Church, they do not always work in the same way. There are some general patterns which can be extracted initially.

For all three Churches the relationships tend to be strongest with perceptions of hierarchy and participation in decision-making. This is what one would expect as problems of authority are at the heart of most organisations, and religious organisations in particular. And we find that clergy, ministers and priests are likely to perceive less hierarchy and to participate more in decision-making the older they are; for the clergy and priests this holds for all four indices of experience. For the Methodists it is age and years ordained which are important. These are in fact the two factors that are important for the other two Churches; the fact that years in the organisation and in the current position are also related in the Anglican and Roman Catholic Churches is a reflection of their static organisational career structure. Because of the movement in the Methodist Church the 'direct' organisational experience variables are uncorrelated with 'general' organisational experience variables. Anyway, this age relationship is basically a reflection of the seniority structure of most organisations and these religious organisations in particular. Older people occupy more senior positions which, by definition, are at the top of the organisational hierarchy and, as such, at decision centres. This is backed up by the fact that the organisational position variables are also linearly related to hierarchy and participation in all three Churches. With regard to these two aspects of organisation structure we see a general organisational process at work.

However, the same is not true for other aspects of structural perception. For Anglican clergy we find that, when examining rules and task specification aspects of organisational perception, the special position of the incumbent becomes a factor. The existence of a freehold and the lack of job definition means that the incumbent perceives least rules and job specification, although the other scores follow the pattern that those highest in the formal hierarchy perceive the fewest rules. While type of ministry is a good predictor of bureaucratic perception for Roman Catholic priests, it operates in a different way. Those working on their own see themselves as most rule-bound, more so than assistants, representing their direct relationship to the bishop and their being recipients of his organisational directives. For the Methodist minister the position changes yet again. Those at the top of the formal chain of command perceive much more bureaucracy than those at the bottom, which is a consequence, we suggest, of the more centralised nature of the Methodist Church as a whole.

With regard to self-conception, again we have both general and particular patterns. As far as occupational conception is concerned we find that in all three Churches the relationship is the same. The more a clergyman, a minister or a priest sees himself as a professional, in all aspects except feelings of autonomy, the more he is likely to see himself operating in a bureaucratic environment. The relationship is the opposite for autonomy aspects of professionalism.

But with reference to theological beliefs we find that essentially they have no impact in the Anglican and Roman Catholic Churches, whereas there are clear relationships in the Methodist Church. The Ecumenicals and Evangelicals amongst Methodist ministers are liable to perceive themselves as working in a bureaucracy, whereas Radicals perceive the opposite. But there is a strong relationship between these self-conceptions and organisational position, Ecumenicalism and Evangelism being central traditions in Methodism. People espousing them are more likely to be in positions of authority, and we have already seen that those in such positions also perceive themselves as being in a bureaucratic environment.

8 Conclusions

The task at this stage is unavoidably one of synthesis, of trying to combine and recreate a whole from a disparate collection of parts which have hitherto been analysed separately. Within each of the chapters we have described the demographic, social and theological characteristics of ministers, priest and clergy and their responses to the problem issues presented, but as yet we possess only fragmented sketches of the denominations as such. The initial task is therefore to draw these descriptive vignettes together in order that the total character of the denominations can be made clear. Yet, as we said in chapter 1, our objective is not merely one of description and classification, of providing an informative narrative, but more essentially one of explanation, of attempting to elucidate those factors which are crucial in the shaping of the conduct, beliefs, sentiments, and intentions of religious functionaries. At the outset we delineated a number of variables which we considered to be central to any explanation of the beliefs and activities of our functionaries. These were: denominational variables, such as organisational position and status, the degree of denominational experience, and the kind of theological college training which a functionary had received; theological belief or cosmology, which for analytical purposes we differentiated from the denominational category, and to accommodate those theorists who have suggested the importance of inter- rather than intra-denominational characteristics; and extra-denominational factors such as social class background, age and professional allegiance. Once more we need to take each factor in turn and see how efficacious it has been in enabling us to account for and predict the attitudes and behaviour of priests, clergy and ministers. This is a dual task in that we have both to review the impact that each factor has had upon each of the dependent variables and, of course, to analyse the relative influence of the explanatory factors themselves; that is to say, we might discover that both belief and denominational experience have an influence upon attitudes towards ecumenical co-operation, for example, but we need to be aware of the relative weight of each factor. Finally, we are then able to reconsider the tentative model which we provisionally elaborated in chapter 1, review whether it remains valid and, if not, the extent to which it will require modification.

I The denominations

The Church of England

The Church of England clergy in our survey were mainly incumbents, that is, responsible for a parish; but their number also incorporated curates, chaplains, deans, archdeacons, bishops and so on. The demographic characteristics of the typical clergyman tend to be rather different than his counterpart in the Roman Catholic and Methodist Churches: he is usually a relatively younger man and comparatively less experienced in that his career within the Church has been rather shorter, he has been ordained more recently, and he has held fewer posts. The experience he has gained of the locality in which he is presently working is also considerably less in that he has held his present position and has worked within his immediate diocese for a shorter period of time.

Clergy have been drawn from a fairly distinctive social background, as they have in all probability been born into homes within the middle and upper reaches of the social hierarchy. The fathers of many clergymen were likely to be professional men, employers or managers, while the fathers of others worked in supervisory roles or in personal service. The kind of education that clergy have received is likely to be in keeping with their social class origins. Thus, a substantial proportion of clergy, for example, has been to public school, while most others have been educated at grammar schools. Following secondary school, most clergymen went to university where they tended to study humanities or theology; most graduated, and a half continued to qualify for a master's degree. At theological college, clergy became more formally initiated in, and tended to accept, a particular branch of churchmanship.

The limits and composition of the clergy's doctrinal inclination appears to have altered little since the mid-nineteenth-century account of W. J. Coneybeare. His distinction between 'High' Churchmen (largely of Catholic persuasion), 'Low' Churchmen (largely Evangelical in persuasion) and 'Broad' Churchmen (those of the centre) still obtains to a great extent. The contemporary churchmanship categories incorporate the 'Anglo-Catholic', the

146

'Prayer-Book Catholic', 'Liberal' and 'Conservative' strains of Evangelicalism, and 'Central or Broad churchmanship'. The proportions of clergy adhering to each kind of theological persuasion also seems to have remained remarkably stable since the nineteenth century; that is, rather less than half sustain a Catholic cosmology, while a quarter continue to adhere to the churchmanship of the middle ground. Where change has occurred, however, it has been within the 'Low' Church perspective. Whereas in Coneybeare's day more than a third of clergymen supported an Evangelical theological cosmology, this brand of churchmanship is now followed by less than 20 per cent of clergy. Evangelicalism within the Anglican faith has been somewhat eroded by the incipient development of a more radical theological persuasion. 'Modernism' and 'New Theology' are progressive theological doctrines which stress, among other things, the importance of making the Church and its message relevant to the experiences of modern man. Yet although the 'Modernists' have been gaining ground they are as yet a rather marginal force within the Church of England. This peripheral shift within a basically stable pattern is, however, significant and is reflected in the way in which clergy are beginning to conceive the relationship of their Church to others. That is, clergy continue to perceive the Church of England 'as having a special relationship to the whole population of an area regardless of the people's religious or other affiliations' an attitude which derives traditionally from the secular 'establishment' of the Church; yet the clergy's ardour for that 'establishment' is clearly diminishing and many are prepared to recommend the disestablishment of the Church of England or at least its revision along the lines of the Church of Scotland.

The way in which clergy define their conception of ministry tends to mirror the traditional doctrinal emphases. Although Leslie Paul has spoken of the undoubted confusion in the minds of Church of England clergy about the roles they should play, our survey has revealed them, as a collective body, still reflecting time-honoured values and beliefs about how they should conduct their ordained ministry. Overarching precedence is still afforded to the clergyman's pastoral role, that loosely woven general imperative which prescribes a broadly based caring for, and responsibilities towards, parishioners. Clergy as a whole, therefore, place pastoralism above their responsibility for the celebration of sacraments. The role of celebrant with its characteristic emphasis upon ritual and visual symbolism provides much of the focus for existing theological controversy about the conception of ministry. Preaching is usually ranked third in the clergy's hierarchy of ministerial values, the presentation and illuminating interpretation of the Word being thus evaluated as of less importance than the solemn re-enactment and sharing in the Spirit. The radical theologians of the day give great sway to the responsibilities of counselling and leadership, the one seeking through sensitive insight, advice and confession, to provide relief to personal problems, the other hoping to provide a source of social energy and initiative for the local community. Whatever the degree of variation within the Church of England, clergy as a whole are inclined to accord the tasks of counselling and leadership rather low priority in their order of preferences. Finally, unanimity is complete in the clergyman's distaste for the mundane and menial tasks of organisational administration and officialdom: *these responsibilities are regarded as a burdensome drudgery, consuming time which could be more profitably spent on crucial vocational work.*

Anglican clergy have the least professional attitudes of our three groups. They stress autonomy and vocation, but give much less weight to colleague relations and judgment. The diversity in conceptions of ministry and theological training make it unlikely that a clear professional/occupational ideology will develop among clergy.

The typical response of clergy to the pressing issues of the day—ecumenism, reform, organisation—is generally guarded. The issue of Church unity, for example, is approached with caution by most clergy. They were willing to countenance organic unity only with those Churches whose structure was similar to their own, such as the Roman Catholic and Orthodox Churches, or those Churches with a relatively familiar theological tradition, such as the Methodist Church. Clergy were much more reluctant to contemplate complete union with radical Protestant Churches such as the Pentecostal Churches. They were more prepared, however, to consider measures of ecumenical co-operation, but again with important qualifications: they willingly accept the tentative and provisional co-operative ventures such as inter-faith meetings, study groups, ventures on joint education, social welfare and community projects. Such measures which attempt to promote a gradual appreciation of another denomination's liturgy, beliefs and myths are warmly accepted, but more radical steps, such as the union of theological colleges or the fusing of ministries, prove more difficult for them to envisage. This deeper resistance to acts which transgress the core tenets of faith, the central articles of theological belief and custom, is particularly manifested in the clergy's practical ecumenical activities: the marked inhibition about participating in services of inter-communion.

Clergy treated the issue of reforming the Church of England with as much reservation as they did the ecumenical issue, even though virtually all the clergy expressed a view that the Church of England required at least some reform. Leslie Paul had assailed the Anglican

Church as being anachronistic in fundamental ways, as being out of phase with crucial changes in twentieth-century society. He believed that the ecclesiastical system developed at the time of St Augustine, with its aim of imposing a territorial grid over the land in order that each bounded community should have a church and parson, was now inappropriate to contemporary needs. The most striking need was to regain control of clergy, to ensure that the parochial deployment of clergy matched the distribution of population throughout the country. With this central preoccupation in view, Paul proposed a number of interrelated measures which would facilitate the process of regaining control of the clergy and of making the Church's structure more symbolically appropriate to the needs of the day. His recommendations included a major parish run by a college of clergy, transforming freeholds into leaseholds, an open central registry, the increased involvement of the laity and so on. Yet, while the clergy clearly believe that their rational re-deployment is an important issue, they are also insistent that it is one which must be resolved by ensuring at the same time that their freehold remains inviolate. They cling firmly to their traditional right of security and autonomy and their attitudes suggest that only persuasion and encouragement and not 'direction' will be tolerated. Clergy are also reluctant to alter the nature of the parish system: they were not enamoured of the idea of a major parish, although they were prepared to encourage existing ideas still in the early stages of development, such as group and team ministries, and the stepping-up of the co-ordination work of rural deaneries. The problems of payment and the position of the laity, however, were approached with a more progressive air, thus their willingness to contemplate a common stipendiary fund for all the clergy and the proposals for a lay pastorate, a pastoral advisory committee and a lay voluntary service.

Finally, clergy work within organisations whose pressing needs and problems increasingly require bureaucratic solutions. We wished to discover the extent to which clergy considered the organisational context in which they worked, bureaucratic or not—that is, the degree to which they perceive their lives as being minutely regulated by rules and procedures, the degree to which they consider their lives to be overspecialised or too intensely overseen by a burdensome system of authority. The Church of England possesses organisational characteristics, seemingly contradictory in nature in that it is episcopal and thus hierarchical; yet the protected freehold symbolises the incumbent's autonomy. These diverse characteristics make for organisational complexity and difficulty of prediction. Our survey shows that Anglican clergy perceive their Church to be less bureaucratic in nature than do priests or ministers—that is, they believe that as an organisation the Church of England is not heavily circumscribed by rules and regulations, that it is not particularly hierarchical and that tasks are not stultifyingly fragmented or specialised. This suggests that the ingrained tradition of the independent parson and freehold is more significant as a structural feature of the Church of England than the 'establishment', or the episcopacy, or the position of the Church Commissioners and so on.

The Methodist Church

The religious functionaries in our survey from the Methodist Church were mainly ministers, although a third were circuit superintendents. This disposition of statuses immediately sets the Methodist ministers apart as having a fairly homogeneous collection of experiences, in that the hierarchy is shallow and the emphasis upon specialised ministries (sector ministers) limited—the common experience is that of serving a geographically based congregation.

Methodist ministers tend to be rather older than Anglican clergy and comparatively more experienced, in that they have been ordained for a longer period. It must be remembered, of course, that the experience of ministers is qualitatively different from that of priests or clergy in the episcopal Churches, in that the emphasis is placed on 'travelling' within and between districts. The likelihood is, therefore, that ministers will have held more positions and have worked in those positions, their circuits and districts, for a shorter period of time than most clergy and priests.

The social class origins of ministers are rather different from those of clergy in that most ministers have grown up in lower-middle-class homes where the father was typically occupied in clerical work, or in personal service, or in some kind of supervisory role. Most ministers went to grammar school, although a substantial number were educated only to an elementary secondary level. Following secondary school, unlike the typical clergyman, most ministers did not continue their education at university, though those who did tended to graduate with a degree rather than a diploma. Whatever the theological college ministers attended, the usual experience was once more relatively homogeneous since the Methodist Church endeavours to impose formal precautions to ensure that their colleges do not develop the kind of distinctive theological stances which characterise the Church of England colleges.

The distinctive kinds of theological cosmology which obtain in the Church of England are not repeated in the Methodist Church, at least not in the same form. Methodism was quite patently a significant component in the eighteenth-century Evangelical Revival with its emphasis upon spiritual experience, conversion, the singular authority of the biblical Word, the importance of oratory and the simplicity of worship. Whatever the developments of Evangelicalism from this period, these themes have remained in some way central. The category 'churchmanship' therefore remains an inappropriate one for the Methodist Church. Nevertheless, we were interested in discovering the types and degrees of variation and we did ask ministers to locate themselves theologically, leaving the category open for the minister himself to complete and describe. The great majority of ministers identified themselves as adhering to an Evangelical or an Ecumenical theological position or some complex of the two. These proportions are an indication of the persistence and continuity of the evangelical doctrine within Methodism and the commitment of the Church to the ecumenical movement. A number of ministers did describe themselves as 'liberal' or 'radical' or 'conservative' yet rather as an adjectival qualification of the central Evangelical/Ecumenical stream. A significant proportion of ministers however did adhere to a theological position which they sought to describe as 'Catholic' or 'Ritualist' or 'Sacramentalist'. The inclusion of this tradition within its Methodism indicates an ability to incorporate a wide diversity of theological ideas as well as a core tradition (this enables us to test with some conviction the proposition that differences within denominations are more important than those between them). Whatever the variations, however, another central preoccupation within Methodism is its concern for social responsibility, its sharing in the responsibility of mission to the community as a whole, and thus its religious egalitarianism, its willingness to regard itself no more than one denomination among others.

Whereas the Anglican clergy present one overall conception of ministry, ministers in the Methodist Church suggest an alternative spectrum of responsibilities. Like the clergy, ministers' ultimate priority is to their diffuse pastoral responsibility; but the role of celebration of the sacraments is considerably downgraded within ministers' doctrinal lexicon because of the general distrust of visual symbolism and ritualism within Methodism. Preaching, counselling and leadership, however, are accorded much greater status and become central features of the Methodist ministry: preaching has traditionally been the pivotal Methodist vehicle for transmitting the biblical message, the truth of the Word, which might permit another personal conversion, another wedge in the process of social regeneration; counselling has been adopted by an increasing number of ordained functionaries, particularly ministers, as a means for 'putting God over', in order that spirituality may be discovered within individuals rather than revered in external symbols; leadership is interpreted as being a necessary adjunct to the concern for a 'social' as well as a religious mission. Finally, the burdens of administration are given more weight by ministers than either priests or clergy, reflecting perhaps the greater preoccupation within that denomination with rules and standardisation.

Ministers have the most professional attitudes, especially with regard to feelings of autonomy, professional reference and colleague control. The stress, then, is more on the group and authority aspects of professionalism, something which is likely to arise from the circuit base of their ministry. Interaction with colleagues is a necessity for the minister.

Methodist ministers are the most ecumenically-minded functionaries in our survey. If there are reservations they exist in the attitudes of ministers towards the organic union of Churches—reflecting ultimately the evolutionary perspective of all the denominations. As with clergy, ministers show that they are more willing to accept unity with those Churches whose traditions are familiar in kind (the Church of England) or whose structures and traditions are similar (the Baptist or the United Reformed Churches). The Roman Catholic and Orthodox Churches appear too alien in religious culture for most ministers to consider thoroughgoing union a practicable proposition. These reservations are important in that they reveal an unwillingness to pursue ecumenicity to its logical conclusion. Ministers, however, do display their ecumenical zeal in their attitudes towards co-operative ventures and particularly well in their active ecumenical participation with functionaries of other denominations. They seem equally eager to tolerate those co-operative activities which seek to clear the ground by way of preparatory meetings and discussions, and also the more radical ventures. Where clergy approach the far-reaching ideas with mistrust and caution, ministers confront them with energy and confidence—thus the responses to the joining of publications, theological colleges and ministries, the sharing of churches and so on, all measures which strike at the core of traditional doctrinal conceptions and assail ecumenical reserve. This much greater willingness to compromise and redefine central articles of faith is reflected in the extent of their ecumenical activities; that is, not only have ministers initiated or been involved in more preaching and joint co-operative events with Churches of other denominations than priests or clergy, they have also initiated more services of inter-communion. This more vigorous putting of ecumenical precept into practice is also revealed in the greater propensity to belong to an ecumenical society of one kind or another.

The Methodist Church, like the Church of England, has been preoccupied with proposals which might facilitate the effective renewal of the Church's organisation and make it more appropriate to its symbolic message. The 'Report on the Restructuring of the Church in the Districts, the Circuits and the Societies' considered that, at a local level, committees should be pruned and restructured to permit greater participation by members, and that in an era of considerable social mobility much could be done to include non-Methodists in the life of the Church, even to the extent of making them eligible for appointment as committee members. The report considered the circuit to be the least effective unit within the Church but one which was nevertheless vital for the work of fostering co-operation between societies: its efficiency could be improved by the introduction of a six-monthly meeting. The report felt that much better use could be made of the district organisation to reinvigorate the necessary process of internal communication. Ministers, like clergy, generally advocated the necessity of at least some 'reform' but, also like their Anglican counterparts, received the detailed proposals of reform rather ambivalently: ministers were unanimous in their approval of those proposals which supported the reduction in number and streamlining of the structure and function of committees at all levels of the Church. Similarly, ministers recommended the notion of extending the executive authority of District Synods and of using the district organisation to facilitate communication. Yet they were not particularly amenable to either the idea of the six-monthly circuit meeting or that of admitting non-Methodists. Among more general matters, the role of the laity was considered to be of considerable importance, and the stationing and travelling of ministers to be a matter of concern.

Ministers, lastly, have a complex attitude towards the nature of their Church as a bureaucracy, its system of rules and its structure of authority. Methodists with their Free Church traditions place considerable emphasis upon the local congregation and the necessity of an educated and theologically informed laity. This makes for a degree of decentralisation which is also a natural consequence of the Methodist idea of a functional ministry: all Christians are seen to be 'ministers' and great stress is laid upon the theological, and thus organisational, equality between 'superiors' and subordinates. This inclination to decentralise in Methodism is, however, counter-balanced by another tendency to lay emphasis upon the uniform pattern of its religious belief. Thus the importance of the national organisation in achieving a well defined system of rules to ensure standardisation. Our survey illuminates the way in which most Methodist ministers have a stronger perception of their Church as more centralised and bureaucratic or routinised than is the case with Anglican clergy. But they do not regard their own Church as being as bureaucratic as do Catholic priests with respect to their Church. This confirms the focal position of the annual conference and the central organisation of the Methodist Church in decision-making and in establishing a clearly defined framework of rules and procedures to regulate local practice.

The Roman Catholic Church

Our survey of Roman Catholic priests contained more functionaries in positions of subordination (assistant priests) than our survey of clergy or ministers. Over a quarter of our priests were assistants to parish priests. Parish priests comprised less than half of the respondents who also incorporated chaplains, deans and bishops. Priests tended to be rather older than clergy or ministers, which is significant when we reflect upon the proportion of 'junior' priests: an indication perhaps that priests can expect to spend longer in positions of 'apprenticeship' than functionaries in either the Anglican or the Methodist Churches. This supposition is confirmed when we look at the experience of priests: most have been ordained for a considerable period, can expect to spend more time in each position than ministers or clergy and much of their career in one diocese.

The parenthood of priests presents a much more heterogeneous picture of social class than is the case in the other denominations: as well as drawing from the professional and employing classes and the middle ranges of the socio-economic order, priests are the only group with a substantial element from manual backgrounds. Most priests were educated at grammar school, although a considerable number were educated at private Roman Catholic schools. Like ministers, few priests proceeded to university, though those that did typically read humanities or theology. Yet probably a greater proportion of priests have studied their subject to a higher level than either clergy or ministers: the theologically gifted are financially supported at home and continental universities or seminaries. At home there is generally a tradition of priests 'belonging' to the local seminary to permit the uniform socialisation.

Priests present no clear and distinct categories of doctrinal belief, no differentiated theological cosmologies. The Roman Catholic Church has tended to adhere to a very distinctive branch of Christianity with its ontological conception of the priesthood—the bestowing of sacred gifts upon ordination—and its ontological conception of the Church, so that those located at pinnacle points in the religious hierarchy are necessarily, intrinsically, more divine in authority. This hierarchical perspective articulates itself through beliefs in the sacraments, creeds and ministry, and presents itself as in some way essential to the persistence of Christianity. The stress upon the divine mystery, ritualism and visual symbolism all fit harmoniously into this highly supernatural scheme. As Fogarty suggested, although the Roman Catholic Church has become rather more flexible, this central and distinctive theology remains entrenched and authority increasingly feels the need to 'confirm, establish and guard the principles emerging from the Church's experience and tradition'. The proposition of a fairly singular uniform and cohesive 'Catholic' theological position, from which the priest is unlikely to stray far, is reinforced by the data we have collated: whereas, for example, ministers tend to perceive their Church as one denomination among others, priests unequivocally tend to attribute theological veracity, authenticity and authority to their particular interpretation of Christianity—'the only authentic Church which continues the work of Christ'; 'the only true Apostolic and Catholic Church' and so on. The persistence of a cohesive, traditional faith is also reflected in the continuing willingness of priests to maintain the privileged organisational position of Rome, granting it the right to define theological policy and, frequently, the minutiae of the priest's working life. This is not to say that priests present a completely uniform face, merely to point out that the radical groups are a very small minority and marginal to the Church as a whole.

The uniformity of belief is illustrated especially in the priest's typical conception of ministry. In contrast to the perspectives within the Methodist and Anglican traditions, the priest's conception of ministry is distinctly and singularly Catholic in form. The pre-eminent responsibility is perceived to be that of celebrant. Whereas clergy and ministers ascribe foremost priority to a generalist conception of ministry, that is of pastor, this role is eclipsed in the Roman Catholic Church by an overarching preference for the particular responsibility of the sacramental ritual. Thus the theological preoccupation with the supernatural is seen here to be reflected in the practical side of the priest's vocation. Thereafter the priest's order of priority for ministerial tasks is exactly the same as those functionaries in the other episcopal Church—the clergy. That is, moderate preferences are accorded to preaching, counselling and leadership, while administration and officialdom are similarly regarded with familiar disdain. Yet, although the ordered positions within an hierarchy of roles is the same, priests do nevertheless grant a rather higher value to the responsibilities of preaching and leadership, indicating perhaps the greater total involvement of the parish priest with his local congregation and his concern to communicate the faith to direct his local Roman Catholic community.

Priests closely follow ministers in terms of professionalism. In particular they emphasise the service orientation and vocation aspects of their occupational role, something which derives from the strong position of the parish priest *vis-à-vis* his congregation. There is also an emphasis on the other aspects of professionalism.

Priests in general treat the ecumenical movement with much more detached circumspection than the functionaries in either of the other two denominations. As with ministers and clergy, priests are willing to accept organic union with those other denominations whose structures and traditions are familiar such as the Church of England and the Orthodox Churches. Paradoxically, priests were much more prepared to countenance union with 'all Christian bodies' than either clergy or ministers. This is accountable, however, when we consider the number of priests who gave their definition of Christian a highly Catholic denotation. The more typical reaction of priests to the ecumenical movement is displayed in their responses to the prospect of co-operative ventures with other denominations. Priests, like clergy, are more eager to participate in the provisional discussions and meetings; but the significant difference is the reluctance even to engage in inter-denominational preaching, and particularly salient is the suspicion of those forms of co-operation which may be seen to strike at the liturgical or doctrinal basis of Catholicism; thus the marked distrust of joint publishing or joint educative activities. Priests, therefore, appear less willing to bend or compromise the central canons of their theological faith. This profound doubt is equally manifested in the practical ecumenicity of priests: they have preached less in inter-faith services and are unanimously against participating in services which celebrate the sacraments (this may well be an edict of the Church, rather than an individual decision, as we discovered in one large metropolitan diocese).

Priests approach the recent attempts of the Roman Catholic Church to search for structural and spiritual renewal with a mixture of enthusiasm and caution: they express enthusiastic response to the idea of certain reforms, yet treat the abstract notion of 'reform' with more suspicion than do clergy and ministers and, more significantly, tend to reject the central themes of the recent reform movement. Vatican II had attempted to inaugurate a new theological epoch for the Roman Catholic Church, to institute a spirit of sympathetic dialogue within the Church and with the modern world outside. We focused upon the report of the Provisional Laity Commission which envisaged itself as implementing the teaching of the Second Vatican Council: to concern itself with priest–laity relationships, lay formation, and the development of structures to facilitate communication. Priests felt able to support a good many of the recommendations of the Laity Commission, particularly those which sought to improve the extent of communication and co-ordination between the various levels in the Church; priests also endorsed those proposals which sought to make the existing structures more open and representative. But notably, they were reluctant to acquiesce in one of the central principles of the Laity Commission's recommendations, that is the need to erode the traditional hierarchical conception of authority—the idea that the supernatural and divine presence is more immanent as the organisational hierarchy is ascended. The admission of the laity to the councils of the Church would have made symbolic inroads into this ontological conception of authority: the time was ripe for the open representation of priests as such, but the wisdom of granting access and influence to the laity was doubted. Among more general items, priests were seen to have a vociferous demand for extra training in order that they might be better equipped to face the realities of a modern society.

Priests perceive themselves as operating in the most bureaucratic of the three denominations. Theirs is an ontological priesthood, in that authority and divinity are bestowed hierarchically, an organisational feature which lends itself naturally to centralisation. The Roman Catholic Church also places great emphasis upon its global responsibilities and the concomitant stress upon the papacy and the 'bishops in concert' inevitably leads to some form of central direction about the standardising of rules and procedures. This relatively bureaucratic structure is reflected in the attitudes of priests. That is to say, they believe there is a clear hierarchy of authority and that power and influence are centralised; they perceive that there is an elaborate division of labour within which tasks are substantially codified by procedures so as to limit the degree of personal autonomy. It must be remembered, however, that although the Roman Catholic Church is perceived to be the most bureaucratic of our three denominations, when compared to other kinds of organisations it is relatively non-bureaucratic.

II Analysis

In this chapter, as in the previous ones, we have been attempting to demonstrate the differences between and within the Churches. We have described the demographic, social, denominational and theological characteristics of ministers, priests and clergy, as well as their beliefs about the problem issues presented—ministry, ecumenism, reform and so on. Yet our aim throughout the book has been much more an explanatory one, of accounting for differences, explaining *why* there should be systematic variations between or within the denominations. We have been looking for factors which will enable us to say why it is that our religious functionaries should differ in their attitudes and conduct towards such controversial issues as Church unity and reform.

The main focus of our explanatory accounts so far has been upon exploring *direct* relationships between factors, for example, the extent to which the age or social class of our religious functionaries can help us to account for the variations in their beliefs and practices. The task now is essentially a theoretical one, of categorising the disparate explanatory factors and elucidating the relative importance of each. Explaining, therefore, why clergy, priests and ministers conceive their ministry in the way that they do becomes a process of unravelling precisely the relative extent to which the theoretical categories dovetail together or operate in a distinct and independent fashion. In chapter 1 we elaborated the three theoretical categories we felt to be crucial:

(1) *Denominational* socialisation; that is, the variations may reflect being a member of a distinctive denomination and commitment to its perspective; explanation is a function of being a Methodist as against a Roman Catholic. The greater experience of membership the greater the commitment. This is because all organisations seek to prescribe the activities of their members: conferring a role upon a person within a hierarchical structure of positions usually succeeds in shaping the outward form of conduct; yet it is left to the lengthy process of socialisation to ensure that the approved values, beliefs and sentiments, which truly weld him to his occupation, are satisfactorily instilled. This might lead us to expect that those clergy, priests and ministers who have been ordained for some considerable period of time and exposed to the familiar rituals of their denomination to have more completely internalised its beliefs and sentiments.

(2) *Beliefs*; theological and professional; although one might expect the theological beliefs held by a religious functionary to be consistent with the denomination to which he belongs, there is an important theoretical distinction to be made between the theological cosmology of functionaries and the denominational cosmology as such. The theological beliefs may be such that their natural allegiances do not lie within the orthodox denominational cosmology; in this situation the Church of England Evangelical may find that he has more in common with an Evangelical in the Methodist Church. Thus for explanatory purposes it may be more important to know whether a religious functionary is a 'Radical', or an 'Evangelical' or a 'Conservative' than knowing whether he is a Roman Catholic, Anglican or Methodist. We are also interested in the extent to which their occupational identity afford beliefs which make the religious functionaries relatively independent of the process of denominational socialisation, the extent to which, for

example, a functionary may adhere to the ideal of functional autonomy when the denomination enjoins collective involvement.

(3) *Extra-denominational*; the explanation of variations in attitude and approach towards the chosen problem issues may, however, lie in the fact that clergy, priests and ministers grew up in a particular social class or were educated in a particular kind of institution. The very age of the religious functionary might dispose him towards more or less conservative or radical beliefs and practices.

The theoretical task, therefore, is one of disentangling the relative degree to which denominational, belief and extra-denominational factors are crucial for explanatory purposes. We began the book by arguing that the Methodist, Roman Catholic and Anglican denominations had widely diverse traditions, beliefs and ritual procedures, and it was because of this that we preferred to use the more specific terms 'minister', 'priest' and 'clergy' to denote semantically the different realms of meaning and relationship, rather than use the generic term 'clergy' to refer to functionaries from all denominations. By taking each denomination in turn we shall be able to test this assumption, that is, to test whether the intra-Church uniformities are more important than the inter-Church similarities.

The Church of England

Accounting for the variations within the Church of England is a relatively complex task. Belief can be seen to exert a relatively stronger overall effect than the variables concerned with denominational socialisation. Those who adopt 'Liberal' or 'Modernist' churchmanship or theological cosmologies lay stress upon the two less orthodox roles of counselling and leadership, relegating the role of celebration of sacraments to a more subordinate position within their ministry. 'Radicals' are also more likely to emphasise the necessity of reforming the structure of the Church, and argue for the exigency of ecumenicalism. Conversely, 'Catholic' and 'Conservative' elements within the Church are traditionalist in ministry and express reluctance about the questions of reform and ecumenism.

The effects of occupational belief and self-image are to distinguish between, on the one hand, the autonomous, service and vocationally orientated clergyman who gives high priority to traditional roles and operating in a non-bureaucratic organisation, on the the other, the occupationally based clergyman who emphasises less traditional roles, wanting union and seeing himself operating in a bureaucracy, no doubt as he feels the pressures of attempting to change it.

The extra-denominational factors contribute in a much more circumscribed way to our understanding of variations in attitude and conduct. Age works predictably—the older and beneficed cling to their traditional rights of security and autonomy, while the young and disadvantaged press for radical changes. Social class works to a different effect: the higher a clergyman's social class origins and the more extended his education the more likely he is to be professionally orientated and occupationally mobile.

By far the most important explanatory variables, however, are the denominational ones. The career patterns, the forms of denominational socialisation, are much more diverse than in the other denominations, reflecting the Anglican Church's greater heterogeneity. The relationship between the various aspects of denominational experience is a complex one. The length of time that one has been ordained has little relationship to other aspects of experience, although it has some link with beliefs. It is experience within the framework of the diocese that is important, as a distinguishing feature. The longer a clergyman has been in the diocese, then the longer he will have been in his present position, that is, relatively immobile. But the longer one has been in one's present position, then the *fewer* positions one will have held; and the *more* positions a clergyman has held, the higher will be his status in the Church. Thus, the clergy at the top of the hierarchy are the 'mobiles' within the organisation. It is the mobility of the career pattern that is fundamental in shaping attitudes towards theological belief and practice. We find that those who have moved around (in terms of job mobility) are ecumenically orientated, operating in a context of organisational participation and autonomy. These are probably the 'organisational men' of the Church, at the top, reflecting and representing its official position on ecumenism, and in an organisational position allowing freedom of expression.

In conclusion we are able to discern three fundamental career paths, three forms of denominational socialisation, which discriminate different groups within the Anglican Church. These are the 'traditionalists', the 'hierarchs' and 'youth'. The traditionalists tend to be older clergy who have not been particularly mobile geographically or socially. They were recruited from higher social classes, but are not necessarily the most highly educated clergy. They espouse a conservative churchmanship and in occupational terms emphasise an ethic of service and feelings of vocation. They will espouse well-established roles, such as pastor, preacher and celebrant, be unmoved by ecumenism, perceive less need for reform and, emphasising their pastoral autonomy, feel that they are involved in a non-bureaucratic organisation.

The hierarchs are also a group of older clergy, but they have trodden a different path. They will have been more highly educated and have occupied a number of positions both within and outside their current diocese. Thus, they are a mobile group and they espouse an occupational identity which is more likely to emphasise colleague groups than clients. As a result they see roles such as administrator and leader as important, they favour a high degree of ecumenical activity and perceive themselves as working in a bureaucratic environment, but with a high level of participation. One might hypothesise that, given the traditions of the Church of England, the initial crucial variable setting them on this organisational path is the receipt of a high level of education. As they proceed through the Church and as they move into administrative hierarchies, so they come to value relationships with colleagues and to represent the 'official' ideologies of the Church. Interestingly, this group does not come out as having a definitive stand on reforming the structure of the Church; after all, they are likely to be its operators.

Finally we have the youth. As one would hypothesise, they have similar views to the hierarchs on role perceptions and ecumenism. They also feel the need for reforms in the operation of the Church. However, the causal path is different. The effect is not arrived at through professionalism (younger clergy will be low on professional attitudes of any kind) or organisational experiences, except that they will have little such experience. The main causal link is through their theological belief-system. They are likely to have a radical theology and to have attended a theological college which backs this up. This modernist, liberal or new theology leads to a definition of a different kind of Church which is reformed and ecumenical.

The Methodist Church

The relative weight of the explanatory categories in the Methodist Church is much the same as in the Church of England; that is, the form of the explanation as against the content of the account shows much similarity. The various categories of belief, theological and professional, reveal *some* independent effect upon the variables we wish to explain: a significant proportion do adhere to a theological position which they sought to describe as 'Catholic' or 'Ritualist' or 'Sacramentalist'. This inclusion of the Roman Catholic tradition within Methodism indicates its ability to incorporate a wide diversity of theological ideas; but it must be said that generally, when ministers described themselves as 'liberal', 'radical' or 'conservative' it was more as an adjectival qualification of the central Evangelical/ Ecumenical tradition.

The occupational beliefs of ministers work to much the same effect as those of Anglican clergy; but, as with the clergy, we find that the two aspects of occupational belief, namely service orientation and colleague control, are important. Colleague control has the same general effects as for clergy: ministers who stress the importance of colleagues being the basic reference group will desire ecumenical emphasis, wish for general reform, espouse roles such as administrator and leader. Those who are service orientated, thus emphasising the roles of clients rather than colleagues, will have opposite attitudes. Thus, those emphasising a long-standing religious orientation are more likely to see the current activities of the Church in a favourable light, suggesting that its activities and organisation are more orientated towards them.

The process of ageing also works to some independent explanatory effect. Age is and can operate in an ambivalent way, either to reinforce the accumulating denominational experience and socialisation or to operate independently through the incipient conservatism of the ageing process. It is the latter conceptual dimension which is particularly important in facilitating an explanation of the reform issue: the older the minister the less likely he will be to countenance reforms of the liturgy or the structure of the organisation, or the welcoming of non-members on the community roll. Conversely, the younger the minister the more increasingly radical the proposals for reform. Generally, however, the advance of age works to sustain and reinforce the experience accumulated, the ingrained beliefs and practices; the older the minister and the longer he has been ordained the more likely he is to espouse traditional role definitions.

The clearly discernible pattern within the Methodist Church, however, is one of the homogeneity of experience and belief, a pattern which illustrates the dominating influence of denominational socialisation. The effects of belief or age or social class are all relatively subordinate in their explanatory power to the overarching influence of denominational belief and practice. There are not the equivalents of the two groups of 'traditionalists' and 'hierarchs', as well as the 'youth'. This is because the Methodist Church sets out to equalise the experience of its ministers and to have only one route to the top of the organisation. The system of stationing and travelling, with the rules for years of service before 'promotion', ensure unity of experience. We find a general set of relationships between the age of a minister, the number of years he has been ordained, the number of positions he has held and the status he occupies. The theological beliefs and sentiments that are gradually internalised are those of Ecumenicalism and Evangelicalism, and a conception of ministry which exhorts the preaching of the message and the pastoral care of a distinct social and religious community. The occupational and

162

professional beliefs of ministers reflect this interrelated pattern; the stress upon serving the community and the feeling of solidarity, cohesion with and commitment to one's colleagues.

There is just one small exception to this picture: the minister who has spent a lot of time in his present district. We have seen that he will be more 'radical'. He is not necessarily older, or younger, nor does he have different beliefs. But what he has done is slip out of the regular Methodist system. He has cut down on his 'travelling'. In this sense he may be more secure, able to flout the system, and not so dependent on finding a congregation that will accept him as their minister.

The Roman Catholic Church

Whereas in the other two denominations beliefs, theological and occupational, contributed some independent influence to the explanation, in the Roman Catholic Church the independent effect of beliefs is negligible. The few who espouse more radical theological beliefs, wishing, for example, more denominational autonomy from the dictates of Rome, are more likely to be favourable to the ecumenical movement and to argue the case for reforming the organisation of the Church. In general, however, there are not the distinct theological cosmologies which potentially tie the priests to similar adherents in other denominations: the uniform pattern is one of believing in a distinctive ontological conception of the priesthood, which holds firmly to the authority and authenticity of the Roman Catholic tradition. We have argued that in the Church of England and among Methodist ministers a professional self-definition has long been part of the overall belief system. In the Roman Catholic Church, with its stronger authority and organisational system, this has not been the case. In that Church the existence of a professional orientation is a relatively new phenomenon and, as Struzzo (1970) and Goldner *et al.* (1972) have pointed out, likely to be associated with a more radical view: those priests who adhere to the notion of professional autonomy being more likely to press the claims of ecumenicalism and reform and espouse less traditional aspects of ministry.

More important than belief as an independent explanatory factor is the influence of age upon the beliefs, sentiments and conduct of priests. Those priests who are young, will be more highly educated, will have been ordained into the Church only for a limited time and will favour ecumenism and reform and stress non-traditional roles. Such priests will have a professional orientation which, in the case of the Roman Catholic Church, generally reinforces ecumenism and reform. This marks the different position of professionalism in this

Church. As in the other two denominations, social class has almost no independent explanatory influence.

The shaping of the theological lives of priests follows much the same mechanisms as in the Church of England and in the Methodist Church: the socialisation of priests into the prescribed and traditional practices of their denomination. The theological cosmologies and professional beliefs of priests conform to the central pattern of the Roman Catholic Church—the stress upon visual symbolism, the ritual of the sacraments and the divinity of the religious hierarchy. The ageing process works more to reinforce and sustain denominational beliefs and sentiments rather than condition any substantial autonomous effect. The priest is generally rooted in a diocese, placing high values upon the roles of celebration, pastoral care, administration and preaching. They will not see any need for internal reform; and they perceive themselves as working in a hierarchical, rule-bound, non-participative organisation. This reflects the overall position and role that such a priest will be in, a long-serving 'officer' of the Church, preaching to his flock, administering Church procedures, building halls, helping to operate schools, embedded in the machinery of the organisation but subject to superior clergy for decisions on many of these matters.

There is thus much less mobility in the Roman Catholic Church than in the other two denominations. It is this organisational position of many years in the same position as a parish priest that gives them their particular outlook. They are men of the Church, administering within a hierarchical rule-bound situation, which they expect and accept, bolstered in that situation by an ethic of service and feelings of vocation.

Those in the Church who have attained positions of some status stress rather different dimensions, but still within the same denominational pattern. The more traditional roles of celebrant and pastor will be emphasised along with the notion of being a leader and representative of the Church. Ecumenicalism will be perceived as sacrificing uniqueness, and reform as unnecessary. While he sees himself acting under prescribed routines, there will be considerable autonomy, little feeling of hierarchy and a high level of participation in decision-making.

III The Model

We began this book by formulating a number of hypotheses and a model of religious orientations, the way, that is to say, the beliefs and attitudes of clergy, priests and ministers towards crucial contemporary issues are typically shaped and conditioned. We began with the possibility that the variations within each denomination were as important as the variations between denominations; Krause (1971) had asserted much more strongly that:

> in all organised religions at present there is a split between the activist clergy and the traditionalists. Both groups but especially the activists, find allies across denominations and are disagreeing radically about the function of the clergyman in a changing scene. At present knowing whether a clergyman is an activist or a conservative is sociologically more important than knowing whether he is a Minister, Rabbi or Priest.

Krause was arguing therefore that the overarching domination of a denominational faith and ritual practice was now moribund and that important theological cosmologies were emerging which cut through the traditional religious divides.

The overwhelming evidence of this research is that this incipient trend does not obtain for the Roman Catholic, Methodist and Anglican Churches: the crucial explanatory factors are overwhelmingly denominational in kind. What has accounted most for the variations in the responses of our religious functionaries has been the way their occupational lives have been moulded by their denominational experience.

There is no doubt that an understanding of the priests', ministers', and clergy's churchmanship and theological cosmologies is central to any explanation of their religious orientation: their faith gives meaning to their idea of ministry and the response that they feel is expected of them in the face of the movements for reform and ecumenicalism. But the theological belief systems which lend meaning to the lives of our religious functionaries are largely denominational in fashion. This does not mean to say that there are not important intra-Church differences in churchmanship and cosmology, only that these are *less* important for our understanding of the general pattern of belief and practice. Theological beliefs are rooted in their denominational context rather than independent and free-floating: the Church of England 'radical' has more in common with his 'Central and Broad Churchman' colleague on the matter of ecumenical preferences than with the Methodist 'Catholic' let alone the Methodist 'Radical'.

We had expected age to be an important factor in our explanatory framework. But age, like beliefs, can work in rather an ambivalent way: it can either reinforce the accumulating denominational experience and socialisation or, conversely, operate independently through the incipient conservatism of the ageing process. Our research illustrates that the growing sense of insecurity that frequently accompanies advancing age has been particularly important in explaining the typical reservations towards certain proposals for denominational reform—the clergy's reluctance, for example, to forgo tenure and autonomy. Generally, however, the ageing contributes to sustaining the religious functionary in his accustomed beliefs and denominational way of life.

The major explanation, therefore, of the priests', clergy's and ministers' responses to the contemporary challenge of Church unity, reform and ministry, lies in the way in which their religious experience has been shaped within their denomination. It is part of the institutional practice of the Methodist Church to equalise the experiences of their ministers, which is reflected in a system of travelling and service before promotion; the greater homogeneity of theological belief within the Roman Catholic Church has already been emphasised, while the Church of England permits a rather more diverse patterning of experience, essentially a distinction between the 'traditionalists'—those clergy whose experience is rooted within the diocese—and the 'mobiles'—whose career path permits a more comprehensive denominational experience, geographical, social and theological.

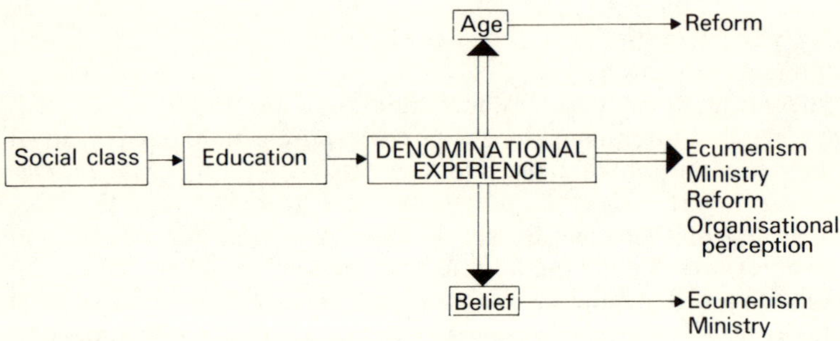

FIGURE 8.1 *A revised model of religious orientations*

The model which we elaborated in chapter 1 thus requires some marginal modification following our empirical odyssey (see Figure 8.1). Our model presupposed both a temporal and an analytical explanation of the dependent variables. The chronological categories of social class origin and educational development shape the choice of denomination and the possible paths of denominational socialisation. The category of denominational socialisation itself is a temporal explanatory variable implying the gradual development of theological belief and practice through time. Age likewise expresses temporal relationships. Yet we were also crucially interested in the analytical properties of the model, its ability to disentangle the relative explanatory weight of three theoretical categories—denomination, cosmology, age. Did they dovetail together in one uniform dependence, or were they analytically independent in their explanatory effect?

166

The model in chapter 1 suggested that the three categories were of equal explanatory importance; our research evidence, however, argues that two of the categories—age and belief—are largely dependent on the third—denomination—for their explanatory influence and are thus theoretically subordinate. The introductory model also suggested that the independent explanatory variables had a uniform effect upon the dependent variables; this too requires modification. The proposition still holds for our dominant explanatory category—denomination—but the other two are rather more specific in their effects: age has more influence upon attitudes towards reform, whereas belief has more effect upon the more theological contentious issues of Church unity and the form ministry should take.

Epilogue

'Today the routines of everyday life challenge religion': thus said
Max Weber, in 1918. Weber's continuing preoccupation had been
with the conditions of this challenge, that is, the progressive rationalisation of life: 'the fate of our times is characterised by rationalisation
and intellectualisation and, above all, by the "disenchantment of
the world".' He depicted societies of the West being transformed
by the ineluctable march of industrial capitalism, science, bureaucracy and political centralisation, each of which was governed by the
pervasive spirit of technical rationality. Whereas in the past conventional routines were set by tradition, revelation or the sentiments,
they were now governed by the dictates of rational calculation and
measurement; personal rules of thumb were replaced by abstract,
systematic and impersonal rules and procedures. 'Hence it means
that principally there are no mysterious, incalculable forces that
come into play, but rather that one can in principle, master all things
by calculation.' Rationalisation instrumentalises everything, drains
the world of its mystery and strips it of charm. Weber had no
illusions about this irresistible 'progress' for, by making the principal
focus the materially calculable, rationalisation necessarily made
central values uncertain, precarious and relative; it gave sway to the
sceptic and created a life which was monochrome and utilitarian.

The conditions which Weber analysed have not receded since his
day. Within such a world the contemporary Church and its functionaries are caught in an ambivalent and vulnerable position in
that they are both in the world but do not really square with it.
In such a situation they are necessarily under challenge: they can
either commit themselves to siege, denying the pervasive sweep of
rationalisation, or undergo a reluctant metamorphosis and attempt
to accommodate themselves to the modern, rational form of things.
Either way, the inevitable consequence is a crisis of identity, a

sense of bewilderment and disorientation and an ensuing struggle to restore some kind of meaning and order. Within each of the major denominations in our survey there has been consideration of the problem of making themselves in some way more symbolically appropriate to the age and, therefore, the possible need to introduce structural reforms, amalgamations and so on: the Roman Catholics have considered the possibility of opening the councils of their Church to more lay participation; the Methodist Church has considered restructuring the districts while the Church of England has contemplated redeploying the clergy. Thus the traditional institutional position and support of the contemporary religious functionary is seen to waver and become less clear.

So the ordained ministry is decidedly an occupation in flux. The parish priest, or incumbent, or circuit minister, occupies a front-line position in an organisation whose secular relevance is questioned from without and whose traditions are threatened from within. This prominence at the same time makes him particularly vulnerable, for he is the person who must acutely experience the frustrations of the Churches' questionable relevance in the modern world.

In response to these disenchanting experiences, he can chose *inter alia* to redefine the nature of his ministry. He can seek to make it 'relevant', either by leaving the ministry and moving into one of the 'helping and caring' professions, or by redefining the nature of his ministry *qua* clergyman or whatever. The first response was found to be evident among American ex-pastors in the United Church of Christ, many of whom had moved into occupations like social work and teaching in response to what they felt to be the irrelevance of the Church in the modern world. The second response is characteristic of those religious functionaries who press for ecumenicalism or denominational reform, or who take up pastoral counselling and similar disciplines. These functionaries, who for example make counselling central to their ministry, want to retain their identities as ordained ministers and yet simultaneously 'tune in' (as Diana Leat has put it) to a 'practical' subject which can be related to theology and which can be validated by a scientific subject such as psychiatry. Such developments are manifestations of what Towler has referred to as 'role-uncertainty'. As the Bishop of Exeter, Dr Mortimer, was reported in the *Church Times* (27 July 1973, p. 2) as saying at his farewell presentation ceremony, he 'detected a certain disillusionment with the parochial ministry, a bewilderment and confusion as to what exactly they were supposed to be doing'. Moreover, what the functionary does do must be carried out in the face of an increasingly sceptical world.

It has been one of the principal purposes of this book to look at some of the ways in which functionaries of three denominations—

Anglican, Roman Catholic and Methodist—have been responding and facing up to this crucial challenge from a 'rational', secular and utilitarian environment, the manner in which they are attempting to cope with the ensuing confusion, the need, that is, to reflect upon the problems of ministry, ecumenicalism, reform and so on. Our study has to a certain extent revealed a reluctance on the part of the clergy, priests and ministers to meet the contemporary challenge. Clearly there has been considerable resistance to the general advocacy of denominational reform: clergy cling to their freehold, ministers challenge the eligibility of non-Methodists for committee membership, and priests resist the advancing claims of the laity. Equally clearly the ecumenical movement has been supported with less than uniform enthusiasm; our emphasis upon the importance of denominational socialisation illustrates the enormous cultural and organisational barriers which work against the movement achieving any significant success. Yet the study has shown the willingness of the younger functionaries, unshackled as yet by the established order, to reform their Church in a manner that is symbolically appropriate to the needs of the day; and it has shown the willingness of 'radicals' across the three denominations to mediate between the Churches in order to achieve a common faith and structure.

Appendix 1
Sample and methods

This study was carried out as part of a research project on the organisational structure of Churches. The clergy, ministers and priests in our sample are from the units that we chose for the purposes of that study.

First of all, nine Church units were chosen. These were three Church of England and three Roman Catholic dioceses, and three districts in the Methodist Church. For each Church, units were chosen which ensured a coverage of important organisational features. Dioceses and districts were chosen as the unit of analysis because they are the major operating level, the overall grouping which is responsible for planning, allocations, etc. The units chosen included large and small, rural and urban. On this basis it can be argued that the units eventually chosen give a good coverage of the various problems which face Churches today.

The initial selection factor was size. For each Church one of the smallest and largest units was chosen, with one in between. This was in order to test one of the main findings of previous organisational research, the relationships between size and bureaucratisation. Size was dealt with on a Church by Church basis, i.e. large size for the Methodists was small for either Anglican or Roman Catholic. Also we ascertained that the particular measure of size used did not matter; a factor analysis of measures such as employees, members, population served, buildings, etc., produced one factor (see Hinings and Bryman, 1974). Within a given size range (in terms of employees) a balance was then looked for in terms of area served. For the Church of England this was relatively straightforward as they have purely urban dioceses, essentially rural ones, and in-between ones. Thus we chose a large, rural diocese, a medium-sized urban one, and a small one covering both a highly urban area and a very rural area. The Methodist Church has no completely urban districts, nor does the Roman Catholic Church have such dioceses. For the Methodists we had a large rural/urban district; a medium-sized rural/urban district, and a small rural one. For the Roman Catholic Church there was a large, mainly urban diocese, a medium-sized mainly urban but with substantial rural, and a small rural/urban diocese.

Having chosen the nine units, the next stage was to draw up a sample from each one. In fact, for the three Methodist districts and the small and medium-sized Anglican and Roman Catholic dioceses a sample was not used but the whole population of full-time working priests, ministers and clergy. The aim was to include all those working in the parishes and societies or in staff positions. This meant that members of religious orders not in full-time parish work were not included in the Roman Catholic numbers. For the two large Anglican and Roman Catholic dioceses all the members of the hierarchy were included, from rural deans up, but a 50 per cent sample of non-incumbents/parish priests and incumbents was taken. Table A1.1

TABLE A1.1   *Numbers and usable responses of questionnaire*

	Sample size	Usable response	% response
Church of England	721	564	78.2
Methodist	275	251	92.6
Roman Catholics	876	412	47.0

gives details of the numbers and usable responses. Information used in this analysis was collected by means of a mailed questionnaire.

The questionnaire used was developed in the usual way. Some of the areas covered (e.g. organisational perception, control structures) were taken from established instruments (Appendix 2 shows the questionnaire used, together with annotations as to the sources of the various questions); others were from once-used questionnaires, e.g. for the Anglicans on role perception (adapted from Leslie Paul); but a considerable number of questions were new ones. As a pre-pilot exercise the first draft of each questionnaire was circulated to clergy of each denomination for them to comment on the extent to which the questions could be understood and also seen to be relevant. This, of course, produced a number of changes. The next stage was a pilot study in each denomination to test the method of distribution, the possible response rates, the extent to which the questions were discriminating in the expected way and the extent to which the questionnaire had face validity. Once this stage was completed the main surveys were undertaken.

A further part of the methodology adopted in the research was, where possible, to construct composite indices. Particularly when dealing with values and attitudes, the sociologist has to be very careful about relying on individual questions or items as indicators. The likely error involved in this is high. To use a pool of items which show strong internal consistency is not only likely to cut down measurement error, it also has the considerable advantages of allowing greater discrimination between individual respondents and the use of a different range of statistics. To examine sets of items for scalability two statistical techniques were used, factor analysis and co-efficient alpha (see McKennell (1970) for an interesting article on their joint use).

There were five particular areas where these two techniques were used, namely:

(1) Professional beliefs
(2) Reform attitudes
(3) Ecumenical perception and operation
(4) Participation in decision-making
(5) Organisational perception

For reform, and ecumenism, the aim was to examine the items in the questionnaire for any structure. In both these cases the items had been chosen on the basis of various sub-conceptual areas as has been outlined in the chapters of the book concerned with them. The *a priori* scales were tested for internal reliability by means of coefficient alpha; a factor analysis was also carried out of all the items, but in the case of both reform and ecumenism no coherent pattern could be discerned by means of the latter technique. Table A1.II gives details of the alpha value for the various scales.

With regard to professionalism, participation, routinisation and organisational perception we were working with items used previously by other researchers who had outlined particular sub-scale structures. Thus an initial aim was to see how far it was possible to replicate those scales. In fact it was only possible to replicate any previous work in the case of the scale of participation in decision-making taken from the work of Hage and Aiken. In the case of all the other areas we were unable to replicate and so turned to factor analysis, using a varimax rotation, to examine the items for scale structures.

TABLE A1.II   *Alpha coefficients for scales*

Professional Beliefs	
Professional reference	0.5162
Service orientation	0.7207
Colleague control	0.5721
Vocation	0.6728
Autonomy	0.6594
Reform Attitudes	
General reform	0.8669
Specific reform	0.9201
Ecumenism	
Organic ecumenism	0.9605
Ecumenical co-operation	0.9064
Ritual co-operation	0.7789
Group membership	0.9073
Organisational Perception	
Routine	0.7572
Job autonomy	0.6938
Rules	0.6904
Hierarchy	0.8172
Participation	0.8384

Appendix 2
The priest and the church

This is the questionnaire distributed to Roman Catholic priests. The structure of the questionnaire for Anglicans and Methodists is the same but questions 1, 2, 35, 61, 63–77, 90–2 are worded appropriately for the Church of England and the Methodist Church.

This questionnaire is organised in sections, each of which is concerned with some aspect of your work, your views of the church, and so on. Most of the questions can be answered by making a simple tick mark in the space provided next to the answer you choose. We should, however, like you to be able to express your true feelings as closely as possible as you answer the questionnaire. If, therefore, you feel that a question is unclear, or does not allow you to say exactly how you personally feel, please say so, and feel free to write your comments in the margins to the left of the questions. We have also left some space at the end of the questionnaire for any further comments you may wish to make. Please ignore the figures in the right-hand column of the page. They are there only to facilitate the processing of the questionnaire and do not represent scores.

	Code	Col.
		LRC2911
I		1,2,3,4,5,6,7

First, we would like to ask you about the nature of your work.

1. Are you a parish priest?

		Code	Col.
Yes		2	8
No		1	

(Please tick only one of the following categories)

2. Are you a

	Code	Col.
Curate or Assistant Priest	1	9
part-time Chaplain (e.g. to students, convent, etc.)	2	
full-time special Chaplain (e.g. to students, convent etc.)	3	
Dean	4	
Curial Official	5	
Auxiliary Bishop/Coadjutor	6	
Bishop	7	
Other (please write in)		
	8	

3. In what kind of ministry do you work? (Please tick only one of the following categories)

	Code	Col.
		10
I am a member of a team ministry	5	
I am in a group ministry	4	
I am assisted by another priest/other priests	3	
I assist another priest/other priests	2	
I work completely on my own	1	
Other (Please write in details if the above categories are inappropriate)		
	6	

4. Would you describe your job as being highly routine, somewhat routine, somewhat non-routine, or highly non-routine? (Please tick only one of the following categories)

	Code	Col.
		11
highly routine	4	
somewhat routine	3	

	Code	Col.

somewhat non-routine 2

highly non-routine 1

5. During the course of your work, how
often do you come across *specific but
important problems* that you don't know
how to solve, and you have to think
them through by yourself or with others
before you can take any action?
(Please tick only one of the following
categories)   12

     daily 5

     2–3 times a week 4

     once a week 3

     2–3 times a month 2

     once a month or less often 1

6. In some jobs things are fairly predictable—
if you do this, that will happen. In others,
you often are not sure whether something
will work or not. What percentage of time
would you say that you are *not* sure
whether something you do will work or not?
(Please tick the figure which comes
closest)   13

     50% or more 5

     40% 4

     30% 3

     20% 2

     10% or less 1

7. If there is something that you don't know
how to handle in your work, can you go to
someone else in the diocese for an answer,
or is it likely to be something that no one
really knows about?   14
(Please tick only one of the following
categories)

     others will rarely know 1

     others will sometimes know 2

     others will often know 3

     others will know most of the time 4

	Code	Col.

Following are some statements that may or may not be true for your job in the diocese rather than the parish. Please circle the category that best applies to your situation in the diocese. Please answer every statement, circling one category only in each.
DT = definitely true; MT = more true than false; MF = more false than true; DF = definitely false.

		Code	Col.
8.	I feel that I am my own master in most matters DT : MT : MF : DF :	1,2,3,4	15
9.	There is a complete written job description for my job DT : MT : MF : DF :	4,3,2,1	16
10.	People are constantly being checked to see that they follow the rules DT : MT : MF : DF :	4,3,2,1	17
11.	Whatever situation arises, we have procedures to follow in dealing with it DT : MT : MF : DF :	4,3,2,1	18
12.	A person can make his own decisions in this diocese without checking with anyone else DT : MT : MF : DF :	1,2,3,4	19
13.	People here do the same job in the same way every day DT : MT : MF : DF :	4,3,2,1	20
14.	People here feel as though they are constantly being watched to see that they obey all rules DT : MT : MF : DF :	4,3,2,1	21
15.	Going through the proper channels is constantly stressed DT : MT : MF : DF :	4,3,2,1	22
16.	There can be little action taken until a superior approves a decision DT : MT : MF : DF :	4,3,2,1	23

			Code	Col.
17.	Everyone has a specific job to do	DT : MT : MF : DF :	4,3,2,1	24
18.	We are to follow strict procedures at all times	DT : MT : MF : DF :	4,3,2,1	25
19.	How things are done is left pretty much up to the person doing the work	DT : MT : MF : DF :	1,2,3,4	26
20.	One thing people like around here is the variety of work	DT : MT : MF : DF :	1,2,3,4	27
21.	A person who wants to make his own decisions would be quickly discouraged here	DT : MT : MF : DF :	4,3,2,1	28
22.	Whenever we have a problem we are supposed to go to the same person for an answer	DT : MT : MF : DF :	4,3,2,1	29
23.	Even small matters have to be referred to someone higher for a final answer	DT : MT : MF : DF :	4,3,2,1	30
24.	Most jobs have something new happening each day	DT : MT : MF : DF :	1,2,3,4	31
25.	People here are allowed to do almost as they please	DT : MT : MF : DF :	4,3,2,1	32
26.	I have to ask a superior before I do almost anything	DT : MT : MF : DF :	4,3,2,1	33
27.	There is something different to do every day	DT : MT : MF : DF :	4,3,2,1	34
28.	Any decision I make has to have a superior's approval	DT : MT : MF : DF :	4,3,2,1	35

	Code	Col.

29. It is impossible to learn enough about the job to handle all the problems that come up DT : MT : MF : DF : | 1,2,3,4 | 36

30. Most people here make their own rules for doing the job DT : MT : MF : DF : | 1,2,3,4 | 37

31. About how often, if at all, do you SEND memos, written reports, notes, or other correspondence to others in the diocese? (Please tick only one of the following categories) | | 38

never	....	1
less than a month	....	2
once a month	....	3
once a week	....	4
more than once a week	....	5

32. About how often, if at all, do you RECEIVE memos, written reports, notes or other correspondence from others in the diocese? (Please tick only one of the following categories) | | 39

never	....	1
less than once a month	....	2
once a month	....	3
once a week	....	4
more than once a week	....	5

33. In the course of your job, about how much would you estimate you use the telephone? (Please tick one of the following categories) | | 40

all the time	....	6
most of the time	....	5
about half the time	....	4
less than half the time	....	3
hardly at all	....	2
never	....	1

	Code	Col.

34. Overall, would you characterise the
diocese as being highly centralised,
centralised, decentralised, or highly
decentralised?
(Please tick one of the following
categories) — **41**

	Code
highly centralised	4
centralised	3
decentralised	2
highly decentralised	1

35. Overall, taking everything into consideration, how
much influence do you think each of the following
individuals or groups have on what happens in
the diocese? Please answer each one, ticking
only one category in each case.

	very great in-fluence	great in-fluence	quite a bit of in-fluence	some in-fluence	little in-fluence	Code	Col.
The Archbishop/ Bishop						5,4,3,2,1	42
Auxiliary Bishop(s)						5,4,3,2,1	43
Vicar General						5,4,3,2,1	44
Dean						5,4,3,2,1	45
Parish Priest						5,4,3,2,1	46
Assistant Priests						5,4,3,2,1	47
Diocesan Council of Priests						5,4,3,2,1	48
Diocesan Pastoral Council						5,4,3,2,1	49

	very great in- fluence	great in- fluence	quite a bit of in- fluence	some in- fluence	little in- fluence	Code	Col.
Deanery/ Area Pastoral Council	....	....	....	....	....	5,4,3,2,1	50
The Laity	....	....	....	....	....	5,4,3,2,1	51

How frequently DURING THE PAST YEAR did you participate in the following for and on behalf of the diocese, as opposed to the parish?

	always	often	some- times	seldom	never	Code	Col.
36. The decision to employ new clergy	....	....	....	....	....	5,4,3,2,1	52
37. The introduction of new areas of work	....	....	....	....	....	5,4,3,2,1	53
38. Direct consultation with the hierarchy	....	....	....	....	....	5,4,3,2,1	54
39. Any decisions concerning past- oral reorganisa- tion	....	....	....	....	....	5,4,3,2,1	55
40. Any of the various diocesan com- mittees	....	....	....	....	....	5,4,3,2,1	56

The following questions are an attempt to measure certain aspects of what is commonly called 'profession-alism'. The statements represent attitudes of priests to their priesthood. There are five possible responses to your own attitudes and/or behaviour. If the item corresponds very well (VW), well (W), poorly (P), or very poorly (VP) please circle the appropriate response. The middle category (?) is designed to indicate an essentially neutral opinion about the item.
(Please circle one category only for each item)

41. Other professions are actually more vital to society than mine	VW : W : ? : P : VP :	1,2,3,4,5	57

		Code	Col.
42.	A person who violates professional standards should be judged by his professional peers VW : W : ? : P : VP :	5,4,3,2,1	58
43.	A person enters this profession because he has a sense of vocation VW : W : ? : P : VP :	5,4,3,2,1	59
44.	I make my own decisions in regard to what is to be done in my work VW : W : ? : P : VP :	5,4,3,2,1	60
45.	I think that my profession, more than any other, is essential for society VW : W : ? : P : VP :	5,4,3,2,1	61
46.	My fellow professionals have a pretty good idea about each other's competence VW : W : ? : P : VP :	5,4,3,2,1	62
47.	Most of the real rewards of my work can't be seen by an outsider VW : W : ? : P : VP :	5,4,3,2,1	63
48.	It is easier when someone else takes responsibility for decision making VW : W : ? : P : VP :	1,2,3,4,5	64
49.	I enjoy seeing my colleagues because of the ideas that are exchanged VW : W : ? : P : VP :	5,4,3,2,1	65
50.	The importance of my profession is sometimes overstressed VW : W : ? : P : VP :	1,2,3,4,5	66
51.	Most people would stay in the profession if their incomes were reduced VW : W : ? : P : VP :	5,4,3,2,1	67

		Code	Col.
52. I don't have much opportunity to exercise my own judgment	VW : W : ? : P : VP :	1,2,3,4,5	68
53. Professional training itself helps assure that people maintain their high ideals	VW : W : ? : P : VP :	5,4,3,2,1	69
54. The most stimulating periods are those spent with colleagues	VW : W : ? : P : VP :	5,4,3,2,1	70
55. A basic problem is the intrusion of standards other than those which are truly professional	VW : W : ? : P : VP :	5,4,3,2,1	71
56. Not enough people realise the importance of this profession for society	VW : W : ? : P : VP :	5,4,3,2,1	72
II			123 456 7
57. The real test of how good a person is in his field is the layman's opinion of him	VW : W : ? : P : VP :	1,2,3,4,5	8
58. When problems arise concerning work there is little opportunity to use your own intellect	VW : W : ? : P : VP :	1,2,3,4,5	9
59. There is not much opportunity to judge how another person does his work	VW : W : ? : P : VP :	1,2,3,4,5	10
60. The profession doesn't really encourage continued training	VW : W : ? : P : VP :	1,2,3,4,5	11

Now we would like you to answer a few questions about the Church. Even though they are complex and difficult questions, please try to answer them.

	Code	Col.
61. How do you think of the Roman Catholic Church?		12

61. How do you think of the Roman Catholic Church?

I think of the Roman Catholic Church as being one denomination among many **1**

I think of the Roman Catholic Church as having special responsibility to the whole population of an area regardless of people's religious or other affiliations **2**

Neither the above statements really represents how I think of the Roman Catholic Church **3**
(Please write in your answer)

I think of the Roman Catholic Church as **4**

....

....

....

....

62. Much is heard today about the need to reform the Roman Catholic Church. Which of the following most nearly indicates your own opinion? The Roman Catholic Church

13

greatly needs reform **4**

certainly needs some reform **3**

needs a little reform **2**

needs no reform **1**

Unless you have answered above that the Roman Catholic Church needs no reform, in which of the following fields do you think reform is most important, quite important, not very important, or not necessary?

	Most important	Quite important	Not very important	Not necessary	Code	Col.
63. Liturgy and forms of worship	....	....	....	....	4,3,2,1	14
64. Appointment of Bishops	....	....	....	....	4,3,2,1	15
65. The role of the laity	....	....	....	....	4,3,2,1	16

185

	Code	Col.
66. Celibacy	4,3,2,1	17
67. Training of Priests	4,3,2,1	18
68. Reform of the paro-chial system	4,3,2,1	19

69. Which of the following categories most nearly
approximates your opinion of the relationship
between Rome and national Churches? ... 20

The national Church should wait for Rome to make
important initiatives 1

The national Church should consult Rome before
adopting any new initiatives and only act with their
approval 2

The national Church should be free to adopt its
own policies except on major issues of faith and
morals 3

The national Church should be completely free to
adopt its own policies 4

Which of the following recommendations, if any,
of the Provisional Laity Commission would you like
to see implemented?

	Yes	No	Code	Col.
70. The laity should be present in all structures to ensure direct lay participation in all decision making			2,1	21
71. A suitable agency for adequate co-ordination should be established			2,1	22
72. Members of all structures should be as representative as possible of the various groupings and shades of opinion within the Church			2,1	23
73. Everybody should have the services of experts, in number never more than the representative membership			2,1	24
74. Links between diocesan structures and national organisations on the one hand and the Bishop's Conference and its Commissions on the other, should be built into the plan			2,1	25
75. The setting up of a professional pastoral research unit			2,1	26

			Code	Col.
76.	The introduction of Christian Stewardship	....	2,1	27
77.	Methods by which people are chosen to serve on the various bodies must be made known and their elections publicised	....	2,1	28

78. Are you in favour of the eventual union of the Roman Catholic Church with any of the following:

	Yes	No	Code	Col.
Church of England	....	....	2,1	29
Methodist Church	....	....	2,1	30
Baptist Church	....	....	2,1	31
United Reform Church	....	....	2,1	32
Pentecostal Churches	....	....	2,1	34
Orthodox Churches	....	....	2,1	35
All Christian bodies	....	....	2,1	36
Others (please specify)			2,1	37

....

79. Union apart, at present in what forms of ecumenical co-operation with other churches would you like to see the Roman Catholic engage more frequently?

	Yes	No	Code	Col.
Clergy preaching in each other's churches	....	....	2,1	38
Jointly organised services with other churches	....	....	2,1	39
Joint meetings of clergy/ministers	....	....	2,1	40
Joint meetings of members	....	....	2,1	41
Joint study groups	....	....	2,1	42
Joint conferences	....	....	2,1	43
Joint publications	....	....	2,1	44
Joint theological colleges	....	....	2,1	45
Joint education, social welfare and community projects	....	....	2,1	46
The sharing of churches	....	....	2,1	47
Joint ministries	....	....	2,1	48
Joint missionary work	....	....	2,1	49

	Code	Col.

80. Have you personally initiated or been involved in any of the following co-operative ventures with another church or churches?

Yes No

	Code	Col.
Preached in a church of another denomination	2,1	50
Invited a minister of another denomination to preach in your church	2,1	51
Celebrated the Eucharist in a church of another denomination	2,1	52
Communication at a service of intercommunion	2,1	53
Planned with a minister of another denomination joint activities other than preaching, joint services, Eucharist, etc. (e.g. meetings of members, study groups, community projects, etc.)	2,1	54

Finally, we would be most grateful if you could answer the following questions about yourself. We ask you for this personal information to assist our understanding of your answers to the above questions. Your answers will be treated in strictest confidence and you will remain completely anonymous.

81. What was your age last birthday? (Please tick one of the following categories) — 55

	Code
under 30 years	1
30–39	2
40–44	3
45–49	4
50–54	5
55–59	6
60–64	7
65–69	8
70 years and over	9

82. How many years have you been working in your present position? (Please tick one of the following categories) — 56

	Code
0–4 years	1
5–9 years	2

	Code	Col.
10–14 years	3	
15–19 years	4	
20–24 years	5	
25–29 years	6	
30–34 years	7	
35–39 years	8	
40 years and over	9	

83. How many years have you been working as a priest in this diocese? (Please tick one of the following categories) — Col. 57

	Code
0–4 years	1
5–9 years	2
10–14 years	3
15–19 years	4
20–24 years	5
25–29 years	6
30–34 years	7
35–39 years	8
40 years and over	9

84. What posts, as a priest, have you held in the Roman Catholic Church, including your present one (both in this diocese and in any other diocese in which you have worked)? Please list them in order, beginning with the first post you held and ending with your present job, e.g. Assistant Priest of . . . . . , Assistant Priest of . . . . . , Parish Priest of . . . . . . Please indicate for each one whether or not it was a post as a parish priest.

Was this as a Parish Priest?

	Yes	No	Code	
(1) First position			1	Posts
			2	58
(2)			3	
			4	
(3)			5	
			6	

		Code	Col.
(4)		7	
		8	
(5)		9	
(6)		1	Incumb.
		2	59
(7)		3	
		4	
(8)		5	
		6	
(9)		7	
		8	
(10) Present position		9	
....			

Total number of positions held including
present one   ....

Total number of positions as Parish Priest   ....

Please circle the appropriate answer

			Code	Col.
85.	Are you a member of a Deanery Council?	YES NO	2,1	60
86.	Are you a member of the Diocesan Pastoral Council?	YES NO	2,1	61
87.	Are you a member of the Diocesan Council of Priests?	YES NO	2,1	62
88.	Are you a member of any ecumenical group?	YES NO	2,1	63
89.	If YES, please indicate those types of group of which you are a member:			
	A Local Council of Churches	YES NO	2,1	65
	A Council of Christian Churches	YES NO	2,1	64
	A Local Clergy Fraternal	YES NO	2,1	66
	Other (please specify)			
	....		2,1	67
90.	Are you currently a member of diocesan commission?	YES NO	1	68

190

		Code	Col.
91. Of how many diocesan commissions are you a member?		2,3,4 5,6,7 8,9	
92. Are you a member of any of the following diocesan commissions?			
Liturgical Commission	YES NO	2,1	69
Ecumenical Commission	YES NO	2,1	70
Schools Commission	YES NO	2,1	71
Youth Commission	YES NO	2,1	72
III			123 456 7
Council of Administration	YES NO	2,1	8
Boundary Commission	YES NO	2,1	9
Other (please specify)			
93. How many years have you been ordained? (Please tick the appropriate category)			10
0–4 years		1	
5–9 years		2	
10–14 years		3	
15–19 years		4	
20–24 years		5	
25–29 years		6	
30–34 years		7	
35–39 years		8	
40 years and over		9	
94. When you were 18 years old, what was your father's occupation?		1,2,3 4,5,6 7,8,9	11
95. At the time you decided to enter the ministry, did you have a relative in the ministry?			
	YES NO	2,1	12

191

	Code	Col.

97. What type of education did you receive? | | 14
(Please tick one of the following types)

    elementary or secondary modern   ……… | 1 |

    technical   ……… | 2 |

    comprehensive   ………. | 3 |

    grammar   ……… | 4 |

    public   ……… | 5 |

    other (please specify)

    ………………………………………………… | 6 |

98. Have you attended any institutions of higher
education (other than a seminary)?   Yes   ……… | | 15

      No   ……… | 1 |

99. If YES, please indicate which of the following
you attended:

    teacher training college   ……… | 2 |

    university   ……… | 3 |

    other (please specify)

    ………………………………………………… | 4 |

100. If you did receive higher education, which of the
following subject categories did you study? | | 16
(Please tick only one category)

    Humanities (not theology)   ……… | 1 |

    Theology   ……… | 2 |

    Social Sciences   ……… | 3 |

    Natural and Physical Sciences   ……… | 4 |

    Technology and Engineering   ……… | 5 |

101. If you did receive higher education, which of the
following types of qualifications did you receive? | | 17

    Diploma, Certificate, etc.   ……… | 1 |

    Bachelor's degree   ……… | 2 |

    Master's degree   ……… | 3 |

    Ph.D.   ……… | 4 |

102. Which seminary did you attend? | 1,2,3
4,5,6
7,8,9 | 18

………………………………………………

	Code	Col.

105. For certain purposes, the main tasks of the
ministry can be summed up under seven general
headings:

the parish priest as *administrator* (of
church affairs);

as *celebrant* (of sacraments and services);

as *leader* (of the local community);

as *preacher* (of the word);

as *official* (of the church);

as *pastor* (and father of parishioners); and

as *counsellor* (adviser and confessor).

Will you now please rank these seven responsibilities in
terms of the order of priorities in which you believe
they *ought* to be placed. (Please number them from 1 to
7, i.e. 1 = first priority)

	Code	Col.
administrator	1,2,3 / 4,5,6,7	21
celebrant	1,2,3 / 4,5,6,7	22
leader	1,2,3 / 4,5,6,7	23
preacher	1,2,3 / 4,5,6,7	24
official	1,2,3 / 4,5,6,7	25
pastor	1,2,3 / 4,5,6,7	26
counsellor	1,2,3 / 4,5,6,7	27

106. Looking back on things—if you had the choice
again—how certain are you that you would enter the
priesthood? Which of the following comes closest
to your feelings?   28

	Code
definitely would do it again	1
probably would do it again	2
not sure whether you would do it again	3
probably would not become a priest	4
definitely would not become a priest	5

Bibliography

ABRAHAMSON, M. (1967) *The Professional in the Organization*, Chicago: Rand McNally.

ALLARDT, E. (1973) 'Structural, institutional and cultural explanations', *Acta Sociologica*, vol. 15/16: 54–68.

ALLEN, P. (1962) 'Growth of strata in early organisational development', *American Journal of Sociology*, 68: 34–46.

BARBOUR, I. G. (1966) *Issues in Science and Religion*, London: SCM Press.

BERGER, P. L. and LUCKMANN, T. (1963) 'The sociology of religion and the sociology of knowledge', *Sociology and Social Research*, 47: 417–27.

BLAU, P. M. (1964) *Exchange and Power in Social Life*, New York: Wiley.

BLIZZARD, S. (1956) 'The minister's dilemma', *The Christian Century*, 73: 508–9.

BRYMAN, A. (1974) 'Sociology of religion and sociology of élites', *Archives de Sciences Sociales des Religions*, 38: 109–21.

BRYMAN, A. and HININGS, C. R. (1973) 'Lay perceptions of church issues', *Research Bulletin 1973*, Institute for the Study of Worship and Religious Architecture, University of Birmingham.

BRYMAN, A. and HININGS, C. R. (1974) 'Participation, reform and ecumenism', in M. Hill (ed.), *A Sociological Yearbook of Religion in Britain 7*, London: SCM Press.

BRYMAN, A., RANSON, S. and HININGS, C. R. (1974) 'Churchmanship and ecumenism', *Journal of Ecumenical Studies* 11: 467–75.

BUDD, S. (1973) *Sociologists and Religion*, London: Collier-Macmillan.

CARLTON, E. (1968) ' "The Call": the concept of vocation in the Free Church ministry', in D. Martin (ed.), *A Sociological Yearbook of Religion in Britain*, London: SCM Press.

CONEYBEARE, W. J. (1853) 'Church parties', *Edinburgh Review*, XCVIII: 273–342.

COULSON, M. and RIDDELL, D. (1970) *Approaching Sociology*, London: Routledge & Kegan Paul.

COX, H. (1967) 'The "new breed" in American churches', *Daedalus* 96: 315–50.

COXON, A. P. M. (1967) 'Patterns of occupational recruitment: the Anglican ministry', *Sociology*, 1: 73–80.

CURRIE, R. (1968) *Methodism Divided*, London: Faber & Faber.

DANIEL, M. G. (1967) 'London clergymen', unpublished M.Phil. thesis, University of London.

DANIEL, M. G. (1968) 'Catholic, evangelical and liberal in the Anglican priesthood', in D. Martin (ed.), *A Sociological Yearbook of Religion in Britain*, London: SCM Press.

DAVIES, R. (1963) *Methodism*, Harmondsworth: Penguin Books.

DEMERATH III, N. J. (1965) *Social Class in American Protestantism*, Chicago: Rand McNally.

DOUGLAS, M. (1966) *Purity and Danger*, London: Routledge & Kegan Paul.

DOUGLAS, M. (1970) *Natural Symbols*, L˒ndon: Barrie & Rockliff.

DOUGLAS, M. (ed.) (1973) *Rules and Meanings*, Harmondsworth: Penguin Books.

DREWETT, A. J. (1966) 'The social status of the ordained minister in the 19th and 20th centuries', *The Modern Churchman*, 9: 127-34.

DUNSTAN, G. R. (1967) 'The sacred ministry as a learned profession', *Theology*, 10: 142–5.

EISTER, A. W. (1967) 'Toward a radical critique of church-sect typologizing', *Journal for the Scientific Study of Religion*, VI, 85–90.

FICHTER, J. H. (1961) *Religion and an Occupation*, Indiana: University of Notre Dame Press.

FOGARTY, M. P. (1963) 'The Catholic Church and change', *New Society*, no. 41, 11 July: 6–8.

GANNON, T. M. (1971) 'Priest/Minister: Profession or non-profession?', *Review of Religious Research*, 12: 66–79.

GILL, R. (1974) 'British theology as a sociological variable', in M. Hill (ed.), *A Sociological Yearbook of Religion in Britain 7*, London: SCM Press.

GLASSE, J. D. (1968) *Profession: Minister*, Nashville: Abingdon Press.

GLOCK, C. Y. and STARK, R. (1965) *Religion and Society in Tension*, Chicago: Rand McNally.

GOLDNER, F., FERENCE, T. P. and RITTI, R. R. (1972) 'Priests and Church: The professionalisation of an organisation', *American Behavioural Scientist*, 14: 507–24.

GREELEY, A. M. (1973) *The Persistence of Religion*, London: SCM Press.

HADDEN, J. K. (1969) *The Gathering Storm in the Churches*, New York: Doubleday.

HAGE, J. and AIKEN, M. (1967) 'The relationship of centralization to other structural properties', *Administrative Science Quarterly*, 12: 72–92.

HALL, R. H. (1963) 'The concept of bureaucracy: an empirical assessment', *American Journal of Sociology*, 69: 32–40.

HALL, R. H. (1968) 'Professionalization and bureaucratization', *American Sociological Review*, 33: 92–104.

HALL, D. T. and SCHNEIDER, B. (1973) *Organizational Climates and Careers*, New York: Seminar Press.

HALMOS, P. (1965) *The Faith of the Counsellors*, London: Constable.

195

HARRIS, C. C. (1969) 'Reform in a normative organisation', *Sociological Review*, 17: 167–85.

HARRISON, P. M. (1959) *Authority and Power in the Free Church Convention*, Princeton University Press.

HARRISON, P. M. (1970) 'Religious Leadership in America' in *The World Yearbook of Religion*, vol. 2, *The Religious Situation*, London: Evans.

HASTINGS, A. and HININGS, C. R. (1970) 'Role relations and value adaptation, a study of the Professional Accountant in Industry', *Sociology*, 4: 353–66.

HILL, M. (1973) *A Sociology of Religion*, London: Heinemann.

HININGS, C. R. and BRYMAN, A. (1974) 'Size and the administrative component in churches', *Human Relations*, 27: 457–75.

HININGS, C. R. and FOSTER, B. D. (1973) 'The organisation structure of churches', *Sociology*, 7: 93–106.

ILLICH, I. (1971) *The Celebration of Awareness*, London: Calder & Boyars.

INKSON, J. H. K., PUGH, D. S. and HICKSON, D. J. (1970) 'Organisation context and structure: An abbreviated replication', *Administrative Science Quarterly*, 15: 318–29.

IRVING, G. (1966) 'The sociology of high and low', *Faith and Order*, 113–15.

JARVIE, I. (1972) *Concepts and Society*, London: Routledge & Kegan Paul.

JOHNSON, B. (1967) 'Theology and the position of pastors on social issues', *American Sociological Review*, 32: 433–42.

JUD, G. J., MILLS, JR., E. W. and BURCH, G. W. (1970) *Ex-Pastors*, Philadelphia: Pilgrim Press.

KRAUSE, E. (1971) *Sociology of Occupations*, Boston: Little Brown.

KUNG, H. (1972) *Why Priests?*, London: Collins.

LATOURETTE, K. S. (1954) 'Ecumenical Bearings of the Missionary Movement and the International Missionary Council', in R. Rouse and S. Neill (eds), *History of the Ecumenical Movement*, vol. I, London: SPCK.

LAUER, R. H. (1973) 'Organisational punishment: punitive relations in a voluntary association', *Human Relations*, 26: 189–202.

LEAT, D. (1973) 'Putting God over: the faithful counsellors', *Sociological Review*, 21: 561–72

LOVELL, T. (1973) 'Weber, Goldmann and the sociology of beliefs', *European Journal of Sociology*, 14: 304–23.

LUCKMANN, T. (1967) *The Invisible Religion*, London: Collier-Macmillan.

MACINTYRE, A. (1962) 'A mistake about causality in social science', in P. Laslett and W. G. Runciman (eds), *Philosophy, Politics and Society*, Oxford: Blackwell.

MACINTYRE, A. (1971) *Against the Self-Images of the Age*, London: Duckworth.

MCKENNELL, A. (1970) 'Attitude measurement: use of coefficient alpha with cluster or factor analysis', *Sociology*, 4: 227–45.

MARSHALL, T. H. (1938) 'The recent history of professionalism in relation to social structure and policy', *Canadian Journal of Economics and Political Science*, 5: 337–50.

MARTIN, D. (1967) *A Sociology of English Religion*, London: Heinemann.

MOBERG, D. O. (1970) 'Theological positions and the institutional characteristics of Protestant congregations', *Journal for the Scientific Study of Religion*, 9: 53–8.

MOLLAND, E. (1959) *Christendom*, London: Mowbray.

MORGAN, D. H. J. (1969) 'The social and educational background of Anglican bishops', *British Journal of Sociology*, 20: 295–310.

MORLEY REPORT (1967) *Partners in Ministry*, Church Information Office.

NAEGELE, K. D. (1956) 'Clergymen, teachers and psychiatrists', *Canadian Journal of Economics and Political Science*, 22: 46–62.

NORTHCOTT, C. (1971) 'A decade of change in the churches', *Contemporary Review*, 218: 292–6.

O'DEA, T. (1963) 'Sociological dilemmas: five paradoxes of institutionalisation' in E. Tiryakian (ed.), *Sociological Theory, Values and Socio-Cultural Change*, New York: Free Press.

PARSONS, T. (1939) 'The professions and the social structure', *Social Forces*, 17: 457–67.

PAUL, L. (1964) *The Deployment and Payment of the Clergy*, London: Church Information Office.

PAUL, L. (1968) *The Death and Resurrection of the Church*, London: Hodder & Stoughton.

PAUL, L. (1973) *A Church by Daylight*, London: Chapman.

PAYNE, R. L. and MANSFIELD, R. (1973) 'Relationships of perceptions of organisational climate to organisational structure, context, and hierarchical position', *Administrative Science Quarterly*, 19: 515–26.

PEEL, J. D. Y. (1973) 'Cultural factors in the contemporary theory of development', *European Journal of Sociology*, 14: 283–303.

PITTENGER, W. N. (1966) 'Catholicism', in M. Halverstan and A. Choen (eds), *A Handbook of Christian Theology*, London: Collins.

RITTI, R. R., FERENCE, T. P. and GOLDNER, F. M. (1974) 'Professions and their plausibility: priests, work and belief systems' *Sociology of Work and Occupations*, 1: 24–51.

ROBERTSON, R. (1970) *The Sociological Interpretation of Religion*, Oxford: Blackwell.

RUDGE, P. (1968) *Ministry and Management*, London: Tavistock.

RUNCIMAN, W. G. (1969) 'What is structuralism?', *British Journal of Sociology*, 20: 253–65.

SMITH A. (1973) '"Ideas" and "structure" in the formation of independence ideals', *Philosophy of Social Science*, 3: 19–39.

SPAULDING, K. E. (1972) 'The theology of the pew', *Review of Religious Research*, 13: 206–11.

STARK, R., FOSTER, B. D., GLOCK, C. Y. and QUINLEY, H. (1971) *Wayward Shepherds*, New York: Harper & Row.

STEWART, J. H. (1969) 'The changing role of the Catholic priest', *Sociological Analysis*, 30, 81–90.

STRUZZO, J. A. (1970) 'Professionalism and the resolution of authority conflicts among the Catholic clergy', *Sociological Analysis*, 31: 92–106.

TANNENBAUM, A. (1968) *Control in Organizations*, New York: McGraw-Hill.

197

THOMPSON, K. A. (1970) *Bureaucracy and Church Reform*, London: Oxford University Press.

THOMPSON, K. A. (1973) 'Religious organisations', in G. Salaman and K. A. Thompson (eds), *People and Organisations*, London: Longmans.

TILL, B. (1972) *The Churches Search for Unity*, Harmondsworth: Penguin Books.

TOWLER, R. (1969) 'The social status of the Anglican minister', in R. Robertson (ed.), *Sociology of Religion*, Harmondsworth: Penguin Books.

VALLIER, I. (1962) 'Church, society and labour resources: an intradenominational comparison', *American Journal of Sociology*, 68, 21-33.

VIDICH, A. and BENSMAN, J. (1958) *Small Town in Mass Society*, Princeton University Press.

WEBER, M. (1947) *The Theory of Social and Economic Organisation*, Chicago: Free Press.

WILLIAMS, D. M. (1966) 'Modernism', *A Handbook of Christian Theology*, London: Collins.

WILSON, B. R. (1966) *Religion in Secular Society*, London: Watts.

WILSON, B. R. (1970) *Religious Sects*, London: Weidenfeld & Nicolson.

WINCH, P. (1958) *The Idea of a Social Science*, London: Routledge & Kegan Paul.

WINTER, J. A. (1970) 'The attitudes of societally-oriented and parish-oriented clergy', *Journal for the Scientific Study of Religion*, 9, 59–66.

Index

Subject Index

Routledge Social Science Series

Routledge & Kegan Paul   London, Henley and Boston

39 Store Street, London WC1E 7DD
Broadway House, Newtown Road, Henley-on-Thames,
Oxon RG9 1EN
9 Park Street, Boston, Mass. 02108

Contents

*Authors wishing to submit manuscripts for any series in
this catalogue should send them to the Social Science Editor,
Routledge & Kegan Paul Ltd, 39 Store Street,
London WC1E 7DD*

● *Books so marked are available in paperback*
All books are in Metric Demy 8vo format (216 × 138mm approx.)

International Library of Sociology

General Editor   John Rex

GENERAL SOCIOLOGY

Barnsley, J. H. The Social Reality of Ethics. *464 pp.*
Belshaw, Cyril. The Conditions of Social Performance. *An Exploratory Theory. 144 pp.*
Brown, Robert. Explanation in Social Science. *208 pp.*
● Rules and Laws in Sociology. *192 pp.*
Bruford, W. H. Chekhov and His Russia. *A Sociological Study. 244 pp.*
Cain, Maureen E. Society and the Policeman's Role. *326 pp.*
●**Fletcher, Colin.** Beneath the Surface. *An Account of Three Styles of Sociological Research. 221 pp.*
Gibson, Quentin. The Logic of Social Enquiry. *240 pp.*
Glucksmann, M. Structuralist Analysis in Contemporary Social Thought. *212 pp.*
Gurvitch, Georges. Sociology of Law. *Preface by Roscoe Pound. 264 pp.*
Hodge, H. A. Wilhelm Dilthey. *An Introduction. 184 pp.*
Homans, George C. Sentiments and Activities. *336 pp.*
Johnson, Harry M. Sociology: *a Systematic Introduction. Foreword by Robert K. Merton. 710 pp.*
●**Keat, Russell,** and **Urry, John.** Social Theory as Science. *278 pp.*
Mannheim, Karl. Essays on Sociology and Social Psychology. *Edited by Paul Keckskemeti. With Editorial Note by Adolph Lowe. 344 pp.*
Systematic Sociology: *An Introduction to the Study of Society. Edited by J. S. Erös and Professor W. A. C. Stewart. 220 pp.*
Martindale, Don. The Nature and Types of Sociological Theory. *292 pp.*
●**Maus, Heinz.** A Short History of Sociology. *234 pp.*
Mey, Harald. Field-Theory. *A Study of its Application in the Social Sciences. 352 pp.*
Myrdal, Gunnar. Value in Social Theory: *A Collection of Essays on Methodology. Edited by Paul Streeten. 332 pp.*
Ogburn, William F., and **Nimkoff, Meyer F.** A Handbook of Sociology. *Preface by Karl Mannheim. 656 pp. 46 figures. 35 tables.*
Parsons, Talcott, and **Smelser, Neil J.** Economy and Society: *A Study in the Integration of Economic and Social Theory. 362 pp.*
Podgórecki, Adam. Practical Social Sciences. *About 200 pp.*
●**Rex, John.** Key Problems of Sociological Theory. *220 pp.*
Sociology and the Demystification of the Modern World. *282 pp.*
●**Rex, John** (Ed.) Approaches to Sociology. *Contributions by Peter Abell, Frank Bechhofer, Basil Bernstein, Ronald Fletcher, David Frisby, Miriam Glucksmann, Peter Lassman, Herminio Martins, John Rex, Roland Robertson, John Westergaard and Jock Young. 302 pp.*
Rigby, A. Alternative Realities. *352 pp.*
Roche, M. Phenomenology, Language and the Social Sciences. *374 pp.*

Sahay, A. Sociological Analysis. *220 pp.*
Simirenko, Alex (Ed.) Soviet Sociology. *Historical Antecedents and Current Appraisals. Introduction by Alex Simirenko. 376 pp.*
Strasser, Hermann. The Normative Structure of Sociology. *Conservative and Emancipatory Themes in Social Thought. About 340 pp.*
Urry, John. Reference Groups and the Theory of Revolution. *244 pp.*
Weinberg, E. Development of Sociology in the Soviet Union. *173 pp.*

FOREIGN CLASSICS OF SOCIOLOGY

●**Durkheim, Emile.** Suicide. *A Study in Sociology. Edited and with an Introduction by George Simpson. 404 pp.*
●**Gerth, H. H.,** and **Mills, C. Wright.** From Max Weber: *Essays in Sociology. 502 pp.*
●**Tönnies, Ferdinand.** Community and Association. (*Gemeinschaft und Gesellschaft.*) *Translated and Supplemented by Charles P. Loomis. Foreword by Pitirim A. Sorokin. 334 pp.*

SOCIAL STRUCTURE

Andreski, Stanislav. Military Organization and Society. *Foreword by Professor A. R. Radcliffe-Brown. 226 pp. 1 folder.*
Carlton, Eric. Ideology and Social Order. *Preface by Professor Philip Abrahams. About 320 pp.*
Coontz, Sydney H. Population Theories and the Economic Interpretation. *202 pp.*
Coser, Lewis. The Functions of Social Conflict. *204 pp.*
Dickie-Clark, H. F. Marginal Situation: *A Sociological Study of a Coloured Group. 240 pp. 11 tables.*
Glaser, Barney, and **Strauss, Anselm L.** Status Passage. *A Formal Theory. 208 pp.*
Glass, D. V. (Ed.) Social Mobility in Britain. *Contributions by J. Berent, T. Bottomore, R. C. Chambers, J. Floud, D. V. Glass, J. R. Hall, H. T. Himmelweit, R. K. Kelsall, F. M. Martin, C. A. Moser, R. Mukherjee, and W. Ziegel. 420 pp.*
Johnstone, Frederick A. Class, Race and Gold. *A Study of Class Relations and Racial Discrimination in South Africa. 312 pp.*
Jones, Garth N. Planned Organizational Change: *An Exploratory Study Using an Empirical Approach. 268 pp.*
Kelsall, R. K. Higher Civil Servants in Britain: *From 1870 to the Present Day. 268 pp. 31 tables.*
König, René. The Community. *232 pp. Illustrated.*
●**Lawton, Denis.** Social Class, Language and Education. *192 pp.*
McLeish, John. The Theory of Social Change: *Four Views Considered. 128 pp.*
Marsh, David C. The Changing Social Structure of England and Waies, 1871-1961. *288 pp.*
Menzies, Ken. Talcott Parsons and the Social Image of Man. *About 208 pp.*

● **Mouzelis, Nicos.** Organization and Bureaucracy. *An Analysis of Modern Theories. 240 pp.*

Mulkay, M. J. Functionalism, Exchange and Theoretical Strategy. *272 pp.*

Ossowski, Stanislaw. Class Structure in the Social Consciousness. *210 pp.*

● **Podgórecki, Adam.** Law and Society. *302 pp.*

Renner, Karl. Institutions of Private Law and Their Social Functions. *Edited, with an Introduction and Notes, by O. Kahn-Freud. Translated by Agnes Schwarzschild. 316 pp.*

SOCIOLOGY AND POLITICS

Acton, T. A. Gypsy Politics and Social Change. *316 pp.*

Clegg, Stuart. Power, Rule and Domination. *A Critical and Empirical Understanding of Power in Sociological Theory and Organisational Life. About 300 pp.*

Hechter, Michael. Internal Colonialism. *The Celtic Fringe in British National Development, 1536–1966. 361 pp.*

Hertz, Frederick. Nationality in History and Politics: *A Psychology and Sociology of National Sentiment and Nationalism. 432 pp.*

Kornhauser, William. The Politics of Mass Society. *272 pp. 20 tables.*

● **Kroes, R.** Soldiers and Students. *A Study of Right- and Left-wing Students. 174 pp.*

Laidler, Harry W. History of Socialism. *Social-Economic Movements: An Historical and Comparative Survey of Socialism, Communism, Co-operation, Utopianism; and other Systems of Reform and Reconstruction. 992 pp.*

Lasswell, H. D. Analysis of Political Behaviour. *324 pp.*

Martin, David A. Pacifism: *an Historical and Sociological Study. 262 pp.*

Martin, Roderick. Sociology of Power. *About 272 pp.*

Myrdal, Gunnar. The Political Element in the Development of Economic Theory. *Translated from the German by Paul Streeten. 282 pp.*

Wilson, H. T. The American Ideology. *Science, Technology and Organization of Modes of Rationality. About 280 pp.*

Wootton, Graham. Workers, Unions and the State. *188 pp.*

CRIMINOLOGY

Ancel, Marc. Social Defence: *A Modern Approach to Criminal Problems. Foreword by Leon Radzinowicz. 240 pp.*

Cain, Maureen E. Society and the Policeman's Role. *326 pp.*

Cloward, Richard A., and **Ohlin, Lloyd E.** Delinquency and Opportunity: *A Theory of Delinquent Gangs. 248 pp.*

Downes, David M. The Delinquent Solution. *A Study in Subcultural Theory. 296 pp.*

Dunlop, A. B., and **McCabe, S.** Young Men in Detention Centres. *192 pp.*

Friedlander, Kate. The Psycho-Analytical Approach to Juvenile Delinquency: *Theory, Case Studies, Treatment. 320 pp.*

Glueck, Sheldon, and **Eleanor.** Family Environment and Delinquency. *With the statistical assistance of Rose W. Kneznek. 340 pp.*

Lopez-Rey, Manuel. Crime. *An Analytical Appraisal. 288 pp.*

Mannheim, Hermann. Comparative Criminology: *a Text Book. Two volumes. 442 pp. and 380 pp.*

Morris, Terence. The Criminal Area: *A Study in Social Ecology. Foreword by Hermann Mannheim. 232 pp. 25 tables. 4 maps.*

Rock, Paul. Making People Pay. *338 pp.*

●**Taylor, Ian, Walton, Paul,** and **Young, Jock.** The New Criminology. *For a Social Theory of Deviance. 325 pp.*

●**Taylor, Ian, Walton, Paul,** and **Young, Jock** (Eds). Critical Criminology. *268 pp.*

SOCIAL PSYCHOLOGY

Bagley, Christopher. The Social Psychology of the Epileptic Child. *320 pp.*

Barbu, Zevedei. Problems of Historical Psychology. *248 pp.*

Blackburn, Julian. Psychology and the Social Pattern. *184 pp.*

●**Brittan, Arthur.** Meanings and Situations. *224 pp.*

Carroll, J. Break-Out from the Crystal Palace. *200 pp.*

●**Fleming, C. M.** Adolescence: Its Social Psychology. *With an Introduction to recent findings from the fields of Anthropology, Physiology, Medicine, Psychometrics and Sociometry. 288 pp.*

● The Social Psychology of Education: *An Introduction and Guide to Its Study. 136 pp.*

●**Homans, George C.** The Human Group. *Foreword by Bernard DeVoto. Introduction by Robert K. Merton. 526 pp.*

● Social Behaviour: *its Elementary Forms. 416 pp.*

●**Klein, Josephine.** The Study of Groups. *226 pp. 31 figures. 5 tables.*

Linton, Ralph. The Cultural Background of Personality. *132 pp.*

●**Mayo, Elton.** The Social Problems of an Industrial Civilization. *With an appendix on the Political Problem. 180 pp.*

Ottaway, A. K. C. Learning Through Group Experience. *176 pp.*

Plummer, Ken. Sexual Stigma. *An Interactionist Account. 254 pp.*

●**Rose, Arnold M.** (Ed.) Human Behaviour and Social Processes: *an Interactionist Approach. Contributions by Arnold M. Rose, Ralph H. Turner, Anselm Strauss, Everett C. Hughes, E. Franklin Frazier, Howard S. Becker, et al. 696 pp.*

Smelser, Neil J. Theory of Collective Behaviour. *448 pp.*

Stephenson, Geoffrey M. The Development of Conscience. *128 pp.*

Young, Kimball. Handbook of Social Psychology. *658 pp. 16 figures. 10 tables.*

SOCIOLOGY OF THE FAMILY

Banks, J. A. Prosperity and Parenthood: *A Study of Family Planning among The Victorian Middle Classes. 262 pp.*

Bell, Colin R. Middle Class Families: *Social and Geographical Mobility. 224 pp.*

Burton, Lindy. Vulnerable Children. *272 pp.*

Gavron, Hannah. The Captive Wife: *Conflicts of Household Mothers. 190 pp.*

George, Victor, and **Wilding, Paul.** Motherless Families. *248 pp.*

Klein, Josephine. Samples from English Cultures.
1. Three Preliminary Studies and Aspects of Adult Life in England. *447 pp.*
2. Child-Rearing Practices and Index. *247 pp.*

Klein, Viola. The Feminine Character. *History of an Ideology. 244 pp.*

McWhinnie, Alexina M. Adopted Children. *How They Grow Up. 304 pp.*

● **Morgan, D. H. J.** Social Theory and the Family. *About 320 pp.*

● **Myrdal, Alva,** and **Klein, Viola.** Women's Two Roles: *Home and Work. 238 pp. 27 tables.*

Parsons, Talcott, and **Bales, Robert F.** Family: Socialization and Inter-action Process. *In collaboration with James Olds, Morris Zelditch and Philip E. Slater. 456 pp. 50 figures and tables.*

SOCIAL SERVICES

Bastide, Roger. The Sociology of Mental Disorder. *Translated from the French by Jean McNeil. 260 pp.*

Carlebach, Julius. Caring For Children in Trouble. *266 pp.*

George, Victor. Foster Care. *Theory and Practice. 234 pp.*
Social Security: *Beveridge and After. 258 pp.*

George, V., and **Wilding, P.** Motherless Families. *248 pp.*

● **Goetschius, George W.** Working with Community Groups. *256 pp.*

Goetschius, George W., and **Tash, Joan.** Working with Unattached Youth. *416 pp.*

Hall, M. P., and **Howes, I. V.** The Church in Social Work. *A Study of Moral Welfare Work undertaken by the Church of England. 320 pp.*

Heywood, Jean S. Children in Care: *the Development of the Service for the Deprived Child. 264 pp.*

Hoenig, J., and **Hamilton, Marian W.** The De-Segregation of the Mentally Ill. *284 pp.*

Jones, Kathleen. Mental Health and Social Policy, 1845-1959. *264 pp.*

King, Roy D., Raynes, Norma V., and **Tizard, Jack.** Patterns of Residential Care. *356 pp.*

Leigh, John. Young People and Leisure. *256 pp.*

● **Mays, John.** (Ed.) Penelope Hall's Social Services of England and Wales. *About 324 pp.*

Morris, Mary. Voluntary Work and the Welfare State. *300 pp.*

Nokes, P. L. The Professional Task in Welfare Practice. *152 pp.*

Timms, Noel. Psychiatric Social Work in Great Britain (1939-1962). *280 pp.*

● Social Casework: *Principles and Practice. 256 pp.*

Young, A. F. Social Services in British Industry. *272 pp.*

SOCIOLOGY OF EDUCATION

Banks, Olive. Parity and Prestige in English Secondary Education: a Study in Educational Sociology. *272 pp.*

Bentwich, Joseph. Education in Israel. *224 pp. 8 pp. plates.*

●**Blyth, W. A. L.** English Primary Education. *A Sociological Description.*
    1. Schools. *232 pp.*
    2. Background. *168 pp.*

Collier, K. G. The Social Purposes of Education: *Personal and Social Values in Education. 268 pp.*

Dale, R. R., and **Griffith, S.** Down Stream: *Failure in the Grammar School. 108 pp.*

Evans, K. M. Sociometry and Education. *158 pp.*

●**Ford, Julienne.** Social Class and the Comprehensive School. *192 pp.*

Foster, P. J. Education and Social Change in Ghana. *336 pp. 3 maps.*

Fraser, W. R. Education and Society in Modern France. *150 pp.*

Grace, Gerald R. Role Conflict and the Teacher. *150 pp.*

Hans, Nicholas. New Trends in Education in the Eighteenth Century. *278 pp. 19 tables.*

●   Comparative Education: *A Study of Educational Factors and Traditions. 360 pp.*

●**Hargreaves, David.** Interpersonal Relations and Education. *432 pp.*

●   Social Relations in a Secondary School. *240 pp.*

Holmes, Brian. Problems in Education. *A Comparative Approach. 336 pp.*

King, Ronald. Values and Involvement in a Grammar School. *164 pp.*
    School Organization and Pupil Involvement. *A Study of Secondary Schools.*

●**Mannheim, Karl,** and **Stewart, W. A. C.** An Introduction to the Sociology of Education. *206 pp.*

Morris, Raymond N. The Sixth Form and College Entrance. *231 pp.*

●**Musgrove, F.** Youth and the Social Order. *176 pp.*

●**Ottaway, A. K. C.** Education and Society: An Introduction to the Sociology of Education. *With an Introduction by W. O. Lester Smith. 212 pp.*

Peers, Robert. Adult Education: *A Comparative Study. 398 pp.*

Pritchard, D. G. Education and the Handicapped: *1760 to 1960. 258 pp.*

Stratta, Erica. The Education of Borstal Boys. *A Study of their Educational Experiences prior to, and during, Borstal Training. 256 pp.*

Taylor, P. H., Reid, W. A., and **Holley, B. J.** The English Sixth Form. *A Case Study in Curriculum Research. 200 pp.*

SOCIOLOGY OF CULTURE

Eppel, E. M., and **M.** Adolescents and Morality: *A Study of some Moral Values and Dilemmas of Working Adolescents in the Context of a changing Climate of Opinion. Foreword by W. J. H. Sprott. 268 pp. 39 tables.*

●**Fromm, Erich.** The Fear of Freedom. *286 pp.*

●   The Sane Society. *400 pp.*

Mannheim, Karl. Essays on the Sociology of Culture. *Edited by Ernst Mannheim in co-operation with Paul Kecskemeti. Editorial Note by Adolph Lowe. 280 pp.*

Weber, Alfred. Farewell to European History: *or The Conquest of Nihilism. Translated from the German by R. F. C. Hull. 224 pp.*

SOCIOLOGY OF RELIGION

Argyle, Michael and **Beit-Hallahmi, Benjamin.** The Social Psychology of Religion. *About 256 pp.*

Glasner, Peter E. The Sociology of Secularisation. *A Critique of a Concept. About 180 pp.*

Nelson, G. K. Spiritualism and Society. *313 pp.*

Stark, Werner. The Sociology of Religion. *A Study of Christendom.*
Volume I. *Established Religion. 248 pp.*
Volume II. *Sectarian Religion. 368 pp.*
Volume III. *The Universal Church. 464 pp.*
Volume IV. *Types of Religious Man. 352 pp.*
Volume V. *Types of Religious Culture. 464 pp.*

Turner, B. S. Weber and Islam. *216 pp.*

Watt, W. Montgomery. Islam and the Integration of Society. *320 pp.*

SOCIOLOGY OF ART AND LITERATURE

Jarvie, Ian C. Towards a Sociology of the Cinema. *A Comparative Essay on the Structure and Functioning of a Major Entertainment Industry. 405 pp.*

Rust, Frances S. Dance in Society. *An Analysis of the Relationships between the Social Dance and Society in England from the Middle Ages to the Present Day. 256 pp. 8 pp. of plates.*

Schücking, L. L. The Sociology of Literary Taste. *112 pp.*

Wolff, Janet. Hermeneutic Philosophy and the Sociology of Art. *150 pp.*

SOCIOLOGY OF KNOWLEDGE

Diesing, P. Patterns of Discovery in the Social Sciences. *262 pp.*

● **Douglas, J. D.** (Ed.) Understanding Everyday Life. *370 pp.*

● **Hamilton, P.** Knowledge and Social Structure. *174 pp.*

Jarvie, I. C. Concepts and Society. *232 pp.*

Mannheim, Karl. Essays on the Sociology of Knowledge. *Edited by Paul Kecskemeti. Editorial Note by Adolph Lowe. 353 pp.*

Remmling, Gunter W. The Sociology of Karl Mannheim. *With a Bibliographical Guide to the Sociology of Knowledge, Ideological Analysis, and Social Planning. 255 pp.*

Remmling, Gunter W. (Ed.) Towards the Sociology of Knowledge. *Origin and Development of a Sociological Thought Style. 463 pp.*

Stark, Werner. The Sociology of Knowledge: *An Essay in Aid of a Deeper Understanding of the History of Ideas. 384 pp.*

URBAN SOCIOLOGY

Ashworth, William. The Genesis of Modern British Town Planning: *A Study in Economic and Social History of the Nineteenth and Twentieth Centuries. 288 pp.*

Cullingworth, J. B. Housing Needs and Planning Policy: *A Restatement of the Problems of Housing Need and 'Overspill' in England and Wales. 232 pp. 44 tables. 8 maps.*

Dickinson, Robert E. City and Region: *A Geographical Interpretation 608 pp. 125 figures.*

The West European City: *A Geographical Interpretation. 600 pp. 129 maps. 29 plates.*

● The City Region in Western Europe. *320 pp. Maps.*

Humphreys, Alexander J. New Dubliners: *Urbanization and the Irish Family. Foreword by George C. Homans. 304 pp.*

Jackson, Brian. Working Class Community: *Some General Notions raised by a Series of Studies in Northern England. 192 pp.*

Jennings, Hilda. Societies in the Making: *a Study of Development and Redevelopment within a County Borough. Foreword by D. A. Clark. 286 pp.*

●**Mann, P. H.** An Approach to Urban Sociology. *240 pp.*

Morris, R. N., and **Mogey, J.** The Sociology of Housing. *Studies at Berinsfield. 232 pp. 4 pp. plates.*

Rosser, C., and **Harris, C.** The Family and Social Change. *A Study of Family and Kinship in a South Wales Town. 352 pp. 8 maps.*

●**Stacey, Margaret, Batsone, Eric, Bell, Colin,** and **Thurcott, Anne.** Power, Persistence and Change. *A Second Study of Banbury. 196 pp.*

RURAL SOCIOLOGY

Haswell, M. R. The Economics of Development in Village India. *120 pp.*

Littlejohn, James. Westrigg: *the Sociology of a Cheviot Parish. 172 pp. 5 figures.*

Mayer, Adrian C. Peasants in the Pacific. *A Study of Fiji Indian Rural Society. 248 pp. 20 plates.*

Williams, W. M. The Sociology of an English Village: *Gosforth. 272 pp. 12 figures. 13 tables.*

SOCIOLOGY OF INDUSTRY AND DISTRIBUTION

Anderson, Nels. Work and Leisure. *280 pp.*

●**Blau, Peter M.,** and **Scott, W. Richard.** Formal Organizations: *a Comparative approach. Introduction and Additional Bibliography by J. H. Smith. 326 pp.*

Dunkerley, David. The Foreman. *Aspects of Task and Structure. 192 pp.*

Eldridge, J. E. T. Industrial Disputes. *Essays in the Sociology of Industrial Relations. 288 pp.*

Hetzler, Stanley. Applied Measures for Promoting Technological Growth. *352 pp.*

Technological Growth and Social Change. *Achieving Modernization. 269 pp.*

Hollowell, Peter G. The Lorry Driver. *272 pp.*

●**Oxaal, I., Barnett, T.,** and **Booth, D.** (Eds). Beyond the Sociology of Development. *Economy and Society in Latin America and Africa. 295 pp.*

Smelser, Neil J. Social Change in the Industrial Revolution: *An Application of Theory to the Lancashire Cotton Industry, 1770–1840. 468 pp. 12 figures. 14 tables.*

ANTHROPOLOGY

Ammar, Hamed. Growing up in an Egyptian Village: *Silwa, Province of Aswan. 336 pp.*

Brandel-Syrier, Mia. Reeftown Elite. *A Study of Social Mobility in a Modern African Community on the Reef. 376 pp.*

Dickie-Clark, H. F. The Marginal Situation. *A Sociological Study of a Coloured Group. 236 pp.*

Dube, S. C. Indian Village. *Foreword by Morris Edward Opler. 276 pp. 4 plates.*

India's Changing Villages: *Human Factors in Community Development. 260 pp. 8 plates. 1 map.*

Firth, Raymond. Malay Fishermen. *Their Peasant Economy. 420 pp. 17 pp. plates.*

Gulliver, P. H. Social Control in an African Society: a Study of the Arusha, Agricultural Masai of Northern Tanganyika. *320 pp. 8 plates. 10 figures.*

Family Herds. *288 pp.*

Ishwaran, K. Tradition and Economy in Village India: *An Interactionist Approach.*
Foreword by Conrad Arensburg. 176 pp.

Jarvie, Ian C. The Revolution in Anthropology. *268 pp.*

Little, Kenneth L. Mende of Sierra Leone. *308 pp. and folder.*

Negroes in Britain. *With a New Introduction and Contemporary Study by Leonard Bloom. 320 pp.*

Lowie, Robert H. Social Organization. *494 pp.*

Mayer, A. C. Peasants in the Pacific. *A Study of Fiji Indian Rural Society. 248 pp.*

Meer, Fatima. Race and Suicide in South Africa. *325 pp.*

Smith, Raymond T. The Negro Family in British Guiana: *Family Structure and Social Status in the Villages. With a Foreword by Meyer Fortes. 314 pp. 8 plates. 1 figure. 4 maps.*

Smooha, Sammy. Israel: Pluralism and Conflict. *About 320 pp.*

SOCIOLOGY AND PHILOSOPHY

Barnsley, John H. The Social Reality of Ethics. *A Comparative Analysis of Moral Codes. 448 pp.*

Diesing, Paul. Patterns of Discovery in the Social Sciences. *362 pp.*

●**Douglas, Jack D.** (Ed.) Understanding Everyday Life. *Toward the Reconstruction of Sociological Knowledge. Contributions by Alan F. Blum. Aaron W. Cicourel, Norman K. Denzin, Jack D. Douglas, John Heeren, Peter McHugh, Peter K. Manning, Melvin Power, Matthew Speier, Roy Turner, D. Lawrence Wieder, Thomas P. Wilson and Don H. Zimmerman. 370 pp.*

Gorman, Robert A. The Dual Vision. *Alfred Schutz and the Myth of Phenomenological Social Science. About 300 pp.*

Jarvie, Ian C. Concepts and Society. *216 pp.*

●**Pelz, Werner.** The Scope of Understanding in Sociology. *Towards a more radical reorientation in the social humanistic sciences. 283 pp.*

Roche, Maurice. Phenomenology, Language and the Social Sciences. *371 pp.*

Sahay, Arun. Sociological Analysis. *212 pp.*

Sklair, Leslie. The Sociology of Progress. *320 pp.*

Slater, P. Origin and Significance of the Frankfurt School. *A Marxist Perspective. About 192 pp.*

Smart, Barry. Sociology, Phenomenology and Marxian Analysis. *A Critical Discussion of the Theory and Practice of a Science of Society. 220 pp.*

International Library of Anthropology

General Editor   Adam Kuper

Ahmed, A. S. Millenium and Charisma Among Pathans. *A Critical Essay in Social Anthropology. 192 pp.*

Brown, Paula. The Chimbu. *A Study of Change in the New Guinea Highlands. 151 pp.*

Gudeman, Stephen. Relationships, Residence and the Individual. *A Rural Panamanian Community. 288 pp. 11 Plates, 5 Figures, 2 Maps, 10 Tables.*

Hamnett, Ian. Chieftainship and Legitimacy. *An Anthropological Study of Executive Law in Lesotho. 163 pp.*

Hanson, F. Allan. Meaning in Culture. *127 pp.*

Lloyd, P. C. Power and Independence. *Urban Africans' Perception of Social Inequality. 264 pp.*

Pettigrew, Joyce. Robber Noblemen. *A Study of the Political System of the Sikh Jats. 284 pp.*

Street, Brian V. The Savage in Literature. *Representations of 'Primitive' Society in English Fiction, 1858–1920. 207 pp.*

Van Den Berghe, Pierre L. Power and Privilege at an African University. *278 pp.*

International Library of Social Policy

General Editor   Kathleen Jones

Bayley, M. Mental Handicap and Community Care. *426 pp.*

Bottoms, A. E., and **McClean, J. D.** Defendants in the Criminal Process. *284 pp.*

Butler, J. R. Family Doctors and Public Policy. *208 pp.*

Davies, Martin. Prisoners of Society. *Attitudes and Aftercare. 204 pp.*

Gittus, Elizabeth. Flats, Families and the Under-Fives. *285 pp.*

Holman, Robert. Trading in Children. *A Study of Private Fostering. 355 pp.*

Jones, Howard, and **Cornes, Paul.** Open Prisons. *About 248 pp.*

Jones, Kathleen. History of the Mental Health Service. *428 pp.*

Jones, Kathleen, with **Brown, John, Cunningham, W. J., Roberts, Julian,** and **Williams, Peter.** Opening the Door. *A Study of New Policies for the Mentally Handicapped. 278 pp.*

Karn, Valerie. Retiring to the Seaside. *About 280 pp. 2 maps. Numerous tables.*

Thomas, J. E. The English Prison Officer since 1850: *A Study in Conflict. 258 pp.*

Walton, R. G. Women in Social Work. *303 pp.*

Woodward, J. To Do the Sick No Harm. *A Study of the British Voluntary Hospital System to 1875. 221 pp.*

International Library of Welfare and Philosophy

General Editors   Noel Timms and David Watson

● **Plant, Raymond.** Community and Ideology. *104 pp.*

● **McDermott, F. E.** (Ed.) Self-Determination in Social Work. *A Collection of Essays on Self-determination and Related Concepts by Philosophers and Social Work Theorists. Contributors: F. P. Biestek, S. Bernstein, A. Keith-Lucas, D. Sayer, H. H. Perelman, C. Whittington, R. F. Stalley, F. E. McDermott, I. Berlin, H. J. McCloskey, H. L. A. Hart, J. Wilson, A. I. Melden, S. I. Benn. 254 pp.*

Ragg, Nicholas M. People Not Cases. *A Philosophical Approach to Social Work. About 250 pp.*

● **Timms, Noel,** and **Watson, David** (Eds). Talking About Welfare. *Readings in Philosophy and Social Policy. Contributors: T. H. Marshall, R. B. Brandt, G. H. von Wright, K. Nielsen, M. Cranston, R. M. Titmuss, R. S. Downie, E. Telfer, D. Donnison, J. Benson, P. Leonard, A. Keith-Lucas, D. Walsh, I. T. Ramsey. 320 pp.*

Primary Socialization, Language and Education

General Editor   Basil Bernstein

Adlam, Diana S., *with the assistance of Geoffrey Turner and Lesley Lineker.* Code in Context. *About 272 pp.*

Bernstein, Basil. Class, Codes and Control. *3 volumes.*
  1. *Theoretical Studies Towards a Sociology of Language. 254 pp.*
  2. *Applied Studies Towards a Sociology of Language. 377 pp.*
● 3. *Towards a Theory of Educatiomal Transmission. 167 pp.*
Brandis, W., and **Bernstein, B.** Selection and Control. *176 pp.*
Brandis, Walter, and **Henderson, Dorothy.** Social Class, Language and Communication. *288 pp.*

Cook-Gumperz, Jenny. Social Control and Socialization. *A Study of Class Differences in the Language of Maternal Control. 290 pp.*
●**Gahagan, D. M.,** and **G. A.** Talk Reform. *Exploration in Language for Infant School Children. 160 pp.*

Hawkins, P. R. Social Class, the Nominal Group and Verbal Strategies. *About 220 pp.*
Robinson, W. P., and **Rackstraw, Susan D. A.** A Question of Answers. *2 volumes. 192 pp. and 180 pp.*
Turner, Geoffrey J., and **Mohan, Bernard A.** A Linguistic Description and Computer Programme for Children's Speech. *208 pp.*

Reports of the Institute of Community Studies

●**Cartwright, Ann.** Parents and Family Planning Services. *306 pp.*
  Patients and their Doctors. *A Study of General Practice. 304 pp.*
Dench, Geoff. Maltese in London. *A Case-study in the Erosion of Ethnic Consciousness. 302 pp.*
●**Jackson, Brian.** Streaming: *an Education System in Miniature. 168 pp.*
Jackson, Brian, and **Marsden, Dennis.** Education and the Working Class: *Some General Themes raised by a Study of 88 Working-class Children in a Northern Industrial City. 268 pp. 2 folders.*
Marris, Peter. The Experience of Higher Education. *232 pp. 27 tables.*
  Loss and Change. *192 pp.*
Marris, Peter, and **Rein, Martin.** Dilemmas of Social Reform. *Poverty and Community Action in the United States. 256 pp.*

Marris, Peter, and **Somerset, Anthony.** African Businessmen. *A Study of Entrepreneurship and Development in Kenya. 256 pp.*

Mills, Richard. Young Outsiders: *a Study in Alternative Communities. 216 pp.*

Runciman, W. G. Relative Deprivation and Social Justice. *A Study of Attitudes to Social Inequality in Twentieth-Century England. 352 pp.*

Willmott, Peter. Adolescent Boys in East London. *230 pp.*

Willmott, Peter, and **Young, Michael.** Family and Class in a London Suburb. *202 pp. 47 tables.*

Young, Michael. Innovation and Research in Education. *192 pp.*

●**Young, Michael,** and **McGeeney, Patrick.** Learning Begins at Home. *A Study of a Junior School and its Parents. 128 pp.*

Young, Michael, and **Willmott, Peter.** Family and Kinship in East London. *Foreword by Richard M. Titmuss. 252 pp. 39 tables.*
The Symmetrical Family. *410 pp.*

Reports of the Institute for Social Studies in Medical Care

Cartwright, Ann, Hockey, Lisbeth, and **Anderson, John L.** Life Before Death. *310 pp.*

Dunnell, Karen, and **Cartwright, Ann.** Medicine Takers, Prescribers and Hoarders. *190 pp.*

Medicine, Illness and Society

General Editor W. M. Williams

Robinson, David. The Process of Becoming Ill. *142 pp.*

Stacey, Margaret, *et al.* Hospitals, Children and Their Families. *The Report of a Pilot Study. 202 pp.*

Stimson, G. V., and **Webb, B.** Going to See the Doctor. *The Consultation Process in General Practice. 155 pp.*

Monographs in Social Theory

General Editor Arthur Brittan

●**Barnes, B.** Scientific Knowledge and Sociological Theory. *192 pp.*

Bauman, Zygmunt. Culture as Praxis. *204 pp.*

●**Dixon, Keith.** Sociological Theory. *Pretence and Possibility. 142 pp.*

Meltzer, B. N., Petras, J. W., and **Reynolds, L. T.** Symbolic Interactionism. *Genesis, Varieties and Criticisms. 144 pp.*

●**Smith, Anthony D.** The Concept of Social Change. *A Critique of the Functionalist Theory of Social Change. 208 pp.*

Routledge Social Science Journals

The British Journal of Sociology. *Editor – Angus Stewart; Associate Editor – Leslie Sklair. Vol. 1, No. 1 – March 1950 and Quarterly. Roy. 8vo. All back issues available. An international journal publishing original papers in the field of sociology and related areas.*
Community Work. *Edited by David Jones and Marjorie Mayo. 1973. Published annually.*
Economy and Society. *Vol. 1, No. 1. February 1972 and Quarterly. Metric Roy. 8vo. A journal for all social scientists covering sociology, philosophy, anthropology, economics and history. All back numbers available.*
Religion. Journal of Religion and Religions. *Chairman of Editorial Board, Ninian Smart. Vol. 1, No. 1, Spring 1971. A journal with an inter-disciplinary approach to the study of the phenomena of religion. All back numbers available.*
Year Book of Social Policy in Britain, The. *Edited by Kathleen Jones. 1971. Published annually.*

Social and Psychological Aspects of Medical Practice

Editor   Trevor Silverstone

Lader, Malcolm. Psychophysiology of Mental Illness. *280 pp.*
● **Silverstone, Trevor,** and **Turner, Paul.** Drug Treatment in Psychiatry. *232 pp.*

Printed in Great Britain by Unwin Brothers Limited
The Gresham Press Old Woking Surrey
A member of the Staples Printing Group